Standard Measuring Equivalents

It comes in handy at times to know the following standard equivalents:

- 3 teaspoons equal 1 tablespoon
- 4 tablespoons equal ¼ cup
- 5 tablespoons + 1 teaspoon equal ⅓ cup
- Pinch or dash equal less than ⅛ teaspoon
- ⅓ tablespoon equal 1 teaspoon
- ½ tablespoon equal 1½ teaspoons
- ⅔ tablespoon equal 2 teaspoons
- ⅛ cup equal 2 tablespoons
- ⅜ cup equal ¼ cup + 2 tablespoons
- ⅝ cup equal ½ cup + 2 tablespoons
- ⅞ cup equal 1 cup less 2 tablespoons

Testing Yeast

When you purchase yeast, pay attention to the expiration date on the package. However, if you're in doubt about the activity of your yeast, you can check by using this easy activity test provided by Red Star Yeast & Products. It's called *proofing* the yeast.

1. **In a 1-cup liquid measuring cup, pour ½-cup warm water.**

   For accuracy, use a kitchen thermometer. The temperature should register 110°F to 115°F.

2. **Stir in 1 teaspoon of sugar and 2¼ teaspoons of yeast (the amount of yeast in one ¼-ounce package).**

3. **Let set for approximately 10 minutes.**

In that length of time, the yeast should have fermented the sugar and produced foam (carbon dioxide bubbles) that have grown to the 1-cup level. If this happens, the yeast is quite active, and you may use it in your bread machine. Pour it into your bread pan and add the other ingredients.

Bread Machines For Dummies®

Temperature Conversions

The recipes in this book use the Fahrenheit system. The following chart can help you make conversions to Celsius.

Fahrenheit	Celsius
80°	40°
100°	50°
200°	100°
300°	150°
325°	160°
350°	180°
375°	190°
400°	200°
425°	220°
450°	230°

Reasonable Metric Replacement Measures

All of the recipes in *Bread Machines For Dummies* use U.S. standard measurements based on teaspoons, tablespoons, and cups. We want you to be able to enjoy these recipes if you use the metric system, so we have included this conversion chart. The measurements given are not exact but have been rounded up or down for easier measuring.

U.S.	Metric
1 teaspoon	5 ml
1 tablespoon	15 ml
¼ cup	60 ml
⅓ cup	75 ml
½ cup	125 ml
⅔ cup	150 ml
¾ cup	175 ml
1 cup	250 ml

The IDG Books Worldwide logo is a registered trademark under exclusive license to IDG Books Worldwide, Inc., from International Data Group, Inc.
The ...For Dummies logo and For Dummies are trademarks of IDG Books Worldwide, Inc. All other trademarks are the property of their respective owners.

IDG BOOKS WORLDWIDE

For Dummies™: Bestselling Book Series for Beginners

 ™

References for the Rest of Us!™

BESTSELLING BOOK SERIES

Do you find that traditional reference books are overloaded with technical details and advice you'll never use? Do you postpone important life decisions because you just don't want to deal with them? Then our *...For Dummies*® business and general reference book series is for you.

...For Dummies business and general reference books are written for those frustrated and hard-working souls who know they aren't dumb, but find that the myriad of personal and business issues and the accompanying horror stories make them feel helpless. *...For Dummies* books use a lighthearted approach, a down-to-earth style, and even cartoons and humorous icons to dispel fears and build confidence. Lighthearted but not lightweight, these books are perfect survival guides to solve your everyday personal and business problems.

> "More than a publishing phenomenon, 'Dummies' is a sign of the times."
>
> — The New York Times

> "A world of detailed and authoritative information is packed into them..."
>
> — U.S. News and World Report

> "...you won't go wrong buying them."
>
> — Walter Mossberg, Wall Street Journal, on IDG Books' ...For Dummies books

Already, millions of satisfied readers agree. They have made *...For Dummies* the #1 introductory level computer book series and a best-selling business book series. They have written asking for more. So, if you're looking for the best and easiest way to learn about business and other general reference topics, look to *...For Dummies* to give you a helping hand.

IDG
BOOKS
WORLDWIDE

1/99

Bread Machines FOR DUMMIES®

by Glenna Vance and Tom Lacalamita

IDG BOOKS WORLDWIDE

IDG Books Worldwide, Inc.
An International Data Group Company

Foster City, CA ◆ Chicago, IL ◆ Indianapolis, IN ◆ New York, NY

Bread Machines For Dummies®

Published by
IDG Books Worldwide, Inc.
An International Data Group Company
919 E. Hillsdale Blvd.
Suite 400
Foster City, CA 94404
www.idgbooks.com (IDG Books Worldwide Web Site)
www.dummies.com (Dummies Press Web Site)

Library of Congress Control Number: 00-105666

ISBN: 0-7645-5241-4

Printed in the United States of America

10 9 8 7 6 5 4 3 2 1

1B/RV/RQ/QQ/IN

Distributed in the United States by IDG Books Worldwide, Inc.

Distributed by CDG Books Canada Inc. for Canada; by Transworld Publishers Limited in the United Kingdom; by IDG Norge Books for Norway; by IDG Sweden Books for Sweden; by IDG Books Australia Publishing Corporation Pty. Ltd. for Australia and New Zealand; by TransQuest Publishers Pte Ltd. for Singapore, Malaysia, Thailand, Indonesia, and Hong Kong; by Gotop Information Inc. for Taiwan; by ICG Muse, Inc. for Japan; by Intersoft for South Africa; by Eyrolles for France; by International Thomson Publishing for Germany, Austria and Switzerland; by Distribuidora Cuspide for Argentina; by LR International for Brazil; by Galileo Libros for Chile; by Ediciones ZETA S.C.R. Ltda. for Peru; by WS Computer Publishing Corporation, Inc., for the Philippines; by Contemporanea de Ediciones for Venezuela; by Express Computer Distributors for the Caribbean and West Indies; by Micronesia Media Distributor, Inc. for Micronesia; by Chips Computadoras S.A. de C.V. for Mexico; by Editorial Norma de Panama S.A. for Panama; by American Bookshops for Finland.

For general information on IDG Books Worldwide's books in the U.S., please call our Consumer Customer Service department at 800-762-2974. For reseller information, including discounts and premium sales, please call our Reseller Customer Service department at 800-434-3422.

For information on where to purchase IDG Books Worldwide's books outside the U.S., please contact our International Sales department at 317-572-3993 or fax 317-572-4002.

For consumer information on foreign language translations, please contact our Customer Service department at 1-800-434-3422, fax 317-572-4002, or e-mail rights@idgbooks.com.

For information on licensing foreign or domestic rights, please phone +1-650-653-7098.

For sales inquiries and special prices for bulk quantities, please contact our Order Services department at 800-434-4322 or write to the address above.

For information on using IDG Books Worldwide's books in the classroom or for ordering examination copies, please contact our Educational Sales department at 800-434-2086 or fax 317-572-4005.

For press review copies, author interviews, or other publicity information, please contact our Public Relations department at 650-653-7000 or fax 650-653-7500.

For authorization to photocopy items for corporate, personal, or educational use, please contact Copyright Clearance Center, 222 Rosewood Drive, Danvers, MA 01923, or fax 978-750-4470.

About the Authors

Glenna Vance (Milwaukee, WI) is director of consumer affairs for a major ingredient manufacturer in the Midwest. A published author, Glenna has been involved in developing consumer recipe programs with major appliance manufacturers and ingredient companies. As a board member of the Milwaukee chapter of the American Institute of Wine & Food, Glenna is instrumental in bringing nationally renowned culinary professionals to Milwaukee for culinary programs and events.

Tom Lacalamita (Long Island, NY) is a bestselling author of five appliance-related cookbooks. Nominated for a James Beard cookbook award, Lacalamita is considered to be a national authority on housewares and has appeared on hundreds of television and radio shows across the country. With a passion for food, cooking, and all sorts of kitchen gadgets, Tom is also a spokesperson for various food and housewares manufacturers.

ABOUT IDG BOOKS WORLDWIDE

Welcome to the world of IDG Books Worldwide.

IDG Books Worldwide, Inc., is a subsidiary of International Data Group, the world's largest publisher of computer-related information and the leading global provider of information services on information technology. IDG was founded more than 30 years ago by Patrick J. McGovern and now employs more than 9,000 people worldwide. IDG publishes more than 290 computer publications in over 75 countries. More than 90 million people read one or more IDG publications each month.

Launched in 1990, IDG Books Worldwide is today the #1 publisher of best-selling computer books in the United States. We are proud to have received eight awards from the Computer Press Association in recognition of editorial excellence and three from Computer Currents' First Annual Readers' Choice Awards. Our best-selling ...For Dummies® series has more than 50 million copies in print with translations in 31 languages. IDG Books Worldwide, through a joint venture with IDG's Hi-Tech Beijing, became the first U.S. publisher to publish a computer book in the People's Republic of China. In record time, IDG Books Worldwide has become the first choice for millions of readers around the world who want to learn how to better manage their businesses.

Our mission is simple: Every one of our books is designed to bring extra value and skill-building instructions to the reader. Our books are written by experts who understand and care about our readers. The knowledge base of our editorial staff comes from years of experience in publishing, education, and journalism — experience we use to produce books to carry us into the new millennium. In short, we care about books, so we attract the best people. We devote special attention to details such as audience, interior design, use of icons, and illustrations. And because we use an efficient process of authoring, editing, and desktop publishing our books electronically, we can spend more time ensuring superior content and less time on the technicalities of making books.

You can count on our commitment to deliver high-quality books at competitive prices on topics you want to read about. At IDG Books Worldwide, we continue in the IDG tradition of delivering quality for more than 30 years. You'll find no better book on a subject than one from IDG Books Worldwide.

John Kilcullen
Chairman and CEO
IDG Books Worldwide, Inc.

Eighth Annual Computer Press Awards 1992

Ninth Annual Computer Press Awards 1993

Tenth Annual Computer Press Awards 1994

Eleventh Annual Computer Press Awards 1995

IDG is the world's leading IT media, research and exposition company. Founded in 1964, IDG had 1997 revenues of $2.05 billion and has more than 9,000 employees worldwide. IDG offers the widest range of media options that reach IT buyers in 75 countries representing 95% of worldwide IT spending. IDG's diverse product and services portfolio spans six key areas including print publishing, online publishing, expositions and conferences, market research, education and training, and global marketing services. More than 90 million people read one or more of IDG's 290 magazines and newspapers, including IDG's leading global brands — Computerworld, PC World, Network World, Macworld and the Channel World family of publications. IDG Books Worldwide is one of the fastest-growing computer book publishers in the world, with more than 700 titles in 36 languages. The "...For Dummies®" series alone has more than 50 million copies in print. IDG offers online users the largest network of technology-specific Web sites around the world through IDG.net (http://www.idg.net), which comprises more than 225 targeted Web sites in 55 countries worldwide. International Data Corporation (IDC) is the world's largest provider of information technology data, analysis and consulting, with research centers in over 41 countries and more than 400 research analysts worldwide. IDG World Expo is a leading producer of more than 168 globally branded conferences and expositions in 35 countries including E3 (Electronic Entertainment Expo), Macworld Expo, ComNet, Windows World Expo, ICE (Internet Commerce Expo), Agenda, DEMO, and Spotlight. IDG's training subsidiary, ExecuTrain, is the world's largest computer training company, with more than 230 locations worldwide and 785 training courses. IDG Marketing Services helps industry-leading IT companies build international brand recognition by developing global integrated marketing programs via IDG's print, online and exposition products worldwide. Further information about the company can be found at www.idg.com. 1/26/00

Dedication

Dedicated with love to my mom, Mildred Weir, who has been a queen in her kitchen all these many years and a positive influence in my life.

—Glenna Vance

I dedicate this book to my mother, Frances Porretta, a woman of great culinary talent, who over the course of my life has given me her unconditional love and support.

—Tom Lacalamita

Authors' Acknowledgments

A book is never the work of a single person. There are many whose contribution make it a success. This book is not an exception.

We would like to especially thank IDG Books and Holly McGuire for asking us to write *Bread Machines For Dummies,* Linda Ingroia for keeping things on track, and Angela Miller for bringing us all together.

We are extremely grateful for our very patient and understanding project editor, Tim Gallan. It was Tim's confidence that this book would be a reality that kept us researching, testing and writing. Every author should, at least once in their lifetime, have an editor as cool, calm, and collected as Tim.

It's amazing how directions can appear to be written clearly until they come under the scrutiny of a skillful eye of one who is quick to question them. For making this book not only grammatically correct, but also make sense, we thank Ben Nussbaum and Gwenette Gaddis, our copy editors.

We are thankful for the luxury of a very professional and competent recipe tester, Patricia Waldoch, who tested, tasted, and tweaked our recipes with extreme carefulness, checking to make sure the ingredient amounts were exact, the oven temperatures were accurate, and the times were correct.

Since a picture is worth a thousand words, we hope that you enjoy as much as we do the quirky, wonderfully descriptive illustrations of artist Liz Kurtzman.

We also want to thank the Production crew at IDG for making this book look so nice.

Publisher's Acknowledgments

We're proud of this book; please register your comments through our IDG Books Worldwide Online Registration Form located at `http://my2cents.dummies.com`.

Some of the people who helped bring this book to market include the following:

Acquisitions, Editorial, and Media Development

Senior Project Editor: Tim Gallan

Senior Acquisitions Editor: Linda Ingroia

Copy Editors: Ben Nussbaum, Gwenette Gaddis

Technical Reviewer: Patricia Waldoch

Editorial Manager: Pam Mourouzis

Editorial Assistant: Carol Strickland

Production

Project Coordinator: Nancee Reeves

Layout and Graphics: Amy Adrian, Joe Bucki, Jacque Schneider, Brian Torwelle, Julie Trippetti, Jeremey Unger, Erin Zeltner

Proofreaders: Laura Albert, Corey Bowen, Melissa D. Buddendeck, David Faust, Angel Perez, Dwight Ramsey

Illustrator: Liz Kurtzman

Indexer: Ty Koontz

General and Administrative

IDG Books Worldwide, Inc.: John Kilcullen, CEO; Bill Barry, President and COO

IDG Books Consumer Reference Group

Business: Kathleen A. Welton, Vice President and Publisher; Kevin Thornton, Acquisitions Manager

Cooking/Gardening: Jennifer Feldman, Associate Vice President and Publisher

Education/Reference: Diane Graves Steele, Vice President and Publisher; Greg Tubach, Publishing Director

Lifestyles: Kathleen Nebenhaus, Vice President and Publisher; Tracy Boggier, Managing Editor

Pets: Dominique De Vito, Associate Vice President and Publisher; Tracy Boggier, Managing Editor

Travel: Michael Spring, Vice President and Publisher; Suzanne Jannetta, Editorial Director; Brice Gosnell, Managing Editor

IDG Books Consumer Editorial Services: Kathleen Nebenhaus, Vice President and Publisher; Kristin A. Cocks, Editorial Director; Cindy Kitchel, Editorial Director

IDG Books Consumer Production: Debbie Stailey, Production Director

IDG Books Packaging: Marc J. Mikulich, Vice President, Brand Strategy and Research

◆

The publisher would like to give special thanks to Patrick J. McGovern, without whom this book would not have been possible.

◆

Contents at a Glance

Cartoons at a Glance

By Rich Tennant

page 5

"...because I'm more comfortable using my own tools. Now-how much longer do you want me to sand the cake batter?"

page 19

"Oooo, what's in here? Is that sun-dried eye of newt? How gourmet!"

page 225

"I'm pretty sure it's pizza dough that gets tossed, not pasta dough."

page 89

Fax: 978-546-7747
E-mail: richtennant@the5thwave.com
World Wide Web: www.the5thwave.com

Table of Contents

Recipes at a Glance

Chapter 13

Chapter 14

Chapter 15

Introduction

● ●

*H*omemade bread — *ummmm* good. Nothing beats it. But who has the time and fortitude to make it anymore? You do, with the help of your automatic bread machine. "But my bread," you say, "doesn't turn out the way I think it should." It can and it will because this is your bread machine handbook. We have written it so you can use it not only as a cookbook filled with wonderful recipes, but also as a resource guide of everything you "knead" to know about your bread machine, the ingredients that you will use, and how to use them. We believe bread machines are easy to use and get bread on your table with minimum time and effort. Trust us, we'll tell you how.

About This Book

Now, we know you would like a guarantee that you'll make a perfect loaf of bread every time, and while we can't promise you that, we share with you our combined 22 years of experience developing recipes specifically formulated for the bread machines. We were there when they were first introduced, working to develop recipes to turn out great bread from the machines. Getting all our experience and knowledge between one book cover has been a challenge, but we've done it.

We'll bet you are anxious to get going, so scan the Table of Contents, check out the recipes, and find one that sounds good. If you have all the ingredients on hand, make it.

Because all of the recipes have been tested, and tested, and then tested again in every machine we could get our hands on, chances are pretty good you will soon be enjoying a wonderful loaf of delicious homemade bread. But be aware, sooner or later, it's bound to happen, you will produce a loaf that doesn't measure up to your standard. Not to fret. You now have all the best resources available to you to avoid that from happening again. Just to be sure, read through Parts I and II and discover what went wrong and why.

Now, if you are of a more cautious nature (and we trust you are), read the first sections to learn more about your bread machine and what to do when. But don't worry about remembering everything you've read on the first reading because this is your bread machine handbook. You will be checking back through it for information, probably as long as you are making bread in a bread machine.

What We Assume about You

There are a privileged few who learned to bake at the elbow of an experienced person: a grandmother, mother, friend, or perhaps even an uncle. Most of us did not. You may know that bread is made with yeast, flour, salt, water, and probably a few other ingredients. But how they are combined is probably a complete mystery to you. We'll tell you what to buy and why. From that point, we will describe the difference between measuring dry and wet ingredients, what *proofing* the yeast means, what dough is supposed to look like during the kneading time, and why a thermometer assures quality control in bread making (even in an automatic bread machine).

How This Book Is Organized

Bread Machines For Dummies is structured first to provide you with the essential information about breads, their ingredients, and how to turn your bread machine into an essential appliance. Then of course, there are recipes — all kinds of recipes, from popular bread machine ones to extraordinary hand shaped. Plus, for those of you who have special dietary needs, we have included breads made with alternative ingredients like rice flour, potato starch, and tapioca flour. For your convenience, we conclude with two nifty, jiffy troubleshooting checklists, sure to get you out of almost any bind.

Part I: Homemade Bread from the Bread Machine

Ever wonder who made the first loaf of bread or how we started eating bread or even who had the idea to make it completely automatic in a machine? Part I gives you the facts.

Part II: Getting the Best Results from Your Bread Machine

Here we provide all of the in-depth ingredient information you'll ever need to know. Plus we tell you everything there is to know about your bread machine — how it works and what the bells and whistles are for. We also include how-to measure tips, and explain why you need to test the liquid temperature, how to bake the bread in the oven if you choose to create an interesting shape, and, of course, how to keep it fresh because there might even be some left over.

Part III: Bread Automatically with the Push of a Button

Now comes the best part. Roll up your sleeves, put on your apron (although you really don't need to because making bread in a machine isn't messy), and get started using these quick and easy recipes for great homemade loaves of bread.

We also show you how to use your bread machine to make the dough that you will shape into bakery-like creations to bake in your oven, thus capturing the admiration of your family and friends.

Part IV: The Part of Tens

Oops! Something isn't right with my bread machine, you say. Quick, see our ready reference of ten troubleshooting tips. Or, if your bread didn't turn out the way it should have, the explanation is in the final chapter, which offers solutions to ten common problems.

Icons Used in This Book

Every ...*For Dummies* book uses little pictures, called icons, to flag certain kinds of information to your attention. Here's what they mean:

This icon indicates a great piece of advice related to cooking or baking.

When we offer tips on buying the right ingredients or equipment, we use this icon.

When we present some general wisdom that you shouldn't forget, you see this icon.

We use this icon to point out potential pitfalls in the bread-making process.

Part I

Homemade Bread from the Bread Machine

The 5th Wave   By Rich Tennant

COOKBOOKS TO AVOID

CLASSIC New England Boiled Desserts

PASTA ON THE GRILL WITH Rolf

HEADCHEESE HEADCHEESE and more HEADCHEESE at the Gilmore Inn

Technique de Manifold

Cooking on your engine block... the French way!

In this part . . .

*E*ver wonder who made the first bread loaf of bread or how we started eating bread or even who had the idea to make it completely automatic in a machine? Part I gives you the facts. And we tell why bread is worth the effort to make at home.

Chapter 1

Why an Automatic Bread Machine?

Commercially made bread is so common today, who would have thought we could go back to homemade bread? And that the trend toward homemade bread wouldn't be a step backward? Bread machines are a step forward — to better bread than there's ever been before.

Eight thousand years ago, when people turned from hunting and fishing to farming and shepherding, they began to cultivate grain to ensure the continuity of a food source. Historians credit Egyptians as the first to grow wheat, barley, and millet, and to capture wild yeast to use in baking and brewing. We also know that as the Roman Empire spread throughout Europe and Great Britain around 2,000 years ago, grain crops, mainly wheat, began to thrive in the conquered territories. Early settlers brought wheat to America and those amber waves of grain grew beyond anyone's wildest hope.

Around the world, the art of making homemade bread became a skill passed down from one generation to the next. Then came the industrial age — commercial bread was mass-produced, sold in the marketplace, and considered superior to homemade bread.

In the 1970s, as Japan was experiencing an economic boom, young Japanese were finding a breakfast of bacon and eggs with orange juice and bread or rolls to be more convenient than fish and a bowl of rice with pickled vegetables. Unfortunately for the Japanese housewife, her family wanted very fresh bread.

What a relief when, in 1987, Shin Ojima, an electrical engineer, manufactured a totally automatic bread machine. Even at prices exceeding $400, automatic bread machine sales took off, and more than 1 million units were sold in Japan in less than 12 months.

This success was short-lived. Within a year, the bottom fell out. Most Japanese live in very small apartments that have sliding, paper-covered partitions for walls. Between the noise of the machine and the aroma of a loaf of fresh bread, many Japanese families found it difficult to sleep. They abandoned the idea of having fresh, homemade bread for breakfast. The machines were trashed.

Fortunately for Japanese manufacturers, the United States and Canada presented a large, untapped market, ready and waiting for such an appliance. The first bread machine reached North America in time for the Christmas of 1988. They originally retailed for more than $400, but prices have dropped dramatically, affording millions of people the opportunity to make delicious, wholesome bread with the push of a button.

Defining a Bread Machine

In this modern, technological age, the bread machine is unlike any other small appliance you have. Microwave ovens, automatic coffee makers, juice makers, and so on, use manual controls that depend on your opening and closing an electrical switch by pushing a button. But your bread machine uses a computer chip that contains the programs for the various cycles the bread machine performs.

For those of you who want to know more about the inner workings of things, you will find the mechanical operation inside the machine to be quite simple. The machine has a small motor that turns a belt-driven drive shaft to rotate a kneading blade inside a bread pan. It also has a thermostat to regulate the temperature inside the machine to the appropriate warmth for rising and baking.

This amazing appliance has changed making bread from an insurmountable task (for many of us) into a simple procedure. It literally kneads, rises, and bakes the bread without the hands-on skill of a human. No wonder the bread machine continues to be a top-selling appliance in the housewares industry. We all love good, homemade bread, and when the process is so easy, we'll make it ourselves.

Use a surge protector strip with your bread machine. The microchips used in bread machines are sensitive to voltage changes. A surge protector strip will guarantee steady voltage and prolong the life of your bread machine.

The Basics on How a Bread Machine Works

With a bread machine, you measure the ingredients, put them into the bread pan in the order they are listed in the recipe, put the pan in the bread machine, select the appropriate cycle, and press Start. Bingo! The bread machine takes over. Is it any wonder that bread machine manufacturers advertise "Homemade bread with the push of a button."

Here is an abbreviated glossary of ingredients to help your understanding of how the ingredients mysteriously change their appearance within the machine, mix with each other, and turn into bread.

- ✔ **Liquids** make the chemical changes happen.
- ✔ **Wheat flour** has protein which, when mixed with liquid, becomes gluten.
- ✔ **Gluten** becomes elastic when kneaded and forms the structure of the dough.
- ✔ **Yeast** is activated when it comes in contact with liquid to ferment the starch in the flour and the sugar in the bread. The fermentation causes gases to form that make the honeycomb structure in the bread dough.
- ✔ **Salt** flavors the bread, controls the yeast activity, and strengthens the dough structure.

Your part in this process is simply to have all the ingredients at room temperature, measure them correctly, and put them into the pan. When you push Start, the machine will begin to mix the ingredients and then knead the dough. For a period of time after the dough is kneaded it will seem like nothing is happening. This is the time when the dough is rising. Most machines then knead the dough a second time and let it rise again before heating up to bake the bread. The machine does the work; you take the credit.

Who and Why? (and What, Where, When, and How)

Early on, the average bread machine purchaser was 55 to 65 years old and somewhat affluent. They were financial risk takers, who had the expendable income to purchase the latest and newest gadget on the market. With the downsizing of corporate America at the beginning of the '90s we also saw many men from this age group, forced out of the work force with incentive retirement packages, picking up bread machine baking as a hobby or as an introduction to cooking. Bread making to them was nostalgic, bringing back memories of the good old days, when they came home to the smell of homemade bread from their mother's kitchen. The smell of bread baking in their own kitchen is comforting, and the taste of homemade bread is wonderful. Eating it is sheer pleasure.

Since the introduction of bread machines over ten years ago, bread machine retail prices have dropped to less than $100, which has initiated a change in who uses them. A recent survey by *Good Housekeeping* showed 43 percent of its readers have bread machines that they use at least once a week. For the most part, today's consumer is a 30- to 39-year old, married, working woman with children. To her the bread machine is a convenience. She's able to prepare nutritious bread with minimum effort that the whole family enjoys. This makes her feel good, because although she works outside the home, her primary concern is the care of her family.

Of course, there's a group of us who just want to eat good food that's good for us. The bread machine makes it possible, with limited effort and time, to make healthy breads for a healthy diet. And did you know that bread machines are now a standard item on the bride and groom's department store shopping guide? Speaking of gifts, bread machine sales are at their highest during the winter holidays. Many grandmothers, who are perceived to have everything, find a big box under the tree for them to open. It's a bread machine! And they love it! Bread machines may make it possible for a grandmom to rekindle her love of baking fresh bread in her kitchen, without the hassle and strain that's a part of making homemade bread without a bread machine. Many people who give a bread machine as a gift receive homemade bread in return.

And let's not forget another group of people using bread machines — kids. They love using them. They are fascinated with how they work and what goes into making a loaf of bread, and kids can use a bread machine with ease. Bread machines are great tools for practical, hands-on learning. Using a bread machine can teach a child how to measure, help them visualize fractions and percentages, and allow them to see organic chemical reactions. Many schools are incorporating the bread machine into their standard classroom equipment, from grade school through high school.

Shapes, Sizes, and Features

In 1989, when we first talked to bread machine owners, we heard, "We love our bread machine, but the cylindrical pan only makes round slices." We'd tell them, "Make baloney sandwiches."

Glenna's preschool story

I took three bread machines, measuring utensils, and the ingredients to make Dinosaur Bread to my grandson's preschool class. I had a small pitcher of water so that the kids could feel the weight of the water and pour it into a measuring cup. I placed the flour in large plastic bowls so that they could measure with as little spilling as possible. Not all of the children were interested in what I was doing, so as they showed interest I let them measure whatever ingredient we were on. By the time I was ready to load the third machine the interest was quite high. I showed the kids how I started the machines, and left the lids open so that they could see the mixing and kneading process.

Because this was not going to be Gourmet Delight Bread, but rather Dinosaur Bread, I saw no need to wait for the dough to rise after the kneading process. Instead, I divided the dough into sections so that each child could make his or her own dinosaur. The teacher had collected a number of dinosaurs from the toys in the school, and we looked at them as we formed the shapes. We used some small tools, like plastic knives and pencils with broken leads, to help shape the dough. Some of the shapes needed a lot of imagination before I could see the dinosaur in them, but who was I to question the validity of the shape? If a child said it was the shape he/she wanted for their dinosaur, it was fine with me. As I sat with them, some told me about making bread at another time with their mother or grandmother. It was so easy to relate to each of them when we were doing something with our hands.

Fortunately, there was a kitchen with an oven in this preschool setting, so after the dinosaurs were placed on cookie sheets and allowed to rest for about 15 minutes, they were baked in a preheated 400° oven for approximately 15 minutes. As the children sat on the group rug for their closing time, they ate their dinosaurs. What fun for a grandma!

Dinosaur Bread

- 1 cup water
- 1 teaspoon salt
- 2 tablespoons sugar
- 2 tablespoons vegetable oil
- 3 cups flour

Place the ingredients in the pan in the order shown, select the Dough or Manual setting and push Start.

But consumers wanted square slices, and the manufacturers responded with vertical pans for square loaves. The comment then was, "The bread is delicious, but it doesn't look like a loaf of bread." Soon, there were slightly rectangular loaf shapes. Now, the shape of many bread machine pans is the traditional loaf. You can also decide how large you want the loaf. Most machines offer 1-, 1½-, and 2-pound sizes.

"Bread machines are easy to use and make great bread, but I can't always remember to start the bread early enough. It takes four hours, you know." So we started seeing the option of shorter cycles, and now all the newer machines have a one-hour cycle. Amazing — bread made in an hour! You can make bread in the same time it takes to put a meal on the table. We still like the longer cycles best, but if you haven't planned ahead (it happens — no big deal) use the short cycle if your machine has it.

If you are the totally organized individual who does plan ahead, you'll love the timer-set feature. (All machines seem to have it.) You put all the ingredients into the pan and select the appropriate cycle. Increase the time to coincide with the time you want the bread to be ready. For example: You have everything in the pan by 8 a.m. but you want fresh, warm Italian bread to accompany the spaghetti dinner at 6 p.m. Therefore, you will probably want the Italian bread done by 5 p.m. to allow enough time for the bread to cool a bit before trying to slice it. There are nine hours between 8 a.m. and 5 p.m. Use the timer to increase the hours already indicated by the chosen cycle until 9:00 appears on the digital screen. Could it be simpler?

Your bread machine may also have a Quick bread cycle. Do not confuse this with a rapid or one-hour cycle. Quick breads are not yeast breads; they use baking powder and/or baking soda rather than yeast to *leaven* (rise) the bread. Chapters 16 and 17 are loaded with delicious quick breads: Apple Bread, Banana Lemon Bread, Orange Date Bread, and Pumpkin Bread, just to name a few. The process for making quick breads is completely different than that for making yeast-leavened breads. The ingredients in quick breads need only to be mixed together just long enough to thoroughly blend; no lengthy rise time is necessary because the baking powder expands the bread when it's heated. Therefore, the Quick bread cycle only has a mix time and a bake time.

The latest addition to bread machines is a cycle that only bakes. It expanded the possibilities for the use of the bread machine. You can make jam, bake meatloaf, and even boil pasta. But, this is a *bread* machine cookbook; we aren't providing you with anything more than the idea that it's possible to make other foods in a bread machine. If you happen to experience a power interruption and you have a Bake cycle on your machine, you're in luck. If the dough is already kneaded and is rising, and the power stops just long enough to make all your digital clocks blink, don't panic. Allow the dough to continue to rise until it is as high as it normally is when it begins to bake. Then select the Bake cycle and push Start. Your bread will be excellent.

For the experienced bread machine baker, there are some pretty sophisticated machines out there that not only have the cycles common to all bread machines, but also can be programmed any way you'd like. You can choose to lengthen or shorten any part of any cycle. One brand even lets you set the baking temperature. Another has a steam feature, which makes the crust crisp (like many European breads).

All bread machines make good bread. When you are making a bread machine purchase, consider the size of loaf you actually will want. Although you can keep bread fresh by freezing it (see Chapter 9), sometimes bigger isn't better. Also, think about where you will store the machine. Do you have the counter space for it or will you be putting it away between uses? The more accessible the machine, the more you will use it. If you have to put it in an out-of-the-way storage space, soon, no matter how much you've enjoyed homemade bread, it will be too inconvenient to bother getting out.

Whether you are buying the machine for yourself or giving the bread machine as a gift, be sure to keep the proof of purchase. If there is any problem with the machine, the sales receipt makes exchanges or adjustments so much easier for the sales department, as well as the consumer.

Using Your Bread Machine

Basic common sense: The more convenient the place is that you keep your bread machine, the more you'll use it. So find a convenient place to keep it. Remember, we want convenience. Bread machines are all about convenience. Don't defeat your purpose by putting the machine on some out-of-the-way shelf, which you have to drag it down from every time you use it.

Stock your pantry and freezer with the basic ingredients: flour, salt, sugar, salad oil, and yeast. Even add a few bread mixes for the time-crunch emergency.

You are starting out on the right path toward your target — homemade bread forever!

You can make White Sandwich Bread, Rye Bread, Egg Bread, French Bread, Hearty Whole Grain Breads — it's your choice and we've supplied many recipes for your choosing. You can even get some of these done in an hour. We've provided a whole chapter with recipes that are especially good when done on the Super Fast cycle.

If it's quick breads that you prefer there are two chapters with nothing but quick breads. Remember how good Banana Bread is with cream cheese? We add lemon juice and grated lemon peel; umm, is it good. If you have zucchini-a-plenty in the fall, you will find our Zucchini Bread recipe to be just what you're looking for.

Wait 'til you experience the Dough cycle and find out how easy it is to make pizza, or sweet rolls, or French baguettes, or coffeecakes. The process is so clean. If you've ever made bread the traditional method, you'll never go back. Not only is the process so unencumbered, there is so little to clean up afterward.

Those grandmothers we mentioned earlier in the chapter rave about the ease of the process. Actually, grandmothers like to use the Dough cycle on the bread machines because often they don't have the strength or endurance to knead the dough, but they still get so much satisfaction from providing dinner rolls at the family gatherings. You can actually use the Dough cycle to knead and rise your family's traditional recipes. If your recipe is too large, you may have to cut it in half.

We've even provided many special, ethnic breads for festive occasions. You may discover one or two from your ethnic background that you haven't had since childhood. Using a bread machine can become a way of life — imagine healthy, nutritious breads at every meal.

Chapter 2

Breads for a Healthy Diet

- -

In This Chapter

▶ Eating bread to make a healthier you

▶ Understanding the value of bread ingredients

▶ Creating the most nutritious breads

▶ Accentuating your menus with bread

- -

*T*o eat, or not to eat, bread is a common dietary question these days —
especially when we hear statistics about how overweight our population
is. Popular magazines for women carry at least one article per issue on
weight loss. Some theories tout the value of high-protein diets, while others
say that we should eliminate sugar or fat.

Those of us who enjoy eating bread may wish that we could increase its protein content or eliminate the sugar and fat. In this chapter, we explain the role
of bread in your diet. When you understand that the primary nutritional purpose of bread is to provide your body with fiber, you realize that although
you can add some protein to your bread recipes, the primary purpose of
bread is not to be a source of protein. And when you realize that the fat in
bread is essential for your body's good health, maybe you won't be so quick
to try to eliminate it from all your bread recipes.

Because breads are a very important part of your diet, we also offer loads of
ideas for making them an exciting part of your menus. Besides the usual
added touch to meals, breads can wrap your entrées, hold your sandwich
ingredients, soak up your stews, garnish your casseroles, accent your salads,
accompany your breakfasts, enhance your hors d'oeuvres, and be a great nib-
bling snack. By the time you finish this chapter, you should be convinced that
bread is good for you and be filled with ideas and inspiration for making your
own bread in your bread machine.

A Healthy Diet Includes Bread

Synergistic is the perfect adjective for bread. Synergistic means having the ability to enhance the effectiveness of an already active agent so that the total effect is greater than the sum of the individual parts. Bread is synergistic because the vitamins, minerals, and proteins in other foods are more readily absorbed when those foods are eaten with bread. In this section, we explain how the fiber and fat found in bread help your body to function properly.

Understanding the function of fiber

The fiber in bread slows the passage of food through the digestive system by holding water and creating bulk. The nutrients are then more completely absorbed. When you eat a slice of bread or a roll with a salad, the raw vegetables or fruit remain in your stomach longer, and your body extracts a higher ratio of vitamins from the food before it is digested. Therefore, bread and salad eaten together have more value to the body than when eaten separately.

The synergism from bread combined with other food continues throughout the digestive tract, allowing carbohydrates to move into the bloodstream at a steady rate. People with diabetes and hypoglycemia find eating bread especially important because it keeps the blood sugar from rising high after a meal and then dropping.

Bread supplies vitamin B and complex carbohydrates, but supplying fiber is its most important function. Many people want to eliminate the white flour found in bread because they have read so much about the value of eating whole grains. Although it's true that whole grain flours contain more insoluble fiber than refined flour, white flours do have some advantages. White flour is milled from the *endosperm* of the grain, which contains the greatest share of protein, carbohydrates, iron, major B vitamins, and soluble fiber.

In the digestive tract, soluble fiber binds with *bile acids* (raw materials from which cholesterol is made) and prevents their absorption into the blood. The result is lower cholesterol. Insoluble fiber, which is found in whole grains, helps to move *carcinogens* (cancer-causing substances) quickly through the body. Fortunately, bread is a food that not only tastes good, but also is good for a healthy diet and lifestyle.

Keeping a little fat in your diet

The claim that bread is fattening is a big, fat myth. The truth is that bread is low in fat and high in long-term energy. On average, one slice of bread has only 1 gram of fat and 75 calories, the majority of which come from complex carbohydrates. As the body's preferred source of fuel, complex carbohydrates contain four calories per gram, compared to fat with nine.

This is not to say that all fat is bad for you, because fat in the diet is absolutely necessary. But not just any fat. The best fats come from natural vegetable oils because they break down during digestion into essential fatty acids, which the body requires to maintain good health. However, vegetable oils that have been hydrogenated, such as margarines and solid shortenings, add only calories and cannot be utilized by the body. So nutritionally speaking, vegetable oils are the best for you, followed by butter.

When you add seeds, such as sunflower or sesame, to recipes, you add the good kind of fat to your bread, because these seeds fall in the category of vegetable fats. (Plus they make bread taste *sooo* good.) Seeds furnish fat, fiber, and flavor. Likewise, adding cracked wheat, wheat germ, or wheat bran brings fat, fiber, and flavor to bread.

Building a Repertoire of Breads

You will want to discover the breads your family enjoys the most. As with every presentation, be it a speech or food for the table, you have to analyze your audience. So, in thinking about using your bread machine to the best advantage, you have to ask yourself, "Who will be eating my bread?"

We have fed our share of young mouths and know they prefer soft and white. If your eaters are primarily children, we'll bet that you will be repeating Good Old American Sandwich Bread several times a week. You can vary their options with Buttermilk Farm Bread and Irish Potato Bread because they are similar in mouth feel. Oh, but wait a minute. What do you think they'll think about the Peanut Butter & Jelly Bread? We can assure you, that will be a keeper in your recipe repertoire for kids of all ages. Little people usually do not like whole grain breads. And that's okay because they primarily eat breads for the complex carbohydrates to give them energy. But if it's fiber you would like them to have, try the Light Wheat Bread or the Buttermilk Oatmeal Bread. Both of these breads offer fiber and yet feel soft in the mouth.

Whether you are a child or a grown-up, you'll find Buttermilk Oatmeal Bread also makes a wonderful breakfast toast. What a healthy way to start a morning — orange juice, an egg or bowl of cereal, and a toasted slice of Buttermilk Oatmeal Bread. Or for a healthy adult breakfast "on the run," try the Five-Grain Bread toasted and spread with a bit of light cream cheese. If you're a muffin stuffer, you'll want to experiment with the muffin mix breads. By using your favorite muffin mix you can make wonderful breakfast breads. Another idea, perhaps best saved for a weekend morning, is French toast made with the leftover Egg Bread.

That is if you can ever have any leftover Egg Bread. Besides serving it with a variety of entrees, you'll also find it is delicious as a sandwich bread. Or, you can make a great sandwich for salami, meatloaf, or other sandwich meat with Beer Rye Bread. Some people like to slice Focaccia to use for sandwiches; it works but we usually serve it by breaking off pieces to accompany soups or salads. We've also included the recipe and directions for Bread Bowls that are popular for serving soups and salads.

If you like to sop your soup or stew, here are some other suggestions: Mushroom Onion, Spaghetti Bread, Chili Bread, and Onion Dill Bread.

We like Onion Dill Bread because it is so versatile. The taste goes well with soups, salads, casseroles, and so on, and it serves as an excellent base bread for small party sandwiches. Also, we often use a variety of quick breads as hors d'oeuvres for a cocktail party, or a bridal or baby shower.

Are you taking bread from your bread machine with you to your workplace to share with fellow employees? You will want to look through the two chapters of quick bread recipes. We are confident that any of them would be a hit. In fact, because they are so quick and easy to make, you'd better take more than one at a time.

Quick breads are also great as desserts. For example, you will find a slice of Pumpkin or Orange Date bread and a dish of canned fruit make a light yet satisfying closure to an evening meal. And for special days, we have included two chapters of Holiday and Ethnic Breads. It is our intent to inspire you to keep your bread machine a hummin' and you and yours enjoyin' the best bread you ever ate.

Part II

Getting the Best Results from Your Bread Machine

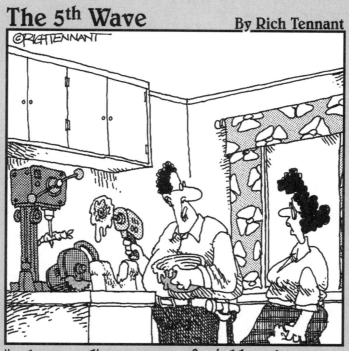

The 5th Wave   By Rich Tennant

"...because I'm more comfortable using my own tools. Now-how much longer do you want me to sand the cake batter?"

In this part . . .

We provide all of the in-depth ingredient information you'll ever need to know. Plus we tell you everything there is to know about your bread machine — how it works and what the bells and whistles are for. We also include how-to measure tips, and explain why you need to test the liquid temperature, how to bake the bread in the oven if you choose to create an interesting shape, and, of course, how to keep it fresh since there might even be some left over.

Chapter 3

Flours for Breads

• •

In This Chapter

▶ Understanding the different wheat flours

▶ Learning the value of other grains

▶ Using alternative flours

▶ Storing flour

• •

*F*lour: a finely ground meal made from wheat, cereal grains, or edible seeds.

Ah, the miracle of flour from the kernel of wheat. When you think about it, it's amazing to get something so light and fluffy from hard kernels of wheat. Yes, you say, I know wheat is ground into flour, but so many terms are used — bleached, unbleached, all-purpose, whole wheat, buckwheat, self-rising, cake flour. What do they all mean? In this chapter, we put meaning into these words used to describe the different flours used in making breads. We tell you which work the best in your bread machine and why; which add nutritional value to your loaves and why; and which to use only in minimal amounts and why.

We also talk about buckwheat, which gets lifted right out of that list of wheat-based products and lands in a completely different category under the other grains like spelt, rye, and oatmeal. Although not the major players among the flours used in breads, they do contribute significantly to flavor and texture.

Another whole category of flours exists, not milled from the common grains most usually associated with breads. These flours hold a very important place in bread machine baking because of the number of people whose bodies cannot tolerate wheat, oats, barley, or rye in their diet. The automatic bread machine opens up the wonderful possibility of delicious breads for those who need to keep to a rigid diet without the common grains. We have included them in this chapter, as well as recipes in Chapter 18, because this bread machine book would not be complete without that information.

From Golden Wheat to Flours

Who hasn't seen a field of golden wheat blowing on the plain, either in real life or in a picture? Evoking prosperity and goodness, this image has even been an inspiration for patriotic songs. Such a simple yet complex gift from the soil to humanity, wheat can nourish entire nations.

The whole, unprocessed kernel of wheat, called a *wheat berry,* has three parts:

- **Bran:** The protective outer coating or skin of the wheat kernel. It's insoluble fiber, meaning it does not dissolve in liquid. Bran is not present in white flour. Many people sprinkle wheat bran on their morning cereal, include it in casseroles, or add 1 or 2 tablespoons to their bread dough to add fiber in their diet.

- **Germ:** The embryo or sprouting section of the wheat seed, the germ contains the majority of the grain's vitamins. It too is removed when white flour is milled.

- **Endosperm:** The substance within the wheat seed that nourishes the embryo, the endosperm is primarily protein and starch. When the endosperm protein is mixed with liquid, it's called *gluten.* Gluten is what makes dough elastic, so that it becomes pliable when kneaded. Gluten also allows CO_2 bubbles created by fermenting yeast to develop a honeycomb of pockets in the dough, causing the dough to rise. Gluten is why wheat flour is almost always used in bread. Other flours can be added for flavor and texture, but wheat flour is normally in the largest proportion.

Wheat Flour Varieties

More than 30,000 varieties of wheat are grown in the United States. These varieties are categorized in six classes: hard red spring, hard red winter, soft red winter, hard white wheat, soft white wheat, and durum. Hard wheats are high in protein and are usually used for yeast breads. Soft wheats have low protein content and are excellent for tender foods like pastries, cakes, cookies, muffins, and so on. The hardest wheat, durum, is used for pastas.

All-purpose bleached or unbleached flour

If you cook at all, chances are you have all-purpose flour in your kitchen or pantry. All-purpose flour is white flour milled from the endosperm of the wheat berry. Both the bran and germ have been removed. Of all the flours available, all-purpose flour has the greatest variety of uses. It's used to make cakes, muffins, pie dough, cookies, cream sauces, gravy, quick breads, and yeast breads.

A bite of English history

In English law the Assize of Bread, in 1266, provided that fine-ground wheat bread (white bread) was for royalty and the clergy. Bread made of whole wheat and part white flour was for the middle class, and breads containing all of the bran were for "all inferior types of people."

While you can use all-purpose flour in your machine, it usually does not have enough protein to make the gluten needed to get dough to stretch when kneaded in a bread machine. This makes for undersized loaves. Therefore, we don't recommend using it. If you are using all-purpose flour in your bread machine and getting small loaves, switch to bread flour the next time you make bread.

Bleached flour is chemically whitened, usually with a chlorine gas or benzoyl peroxide. It is thought that bleaching flour strengthens the protein and gives it a longer shelf life. Bleached flour is preferred by American bakers because of the esthetics associated with white bread. Unbleached flour, on the other hand, is creamier in color although it does whiten with age.

Bleaching flour does not change the flour's nutritional value or functional use. Whenever you hear the word *chemical,* it may be an alert word that sparks a watch-out, avoid, or do-not-use thought pattern. However, chemicals are part of food production and are not necessarily harmful to your health. In the chemical whitening of flour, the bleaching agent evaporates and no harmful chemical residues remain in the flour.

Self-rising flour

Never use self-rising flour in a bread machine. Milled from soft wheat, it has baking soda and salt added and is used for dumplings, biscuits, and pancakes. Even if you think you can use it by omitting the salt in the recipe, your bread will not turn out okay. Self-rising flour doesn't withstand the rigorous mixing or kneading of the bread machine, and the bread will not rise well. Don't disappoint yourself unnecessarily.

Cake and pastry flours

Made from soft wheat, cake or pastry flour is very low in protein and is ideal for making flaky pastries and light-as-air cakes. Do not use it to make bread, however, as it produces too little gluten.

Bread flour

Bread flour is milled from hard wheat and produces the largest loaves of any flour, because it has a high amount of protein. Protein becomes gluten and forms an interlocking network of elastic strands that trap the gases produced by yeast, causing the dough to rise. As the dough is kneaded in your bread machine, the gluten network increases and strengthens. You can easily find bread flour in supermarkets, specialty stores, and ingredient catalogs.

Whole-wheat flour

As the name implies, flour producers use the entire wheat berry to make whole-wheat flour. When you make breads with whole-wheat flour, you will find them to be shorter and denser than breads made with bread flour. This may be true for two reasons:

- The whole-wheat flour may not be from a hard wheat, so the protein content is low and not enough gluten is produced.

- The bran and germ in whole-wheat flour make it more difficult for the elastic network to develop.

If you use whole-wheat flour, the dough in the bread machine may look too wet at first. This happens because the bran in the flour resists absorbing the liquid. Therefore, it takes longer for the whole-wheat flour to absorb the moisture than it does for bread flour. Be sure to check the dough in your bread machine after about five minutes of kneading. If the dough is still too wet, add more flour, 1 tablespoon at a time. However, if the dough is quite dry looking, add more liquid, 1 tablespoon at a time.

You can make 100 percent whole-wheat bread in almost every bread machine, but most recipes use a combination of whole-wheat flour and bread flour. Blending these flours makes the texture softer and the bread more palatable, while at the same time providing the fiber and flavor of the entire wheat berry. The whole-wheat flour found in most supermarkets is only of average quality for making bread. For you purists, purchase whole-wheat flour especially milled for bread making. It is available in some specialty food stores or mail-order catalogs. Also, there is a blend of whole-wheat and white flour on the market, which works beautifully in your bread machine.

White whole-wheat flour

This is a fairly new flour, milled from a new variety of hard winter-white wheat grown in Kansas. It has the same nutrient value as other whole-wheat flour but is milder and sweeter in flavor and lighter in color than flour obtained from hard red wheat. You may use it in any of our recipes that call for whole-wheat flour. We think it performs very well in a bread machine, either on its own or mixed with bread flour.

Wheat germ

The germ is the embryo of the wheat kernel and is milled out of white flours. When it is added to bread, it provides fiber and gives a slightly nutty flavor. Wheat germ tastes better lightly roasted than raw. Usually, wheat germ is in the cereal aisle at the grocery store, but we have also found it with the dietetic health foods. After you open a jar of wheat germ, be sure to refrigerate it, as it will go rancid quite easily because of its high fat content.

Rancidity is the result of a chemical change in fat caused by exposure to air and age. Rancid fat has an unpleasant odor and taste. Whole grain flours, wheat germ, and wheat bran are susceptible to rancidity because of their natural oils. If you are in doubt as to whether your flour is rancid, wet your finger and touch the flour. A bit will stick. Taste this flour. If it's bitter, your flour is rancid and should be discarded. ***Note:*** Refrigeration prevents rancidity.

Wheat bran

Wheat bran is the outer layer of the wheat kernel. Like wheat germ, it is milled out of white flours. You can add it to bread dough in very small amounts to increase the amount of fiber. Do not confuse wheat bran with bran breakfast cereal, as they are not the same. Wheat bran is a very small, thin flake. We usually find it in the dietetic health food section at the supermarket. Although wheat bran does not contain the amount of oil wheat germ does, it should still be stored in the refrigerator.

Vital wheat gluten

Millers are actually able to use white flour from hard wheat, remove the starch, and leave only the protein. They call this product *vital wheat gluten* (some call it *wheat gluten* or even just *gluten*). When you add it to bread, the dough becomes more elastic and expands easier. Although it is not absolutely necessary, vital wheat gluten definitely contributes to a higher volume and better texture in whole-wheat breads. We recommend 1 teaspoon for each cup of whole-wheat flour.

Do not confuse gluten flour with vital wheat gluten. Gluten flour is usually about 50 percent gluten and 50 percent starch. Professional bakers use it for bread, mixing it with low-protein flour. When we experimented with gluten flour in a bread machine, the bread was tough, so don't use it. See Table 3-1 for information on the protein content of different types of flour, and remember that adding vital wheat gluten can increase the amount of protein.

You can add vital wheat gluten to all-purpose flour as a substitute for bread flour. It increases the protein content and contributes to a higher volume than you would get by using only all-purpose flour. Directions for how much to use are on the vital wheat gluten package. We have found that 1 teaspoon per cup of all-purpose flour is adequate.

Table 3-1	Protein Content of Flours
Type of Flour	*Protein Content*
All-purpose national brands	10–11%
All-purpose Southern brands	2–6%
Bread flour	11–12%
Semolina flour	12.3% and up
Cake flour	7–9%
Pastry flour	8–9%

Flours from Other Grains

Wheat isn't the only grain that's used to make flour. Some other bread flours that you've probably heard of follow.

Rye flour

Rye is grown primarily in northern Europe, often in conjunction with wheat. It is considered an inferior grain compared to wheat because it is harder to grow and has a lower gluten content. Just as France has white, fat-free, crusty breads, Russia and Poland traditionally serve heavy, dark rye breads. However, French bakers sometimes add small amounts of rye flour to their white breads. You may want to try this technique, because rye flour ferments easily. This means it increases the yeast activity in the bread and enhances the texture by strengthening the dough's honeycomb-like structure. A small amount of rye flour can also help to reduce the incidence of wrinkled tops that sometimes occur in bread machines. We recommend 2 teaspoons of rye flour per cup of bread flour or whole-wheat flour.

Did you know that your favorite rye bread is made primarily with wheat flour? That's right. Although rye flour has protein, it does not become elastic when kneaded. Therefore, it does not form an expandable structure in bread dough. So without wheat flour in the recipe, the loaf would rise very little. Rye flour does contribute some to the flavor of the bread, but most of the flavor we associate with rye bread comes from spices such as caraway, fennel, or anise.

Medium rye

Several grinds of rye flour exist; the most common found in supermarkets is medium rye. The color is very light gray. In a bread machine, the ratio of rye flour to bread flour is never more than 1:2 (1 cup of rye flour to 2 cups of bread flour).

Pumpernickel rye

The same ratio of rye to bread flour holds true for pumpernickel rye flour. However, pumpernickel rye flour is much coarser because it is ground from the whole kernel. Therefore, a loaf of pumpernickel bread is shorter and denser than one made with medium rye flour.

Semolina flour

Italians love to use semolina flour to make pasta and noodles. It looks coarser than bread flour and has a yellowish cast. Although semolina flour is milled from the hardest wheat, known as durum wheat, it does not have the type of protein that becomes elastic when kneaded. Therefore, semolina flour can be used only in combination with bread flour in a bread machine. It makes the loaves golden brown and adds a nutty flavor to the bread.

Oatmeal

Although oatmeal contains gluten, it does not become elastic when it's kneaded. So, oatmeal is always used in bread as an add-on. Put just a bit of dry oatmeal (1 or 2 tablespoons will do) in a whole-wheat dough and it will make the bread taste a bit sweeter with a mellow richness. If you ever have leftover oatmeal cereal, save it and use it in your next bread. You'll love the bread; it will be higher and lighter because of the cooked oatmeal. Be sure to deduct some of the liquid in the recipe because the cooked cereal contains liquid. For example, if you have about ½ cup leftover cooked oatmeal, deduct about ¼ cup from the liquid amount called for in the recipe. Check the dough for consistency after your bread machine has been kneading for about five minutes. The dough should be in one slightly tacky ball, not stiff. You may have to add more liquid if it appears dry. If it seems too wet, add flour, one tablespoon at a time until the dough has the right degree of firmness.

When a recipe calls for oatmeal, it doesn't matter whether you use instant oatmeal or the old-fashioned rolled oats, and remember, it doesn't mean cooked unless it says cooked.

Buckwheat

The name buckwheat is misleading because buckwheat is not a wheat product. Wheat, corn, rice, and rye are in the grass plant family, whereas buckwheat is related to the rhubarb family — go figure. Buckwheat seeds are ground into flour and commonly used in pancakes. Buckwheat flour has a strong flavor; used in small quantities, it gives a pleasant twist to bread.

Spelt

Spelt, a grain mentioned in the Bible, has gained popularity because it can be grown without the use of chemical herbicides or pesticides. An ancestor of modern hybrid wheat, it has a good gluten content and is well suited for making yeast breads. You can use spelt as a substitute for whole-wheat flour in any bread recipe.

Whole-grain flours turn rancid over a short period of time. Keep all flours fresh by storing them in the refrigerator or freezer. Be sure to use airtight containers. If you use heavy, plastic, self-sealing freezer bags, the flour will not clump. Measure the amount you need and allow it to come to room temperature before making bread. If you're in a hurry, use the automatic defrost on your microwave.

Alternative Flours without Gluten

Many alternative grains exist that you may want to try in your bread machine. We can guarantee a unique tasting experience, and you may find a new favorite. One thing these flours have in common is there is no gluten. Many supermarkets have these flours in their dietetic health food section. They are also available at health food stores.

If you have been reading through this book, you are probably wondering how these doughs expand without gluten. The answer is xanthan gum, a bonding agent that also becomes elastic and holds the ingredients together.

When we make yeast breads with alternative flours, their textures are closer to quick breads than yeast breads. However, the pizza crust is very close to pizza crust made with all-purpose flour.

The most common need for alternative flours comes with the diagnosis of Celiac Sprue Disease. It is a chronic digestive disorder caused by a toxic reaction to the gluten found in all forms of wheat, rye, oats, and barley. The only treatment is a lifelong dietary restriction of living without those grains. You can make delicious gluten-free breads in a bread machine by using combinations of the following alternative flours and ingredients. The recipes using these flours are in Chapter 18. You won't want to overlook them.

- **Rice flour:** When wheat, oats, barley, and rye have to be eliminated from the diet, rice flour is the most common flour used. Like white flour made from wheat, rice flour does not contain the outer layer (the bran) of the rice kernel. Don't confuse rice flour with sweet rice flour, which is primarily used for thickening.

- **Brown rice flour:** As the name implies, brown rice flour is milled from the whole rice kernel, as whole-wheat flour is milled from the whole wheat berry.

- **Potato starch or potato starch flour:** This is made from the starch in potatoes. Do not confuse this product with potato flour, which is used primarily for thickening.

- **Tapioca flour:** This extremely fine flour comes from the roots of the cassava plant and is used in combination with rice flours and/or potato flour.

- **Soy flour:** Although soy flour is very nutritious, it's also quite heavy and can be used only in small amounts in gluten-free breads.

- **Bean flours:** You can find many bean flours, which provide nutrients as well as good flavor to otherwise bland-tasting breads.

- **Xanthan gum:** Because alternative flours do not have the protein to create the gluten to hold moisture and support the structure of bread, xanthan gum is needed. In food science terminology, xanthan gum is known as a *structure builder* and a *binding agent*. Xanthan gum works great for gluten-free breads in a bread machine. We've tried other ingredients like gelatin, but they don't work nearly as well. Guar gum is equal to xanthan gum but sometimes has a laxative effect, so we do not recommend using it.

  Some health food stores carry xanthan gum. Our most reliable source has been to mail-order it through Ener-G Foods in Seattle, Washington. It has a toll-free number, 1-800-331-5222.

A gluten-free experience

Several years ago, when bread machines had been in the United States for approximately two years, Glenna had the opportunity to attend a Celiac Sprue seminar aboard a cruise ship. It was certainly a rare occasion for her as well as for the Celiacs who were attending. Eliminating all forms of wheat, rye, oats, and barley from the diet can be socially debilitating. Not only do Celiacs have to avoid wheat-based bread, but also those cereal proteins that are often hidden in foods one would not even think to ask about. Eating out is difficult; a vacation cruise is almost unheard of.

However, the Celiac support group in Orlando, Florida, made the arrangements with a cruise line to have gluten-free meals and snack foods for the entire trip. Glenna went to learn about the disease and to learn about the ingredients used to make gluten-free breads. Several of the Celiacs knew how to make gluten-free breads in bread machines.

Glenna has worked through Red Star Yeast to develop gluten-free bread recipes for the bread machine, and several are available upon request. We have included some new recipes in this book because we feel strongly that no one should have to go without good bread. Bread machines make it so easy.

For more gluten-free recipes than what we've provided in Chapter 18, contact Red Star Yeast at 1-800-423-5422.

Storing Flour

You can keep all-purpose, self-rising, and bread flour for six months to a year if you store them in airtight containers in a cool, dry place to preserve moisture, freshness, and baking quality. Do not store near heat. If you do not keep them in airtight containers, the relative humidity of the air will affect the flour's moisture content. In humid conditions, the flour absorbs moisture; in arid conditions with low humidity or high temperature, the flour loses some of its natural moisture.

Store whole-grain flours in airtight containers in the refrigerator or freezer. Whole grains contain oils that can turn rancid if not refrigerated. You can safely freeze whole-grain flours for a year. Be sure to freeze them in moisture-proof and vapor-proof containers designed for freezer use. We use heavy, self-sealing freezer bags.

Allow flours to come to room temperature before placing them in your bread pan. Because the yeast needs a warm, moist dough to be active, cold flours make the yeast perform sluggishly, and your dough will not rise adequately.

If you're in a hurry and you have cold flour, try microwaving it by using the Automatic Defrost setting. Measure the amount you need, cover it with wax paper, and microwave for a few minutes; then stir the flour and continue to microwave. Repeat this process until the flour has the chill out of it but is not hot. Stirring the flour helps to eliminate hot spots.

Chapter 4

The Miracle of Yeast

*I*n this chapter, we tell you everything you ever wanted to know about yeast — and why it's important to be knowledgeable regarding different types of yeast. We talk about how to decide which yeast to use; whether the yeast should be active dry yeast, fast-acting yeast, or bread machine yeast; how much yeast to use; how to store it; what factors affect its ability to ferment; and how to tell whether it is still active. We even talk about other agents that make bread rise: baking soda and baking powder.

A Feast of Yeast Facts

Even though yeast cells exist all around us, you need a microscope to see them. Yeast is a tiny plant organism with only one cell, about the size of a human red blood cell. It may be hard for you to believe that this microorganism actually causes bread dough to rise, but it's true. Yeast breaks down sugar into carbon dioxide gas. In bread dough, the gases form bubbles, which honeycomb the mass of dough and puff it out until it rises.

Louis Pasteur, the father of modern microbiology, discovered how yeast works and labeled this natural process fermentation; it happens when vintners make wine, when brewers make beer, and when you make bread in your bread machine.

Yeast reproduction

Did you know that yeast is both asexual and bisexual? That's right. Those little one-celled plants (fungi) will divide and multiply or get together, so to speak, and multiply. They aren't fussy as long as they have food (sugar to ferment), are warm and moist and have plenty of oxygen. Their reproduction is called *budding,* a process in which a protrusion grows out the side of the cell wall and then breaks off to form a separate daughter cell. Under ideal conditions, the yeast cell reproduces every two to three hours. In the manufacturing of yeast, they are fed molasses and nutrional supplements and given plenty of oxygen through an ariation process.

Sometimes people ask if they can use baker's yeast to make wine. We explain that baker's yeast will ferment their fruit, but they may not end up with the flavor they had anticipated. Scientists have discovered that some strains of yeast enhance the flavor of fruits during the fermentation process much better than the active dry yeast normally used to make bread. And we don't recommend using yeast intended for winemaking in your bread machine!

We've heard people say, "Oh, yeast is yeast — it's all pretty much the same." This just isn't true; the only sameness about it is the basic fermentation action. Scientists have actually "fingerprinted" various yeast strains and categorized them so that vintners will be able to select a particular strain of yeast to produce the desired wine flavor from their fruit. The yeasts used to make bread haven't yet been categorized as minutely as those used for wines, but it's only a matter of time.

Another question we often get is whether one can eat fresh yeast for nutritional purposes. We've heard it said that during the cold winter months, miners in the northern Midwestern states would take approximately an ounce of fresh yeast in their lunch box to prevent them from catching a cold. Today, no dietician or food scientist would recommend eating fresh yeast, as it would cause gastrointestinal distress. But it's true that yeast is very high in the B vitamins. That's why people use brewer's yeast as a nutritional supplement.

Some brewer's yeast is a byproduct of the brewing industry. After five to ten beer fermentations, the yeast loses its vitality and is no longer acceptable for making beer. It's then dried and sold as brewer's yeast, a nutritional food. Over the years, the term has become generic, and baker's yeast is often sold as brewer's yeast. The processing and drying of this yeast is carefully controlled so that it's biochemically uniform and remains inactive; the life enzymes that ferment sugar are dead, but the nutritional value remains. This "brewer's yeast" provides valuable amounts of B complex vitamins and protein when taken as a nutritional supplement. It has a naturally pleasant, toasted, nutty flavor as compared to the bitter aftertaste of the brewer's yeast that is a byproduct of the brewing industry.

Inactive dry yeast is used in animal feed formulations as well. Biochemists and food scientists have also discovered that yeast enhances food flavors. Inactive yeast is used in seasoning many food products, such as cheese-flavored popcorn, canned soups, and even ice creams. If you're into reading labels for ingredient contents, you often see yeast as an ingredient. Unless you're reading the label of a bakery product, the yeast is being used as a flavor enhancer.

Now that we've given you enough yeast information so you will get a blue ribbon for your science fair yeast project, the next few pages provide you with practical, bread-related yeast information.

The Types of Yeast You Can Use for Bread

Yeast is a *leavening agent*. A leavening agent puts air into a mixture, thereby increasing its volume. In baking, the leavening action may be produced by chemical or biological means.

We like to think of yeast as similar to the seeds we plant in the garden. We plant seeds in warm, moist soil and they sprout and grow. Both yeast and seeds need food and warmth. While seeds flourish on soil and sunlight, yeast thrives on sugar and warmth. Seeds eventually produce more seeds, and yeast cells reproduce to form more yeast cells.

Compressed yeast (cake yeast)

Every now and then, a consumer will want to know, "Can I use cake yeast in my bread machine?" The answer is yes — just crumble it on the top of the flour like you would sprinkle on the dry yeast. Cake yeast, or compressed yeast (the terms are used interchangeably), is still available in some sections of the country. It's fresh yeast that has not been dried and therefore contains 70 percent moisture.

Cake yeast is sold in small cakes in the dairy section of the supermarket. Unlike squares of chocolate, which have been standardized in size (a square of chocolate is equal to 1 ounce of chocolate, no matter what the brand name), cakes of yeast are not all the same size. The common weights are 0.6-ounce, 2-ounce, and 8-ounce.

To determine the amount of cake yeast you need from an active dry yeast amount in your recipe, use the following conversions:

- ¼-ounce of active dry yeast equals ⅔-ounce of cake yeast
- 2¼ teaspoons of active dry yeast equals ⅔-ounce of cake yeast
- 3 packages of active dry yeast weighing ¼ ounce each equal 2 ounces of cake yeast

Active dry yeast

Active dry yeast is processed one step further than compressed yeast. It is extruded into noodle form, loaded onto a conveyor belt, and passed through a series of drying chambers where warm air is blown through the yeast. The yeast emerges with moisture content of about 8 percent, as compared to the 70 percent moisture in compressed yeast. Due to the low moisture content, the yeast is in a semi-dormant state. Therefore, it has a longer shelf life with little effect on its baking activity. It's highly stable and known for its consistent performance.

We use active dry yeast in all our recipes except those designed for the one-hour cycle.

Active dry yeast is the most common form of yeast available. It's granular in form because it has been dried at controlled temperatures and then ground. You find it in the baking aisle at your grocer in either 4-ounce jars or strips of ¼-ounce packages. Each ¼-ounce package contains approximately 2¼ teaspoons of yeast. Because yeast loses potency when exposed to oxygen, moisture, or warmth, both the jars and the packages have been nitrogen flushed and sealed.

Active dry yeast is available in warehouse clubs and restaurant supply houses in large 1- and 2-pound foil-lined packages that are vacuum-sealed. Unopened packages may be kept at room temperature, but be careful not to keep them next to the oven.

After opening a package of yeast, you may keep it in the refrigerator or freeze it. The yeast should be good for about six weeks if kept tightly closed and refrigerated. In the freezer, it will stay active for approximately six months.

World War II expanded the development of yeast

The industrial production of baker's yeast first began in Europe about 150 years ago. During World War II, the United States government prompted Fleischmann Laboratories and Red Star Yeast & Products to develop a stable yeast product that could be readily transported and stored so the armed forces could enjoy fresh bread. The government needed a dry yeast that did not require refrigeration and required only rehydration with warm water prior to being used in bread dough. The active dry yeast that we use today is the result of this wartime innovation.

Fast-rising yeast

As bakery production became automated, an incentive to develop fast-acting yeast existed. In the early 1980s, yeast companies began offering instant yeast to bakeries. Fast-acting yeast also showed up on the shelves of the local grocery store. As the yeast names (Quick Rise, Rapid Rise, Instant) imply, fast-acting yeast shortens the rising time for dough.

Although bread machine owners aren't necessarily concerned about the length of rising time, you can use fast-acting yeast in your bread machine. If you are substituting a fast-acting yeast for active dry yeast in a bread machine recipe, use less. A general rule is to use ½ teaspoon of fast-acting yeast per cup of flour. However, it's best to check the yeast label for the manufacturer's recommendation. If you're in doubt, call the customer-service hot line written on the packaging or check the manufacturer's Web site.

Fast-acting yeast is a must for one-hour cycles; use 1 teaspoon per cup of flour.

Like active dry yeast, fast-rising yeast is sold in grocery stores in ¼-ounce packages and 4-ounce jars. It's also available in 1-pound vacuum packages. The larger package is marketed for the food industry, but buy it if you can find it. After opening, freeze the yeast in the original bag. These bags are lined with foil and are not porous, so the yeast will stay fresh for at least six months. Still too much yeast for you and your family? How about sharing with a friend?

Bread machine yeast

Bread machine yeast is also available. It's a fast-acting yeast with ascorbic acid added. The ascorbic acid acts as a dough conditioner; therefore, the dough stretches much more easily. We have found that ½ teaspoon of bread machine yeast per cup of flour works quite well. Because bread machine yeast is fast acting, it works well in the one-hour cycle.

But I didn't want flat bread!

When your bread doesn't rise, quite naturally you blame the yeast or the bread machine. But other factors can also adversely affect yeast activity.

In some areas, the source of the water supply changes depending on the availability of water. When the change occurs, bread machine owners see either a decrease or an increase in the size of their loaves. I know this happens in areas of Florida. If you live in an area like that, rely heavily on bottled water for your bread making.

In the Southwest, the water is often unusually hard. That hardness adversely affects yeast activity, as does very soft water. This is especially true if you have a water softener, which increases the salt in the water.

Then there's the case of winter dryness, especially in northern climates. Just as your home becomes drier when you use your heating system, so do your flours. Even when you store your flour in an airtight container, it can dry out. Remember to check the consistency of the dough while it kneads to see if it needs more moisture.

Altitude dryness also occurs. Flours are naturally drier at higher altitudes. Often, increasing the liquid amount in the recipe is the simple solution to using a bread machine at a high altitude. Start with the given amount, but open the lid after the dough has been kneading about five minutes to look at the dough. It will probably be quite dry, so begin adding liquid, one tablespoon at a time, to let it work into the dough. Continue adding until the dough ball is soft and a bit tacky. Count your added tablespoons to give you a good idea of how much more liquid you will usually need in your recipes.

If you're in a very warm, moist climate, like the Gulf of Mexico area during the summer, you have to cool the water you use in your bread-machine recipe to as low as 40°. Yeast, like humans, is very sluggish in temperatures over 100°. So you have to begin with very cool water so that the dough doesn't get too warm. And you have to decrease the amount of water because the flour will have acquired moisture from the environment and will not be able to absorb all the liquid called for in the recipe.

Testing Yeast

When you purchase yeast, pay attention to the expiration date on the package. However, if you're in doubt about the activity of your yeast, you can check by using this easy activity test provided by Red Star Yeast & Products. It's called *proofing* the yeast.

In a 1-cup liquid measuring cup, pour ½-cup warm water. For accuracy, use a kitchen thermometer. The temperature should register 110° to 115°. Stir in 1 teaspoon of sugar and 2¼ teaspoons of yeast (the amount of yeast in one ¼-ounce package). Let set for approximately ten minutes. In that length of time, the yeast should have fermented the sugar and produced foam (carbon dioxide bubbles) that have grown to the 1-cup level. If this happens, the yeast is quite active, and you may use it in your bread machine. Pour it into your bread pan and add the other ingredients.

Be sure to decrease your liquid ingredients to adjust for the ½-cup water that you used to test the yeast.

Other Leavening Agents

While yeast activity is a biological happening that produces gases to expand dough, there are also chemicals that will react in a dough system to produce gases and expand the dough. You can use chemicals, either in conjunction with yeast or in place of it, to cause dough to rise. Here are just a couple:

- **Baking soda:** Baking soda is one of the main chemical leavening agents used in baking. You have to have a wet ingredient that is acidic, such as buttermilk, sour cream, or molasses, to activate the baking soda. As soon as baking soda combines with an ingredient like buttermilk, it starts producing carbon dioxide bubbles. The leavening action increases considerably when the dough is heated, so the greatest rise comes when it begins to bake.

  If you have a Quick Bread cycle on your machine, you'll want to try our Irish Soda Bread recipe (see Chapter 16).

- **Baking powder:** You may already have baking powder in your cupboard, as it's the most common chemical leavener for home bakers. Baking powder has a double-acting reaction because its leavening agents produce carbon dioxide twice. The initial reaction occurs at room temperature when the baking powder is mixed with liquids, and the most volatile action occurs as the batter is heated and a huge amount of carbon dioxide bubbles are created.

If you have a Quick Bread cycle on your machine, you use baking powder instead of yeast. Because the chemistry of baking powder reacts instantly with liquid and then again with heat, the development time of the dough is much shorter. The dry ingredients get moistened and mixed only shortly before the bread machine begins heating to bake the bread.

Chapter 5

Liquids: The Ingredients That Make It All Come Together

• •

In This Chapter

▶ Making sure your dough has the right moisture

▶ Evaluating water and milk

▶ Adding eggs for tenderness

▶ Assessing liquid substitutions

• •

*I*t doesn't take a rocket scientist (or a food scientist) to know that everything changes when you add liquid to dry ingredients. In bread dough, the dry ingredients get moistened, the yeast dissolves, and the formation of gluten is stimulated. In this chapter, we'll give you the lowdown on all the yummy liquid possibilities, but remember: It's the degree of moistness that's crucial. In fact, it's the key to making good bread in a bread machine. If there's too much liquid, the dry ingredients don't get moistened, they get soaked. The growth of gluten is stimulated, but to a point where the dough will not hold a structure when it's baked. On the other hand, if there is not enough liquid, the bread won't rise as the gluten won't develop enough elasticity to stretch.

Doh! Avoiding Moisture Mistakes

Even though recipes are honed to perfection, there always remains the variable of the flour's absorption quality. In other words, how much liquid will the flour absorb and still be able to maintain a honeycomb structure when baked? This is where you will want the quality control dough-consistency test. If it takes five minutes to assemble the ingredients in the pan, why not take another five to be sure your dough has the correct balance between wet and dry ingredients? Doing so will make all the difference between a small, dinky loaf (too dry), or a nice size loaf with a beautifully rounded top (right balance), or a flat-topped loaf (too wet), or a loaf that has a sunken, concave top (much too wet).

Dough consistency test: You can tell if there is a good balance between the liquid and the dry ingredients just by looking at the dough during the first kneading time. And yes, you can open the lid and look at the dough; opening the lid does not interfere with the dough's development.

- ✔ Check the dough about five minutes after the machine starts kneading; the dough should be a soft, slightly tacky ball.

- ✔ Go ahead, touch the dough.

- ✔ Just a tab bit should come off on your finger. If the dough is too wet, it will still be clinging to the sides of the pan. You need to add more flour, one tablespoon at a time. Let that flour work into the dough, and if that doesn't help the dough come off the sides and into a ball, keep adding flour, one tablespoon at a time, until it does.

- ✔ On the other hand, you may need to add water, one tablespoon at a time, if the dough is too dry. (If the dough is in small clumps or it's in a ball, but the ball's stiff or not tacky, it's too dry.)

Your choice of liquid will affect the flavor and texture of the bread. Water, the most common liquid used in bread dough, brings out the flavor of grains and creates a crisp crust. You can also use a vegetable water, like potato water for example, and the bread will be sweeter than if you had just used plain water. (Potato water is the water left in the pot when you're done boiling potatoes.) Milk and milk products like yogurt, cottage cheese, or sour cream are common in breads and make the texture finer and more velvety and the crusts quite chewy. Buttermilk gives a characteristic sour taste and beer is sometimes used for a tangy, sourdough-like taste. And don't forget that eggs are a liquid, too.

Water

No matter where you go the drinking water will taste different and for all sorts of reasons. Although water appears to be a rather simple substance, it can be highly complex, with many unique properties depending on its source. Fresh water is generally divided into two broad categories, *surface water* and *ground water*. The source of surface water could be rain or snow or it could come from rivers, streams, or lakes. Ground water is obtained from springs, shallow and deep wells, or is water reclaimed by removing the salt minerals from seawater.

Whether water comes from the surface or the ground has a major impact on its character. Surface waters usually have higher levels of organic, chemical, and microbial contaminants than ground waters. In urban areas you can count on the surface water being chemically treated for your safety. Rural areas with wells (a source of ground water) have water that is rich in mineral substances. We call this water *hard water*. Hardness in water is attributable almost totally to the presence of calcium and magnesium. *Soft water* has almost no calcium and magnesium, and many people have water softeners to counteract the mineral content. If your water is ground water, here are some things to keep in mind:

- In the Southwest, primarily Arizona and New Mexico the water is quite hard.

- Other areas known to have hard water are the states of North and South Dakota, Nebraska, Kansas, Iowa, Illinois, and Indiana.

- The southern states of Mississippi, Alabama, Georgia, Virginia, and North and South Carolina have very soft water.

- In some areas, like Florida, the source of the water supply changes during certain seasons of the year so the range varies from slightly hard to somewhat soft water.

Why should you care? Because water characteristics dramatically affect yeast activity. A water of medium hardness is considered most suitable for baking bread because some of the minerals in it have a strengthening effect on the gluten of the dough. Excessively hard waters are undesirable because they slow fermentation by tightening the gluten structure too much, so the dough is unable to stretch easily. Soft waters are objectionable because they lack gluten-strengthening minerals and, as such, tend to yield soft, sticky doughs. Waters softened with water softeners will inhibit or slow down yeast activity. Both too hard and too soft water, as well as water high in fluoride and chlorine, will result in short stubby loaves. If you suspect you have a water problem, try substituting bottled water or milk. If you get better results, you can bet that the local water is causing your problem.

Milk

In different parts of the world, milk from various animals is used for food. In the United States, however, the dairy cow produces almost all of the milk on the market. Therefore, when we use the term "milk" in *Bread Machines For Dummies* we mean cow's milk. This food is among the most perishable of all foods due to its excellent nutritive composition and its liquid form. Pasteurizing milk solved a multitude of health problems, as raw milk was a carrier of bacteria that caused gastroenteritis, tuberculosis, diphtheria and even typhoid, undulant fever, and scarlet fever. Progress in dairy technology and public health has resulted in milk that can be depended upon to be safe, nutritious, and a pleasing food, even though it may be produced hundreds or thousands of miles away from the point of consumption. Protecting the quality of milk is a responsibility shared by public health officials, the dairy industry and you, the consumer.

Keep your milk and milk products safe and fresh by following these precautions:

- ✔ Keep milk and milk products in containers that will protect them from exposure to bright daylight and strong fluorescent light. This will prevent a reduction in riboflavin, ascorbic acid, and vitamin B6 content as well as the development of an off flavor.

- ✔ Store milk in a refrigerator (40°F or less) as soon as possible after purchasing.

- ✔ Return milk to the refrigerator immediately after pouring to prevent bacterial growth.

- ✔ Keep the container closed to prevent undesirable odors and flavors from developing in the milk.

- ✔ Keep canned evaporated or sweetened condensed milk in a cool, dry place. Once opened, transfer any unused portion to a clean opaque container and refrigerate.

- ✔ Store dry milk in a cool, dry place and reseal the container after opening. Humidity causes dry milk to lump and may affect the flavor and color. If such changes occur, the milk should not be consumed. When the dry milk has been reconstituted (by mixing with water) it should be stored in an opaque, tightly covered container and refrigerated.

- ✔ Freezing milk and milk products does not influence their nutritional properties. However, when thawed they may be susceptible to the development of an oxidized flavor and not be entirely satisfactory. Some people will use them for cooking and baking with no noticeable detrimental effect. Our suggestion is to use them with caution. Be sure to taste the thawed product before using it in a bread dough. Any off-taste does not necessarily go away by mixing it with other ingredients and baking it.

- ✔ Do not use the delayed timer on your bread machine when any milk product is an ingredient in the recipe.

- ✔ It used to be that scalding milk was necessary to kill bacteria that might affect the yeast activity and to alter a protein in the milk that played havoc with the gluten structure in bread. However, pasteurization has protected us from harmful bacteria and has altered the proteins, so scalding milk is no longer necessary.

Milk in recipes

In general, adding milk to bread significantly increases its protein and mineral content. You'll love the subtle sweetness and the soft, delicate texture milk adds to bread. The crust will have a rich color and be oh, so very tender. And, there's one more benefit in adding milk to breads: The bread stays fresh longer. Much of these attributes come from lactose, the sugar in dairy products. Yeast does not ferment lactose. Therefore, when milk is used in bread, the lactose will make the bread taste sweet, and the crust will be a golden brown, because of the presence of unfermented sugar. The fat in milk, as well as the lactose, makes the texture of the bread and the crust softer. And to make this even better, you can use whole or reduced-fat milk — with equally good results.

If someone is lactose intolerant, replacing milk with water is the simplest solution. Of course, the texture of the bread will be different without milk. There are other substitutions available, such as soy-based formulas, where the bread texture is very similar to bread made with milk.

Kinds of milk

There are all kinds of milk, as a quick glance at any grocery-store refrigerator case will tell you. Most milk currently sold, including whole, lowfat, and skim is fortified with vitamin D at a level of 400 International Units (IU) per quart.

Here are the types of milk commonly available:

- **Whole milk:** In order for whole milk to be legally shipped in interstate commerce, it must be: (a) pasteurized, ultra-pasteurized, or UHT processed; (b) contain a minimum of 3.25% milkfat; and (c) contain 8.25% milk solids not fat.

- **Lowfat milk:** Some of the fat is removed and the milk is named according to the amount of fat remaining, such as 0.5%, 1.0%, 1.5%, or 2% milk. All must contain at least 8.25% milk solids not fat. Because vitamin A is removed with the milkfat, vitamin A is added to lowfat milk at a level of 2,000 IU per quart.

- **Skim milk:** As much fat is removed as is technologically possible in nonfat or skim milk. The fat content is therefore less than 0.5%. It must contain at least 8.25% solids not fat and must be fortified with 2,000 IU of vitamin A per quart.

- **Evaporated milk:** Sweet whole cow's milk is evaporated so that it contains not less than 7.5% by weight of milk fat and 25.5% of total milk solids. About 60% of the water is evaporated from whole milk under vacuum to reduce the volume by half. The resulting concentrate is homogenized, fortified with vitamin D (400 IU per pint), canned, and heat sterilized.

✔ **Evaporated skim milk:** Must contain less than 0.5% fat and a minimum of 20% total solids and be fortified with 2,000 units of vitamin A per quart. It is produced like evaporated milk and vitamin D is added.

✔ **Sweetened condensed milk:** Processed in the same way as evaporated milk except that sugar is added before the evaporation takes place and the heated mixture is cooled rapidly, with agitation. Sweetened condensed milk cannot be interchanged for evaporated milk in recipes because evaporated milk does not have sugar added.

Buttermilk, Yogurt, and Sour Cream

If your American ancestors were farmers, chances are pretty certain that your great-great-grandmother used buttermilk in her breads and other baking. Buttermilk, though it has no fat in it, originally came about as the by-product of churning cream into butter. Because our foremothers wasted nothing, they used the butter-flecked liquid in their recipes. The baked goods were so light and fluffy that buttermilk became a treasured ingredient.

Today, buttermilk, sour cream, and yogurt are each made with bacterial cultures, incubating until the desired level of lactose is turned into lactic acid. Buttermilk begins as skim milk; sour cream as cream; yogurt as skim milk, milk, and/or cream. The presence of lactic acid gives a more tender curd to the milk products; thus they produce a tender crumb in breads. Usually baking soda is added to the recipe to balance the acidity when buttermilk, sour cream or yogurt are used.

Although there is no true substitute for fresh buttermilk, adding 1 tablespoon of lemon juice or vinegar to 1 cup of milk is an acceptable pinch-hitter.

Because buttermilk is not a popular beverage, it may be helpful for you to know that it can be frozen. If it has separated when thawed, just give it a good shake, and it will go back together.

SACO Cultured Buttermilk Blend is a dry buttermilk powder that is handy to have on your pantry shelf when your recipe calls for buttermilk. It is packaged in a moisture-proof canister that has an easy-open pull top and a convenient, resealable plastic lid, and is sold in either the baking supply aisle or where other dry milk products are sold. There is a simple conversion table on the package; for 1 cup of buttermilk, use 4 tablespoons of dry buttermilk and 1 cup of water. To use in a bread recipe, you do not need to reconstitute the buttermilk. Simply measure the amount of water equal to the amount of fluid buttermilk stated in the recipe and pour into your bread pan. Then add the appropriate amount of dry buttermilk with the other dry ingredients.

Eggs

You won't have "egg on your face" or feel like you're "walking on egg shells" if you add an egg or two to your favorite bread recipe. Eggs can transform a ho-hum dinner roll into a fine, rich, delicate treat. Eggs add protein and make bread rise higher. A large egg should contain ¼-cup of liquid. Lately, however, we think the chickens are becoming stingy, because large eggs often measure less. If you encounter the same, then use extra-large. When you are feeling creative and want to add an egg to a recipe that doesn't call for one, be sure to deduct ¼-cup of some other liquid.

If you can't eat eggs, you can use liquid egg substitutes. Or, you can eliminate the eggs altogether and replace the liquid amount with water (¼-cup water for each egg). Of course, the texture will not be as the same, but the bread will still be very good.

The egg is one of nature's most nutritious, economical, and versatile foods. With proper care and handling, it poses no greater food safety risk than any other perishable food. Follow these important guidelines:

- ✔ Buy Grade AA or A eggs from refrigerated cases only. As soon as possible after purchase, refrigerate them again, in their cartons on a middle or lower shelf, not in the door where temperatures fluctuate widely.

- ✔ If possible, do not buy cartons of eggs where one or more are cracked. Do not use cracked eggs. If they are in your egg carton, discard them.

- ✔ When you are preparing to bake and need eggs at room temperature, place cold eggs in a bowl of very warm (not hot) water. This will remove the chill quickly and bring them to room temperature without the danger of prolonged exposure to room temperature.

- ✔ Wash your hands for at least 20 seconds before cracking eggs into clean utensils.

- ✔ Do not use the delay timer on the bread machine when eggs are an ingredient.

Juices, Purees, and Beer

For those of you who color outside the lines, use your creative nature, or think thoughts like, "Hmm, wonder how that would taste," we say, "Go for it. It will make for interesting eating, or at least, interesting conversation." Here's some information that will prevent unnecessary frustration.

If you decide to use vegetable waters to replace another liquid, ask yourself, "Is there salt in this vegetable water?" While it is true vegetable water, potato water for example, enhances flavor; the salt in the water will unbalance the recipe formula. The best solution: Don't salt the vegetables before boiling or steaming. Besides, it's better for the nutrient content of the vegetables, as salt pulls vitamins and minerals out of the vegetables and into the water.

Likewise, vegetable juices usually have salt added. This doesn't mean you have to give up and not add vegetable juices. It does mean, however, that you'll have to reduce the amount of salt given in the recipe. How much? You'll probably have to guess. Start by reducing the salt in the recipe by ½ teaspoon. For example, if the recipe uses 1½ teaspoons salt and you want to replace the water with a canned vegetable juice, use only 1 teaspoon salt. If the texture is coarse, or the top is flat or concave, there wasn't enough salt. If the loaf is short with a dense texture, there is still too much salt.

Fruit juices add sugar to the bread. Sometimes the amount of sugar isn't enough to make any significant difference, but if the loaf turns out short and dense, make a note to yourself. Next time reduce the sugar the recipe calls for by a tablespoon.

A recent trend is to replace the fat in a bread recipe with unsweetened fruit purees. Although we don't think this is necessary, it can be done. Here's how: Replace the fat with an equal amount of puree, and decrease the liquid in the recipe by the same amount. For example, say a recipe calls for 3 tablespoons of oil. You could omit the oil and use 3 tablespoons of unsweetened applesauce. You would also have to reduce the liquid amount by 3 tablespoons. Therefore, if the recipe has 1½ cups water, you would measure 1½ cups water. Then, with your measuring tablespoon you would remove 3 tablespoons of the water. Depending on what your tastes are, you can use this method to eliminate fat. We have not included any recipes calling for a puree in place of fat because we're not really satisfied with these breads. But some people think they're great, and you can use the above method with any of the bread recipes in this book.

One more optional liquid some people use is beer. Beer makes a smooth-textured bread and adds flavor. The added sugars and starch provided by the beer give the yeast a little something extra to feed on and cause the bread to rise a little higher. You won't get a buzz from the beer in bread; the alcohol evaporates as the bread bakes.

Chapter 6

Sugar 'n' Spice and All Things Nice

· ·

In This Chapter

▶ Sweetening for fermentation and flavor

▶ Salting for structure and seasoning

▶ Spicing things up

▶ Using herbs for extra flavor

▶ Adding fruits and nuts

· ·

*B*read is the warmest and kindest word in any language. It means life, hope, and comfort. Throughout literature one can find endless metaphors and analogies that use bread as their object of comparison. Because bread is regarded as necessary for sustaining life, you commonly hear of one's monetary means of support referred to as *my bread and butter*. The one who works and supports a family is regarded as the *bread winner*.

We not only sustain our life by including bread in our diet, we also enjoy abundant living when we discover the fabulous flavors that can enhance bread. When we delicately use sugars and spices, fruits and nuts, herbs and dried vegetables we can transform ordinary breads into delights of the palate — hallmarks of prosperity on our table.

Sugar and Other Sweeteners

Sugar furnishes food for the yeast, tenderizes the dough, promotes a good crust color, aids in the retention of moisture in the baked bread (thus prolonging freshness), and, of course, adds flavor. One can hardly eliminate sugar from bread and still say, "Umm, this bread is sooo good."

Unless, of course, it's French bread, which uses no sugar. That's right, there is no sugar in French bread. While it is true that as yeast ferments sugar, gases are formed that cause the bread to rise; it is also true that yeast will ferment the starch in flour. However, it takes a longer time for yeast to ferment the starch than it does for yeast to ferment sugar. That's why most bread machines have a French Bread cycle with a longer rising time. Also, the baking temperature is higher on a French Bread cycle because without sugar the crust will not get too dark with a higher heat.

Sugar browns easily and gives the crust a golden-brown color. For this reason, most bread machines have a Sweet Bread cycle with a lower baking temperature. Always use this cycle if the ratio of sugar to flour is higher than 1 tablespoon of sugar for each cup of flour or if you've added dried or candied fruits.

If a little sugar is good, a lot of sugar must be better — *wrong*. Don't overwhelm your yeast with too much food. The yeast will get sluggish, just like we do when we overeat, and you will end up with a small bread. Adding more sugar to your recipes is not the way to get creative; you will just upset the important balance among the ingredients.

Store all sugars in airtight containers to prevent them from absorbing water from the environment or drying out.

White granulated sugar

Common table sugar has fine, granulated crystals that dissolve easily into the bread dough. Although it has little nutritive value (no vitamins, minerals, or fiber), it is the most commonly used sugar in breads.

Where sugar comes from

Sugar cane stalks are the chief source of the world's sugar. They resemble a corn stalk and grow about 15 feet high and 2 inches thick. Sugar beets are also a source of sugar.

A sugar mill removes the juice from the stalks or beets, heats the juice, and then runs it through clarifiers and filters to remove impurities. Next, the juice is reduced to a heavy mixture of crystals and syrup. After the crystals and syrup are separated, the syrup is made into molasses and the crystals are refined into sugar.

Confectionery sugar

Confectionery sugar is also called powdered sugar. It contains approximately 3 percent cornstarch to retard lumping or crystallization. The fineness of this sugar lends itself to blending, and it's used primarily in frostings, icings, and glazes.

Do not use confectionery sugar in bread dough. The small amount of cornstarch it contains is enough to give bread a peculiar taste.

Brown sugar

Originally brown sugar was not as refined as white sugar — it had not been purified of molasses and moisture. Today, brown sugar is refined white sugar with a bit of molasses added; the darker the sugar, the more molasses was re-added to the sugar. This bit of molasses has no significant effect on the nutritional value of the sugar. However, the molasses in the sugar changes the flavor of bread and adds color. It's especially desirable in fillings and toppings, and blends well with spices such as cinnamon and nutmeg.

Always measure brown sugar by packing it into the measuring spoon or cup.

Honey

Although honeys may vary in their sweetness depending on the bees' source of food, it takes a very trained palate to detect the difference once the honey has been used in bread. Ounce-for-ounce, the nutrient content of honey is about the same as table sugar, although honey may taste a bit sweeter. It's been our experience that we can exchange an equal amount of honey for table sugar or brown sugar and still have the recipe ingredients in balance.

We choose honey for whole-wheat breads because the flavor harmonizes well the wheat. See the recipes for Granola Wheat and Light Wheat (in Chapter 11).

When honey crystallizes in the jar, you can return it to the liquid state by placing it in a container of hot water or using the Automatic Defrost setting on your microwave. (Be sure to remove the metal cap before putting the jar in the microwave.)

Molasses

Molasses is the byproduct of white sugar production and is not as sweet as sugar. Sugar cane is pounded and squeezed, the juice is extracted, and boiled. The sugar crystallizes and molasses remains in a syrup form and is separated from the sugar crystals. What remains after the first extraction is the lightest molasses. Further boiling of the molasses produces more crystallized sugar and darker molasses that is less sweet because more sugar has been removed. Black strap molasses has the least amount of sugar and is not practical to use for baking. As with honey, we've substituted molasses (a mild-flavored, unsulfured molasses) for sugar in bread recipes and gotten the same size loaf. Often, molasses is added to rye-flour breads, as in the Dark Pumpernickel Rye and the Five-Grain Bread (both in Chapter 11).

White sugar, brown sugar, honey, molasses, and maple syrup may be substituted for each other in a recipe with fairly equal results. Always remember to check the dough after five minutes of kneading for dough consistency. At that time, the dough should be in a soft, tacky ball with none left on the sides or bottom of the pan.

Maple syrup

Pure maple syrup is one of the most delicious sweeteners. The sap from maple trees is boiled down to a sweet syrup. Opened bottles should be stored in the refrigerator. Don't panic if you find mold on the top of your maple syrup. Even though you won't want to eat the mold (of course), the syrup is still good. Simply strain the syrup and bring it to a boil, and then put the syrup back into a clean container.

A greased spoon will allow molasses, honey, or maple syrup to glide off without leaving a residue.

Sugar substitutes

Most sugar substitutes on the market are proteins. Although there are some sugar substitutes that claim they can be used for baking, they are not food for yeast. Therefore, you can't use them in bread to perform the same function that a sugar does.

You can use fructose, found naturally in fruit and corn, in bread. But the truth is, it's not any more healthy to eat fructose than white sugar. Fructose, like table sugar, is a simple carbohydrate that nourishes your body in the same way. It is usually manufactured from corn syrup, which is as highly refined a sugar as that from the sugar cane. Teaspoon for teaspoon, fructose has 3 calories less than table sugar.

Salt

Salt controls yeast activity. With salt in the dough, the yeast will ferment the sugar at a steady pace. Without salt, the yeast will work like crazy and then burn out before the rising time is complete. You can suspect that you probably forgot the salt if the bread rises beautifully and then collapses as it begins to bake.

In addition to controlling yeast activity, salt strengthens the dough structure and adds flavor. Because many of the people who buy *Bread Machines For Dummies* are trying to keep their sodium intake in check, the recipes in this book use modest amounts of salt. If you do use a salt substitute, read the ingredients of the product. It must contain some sodium. Potassium chloride alone will not control yeast activity. If you must cut out all sodium in your diet, you will need to do some experimenting, reducing the sugar as well as the salt, so that the yeast is not overstimulated. The shorter yeast-bread cycles work well when you have to completely eliminate salt.

Herbs and Spices

What makes an herb different from a spice? Herbs are generally leaves and can be grown on one's own windowsill. Spices can be flower buds, such as cloves; fruits, such as pepper, nutmeg and vanilla; seeds, such as anise, caraway, cardamom, coriander and mustard; or rhizomes that spread underground, such as ginger and turmeric. And then there's saffron, in a class of its own, derived from the stigmas of a crocus plant. Some plants like celery and coriander provide both herbs from the leaves and spices from the seeds. Spices come from all over the world — usually a long way from our kitchen windowsill.

The wonderful part is that today we can find them at our local markets. Buy small amount of spices at a time as their flavor diminishes with age. If possible buy whole spices and grind or crush your own as needed. Always store spices in containers that protect them from air and light. Here are descriptions of some of the spices we love to use in our breads.

The Spice House

In Milwaukee, Wisconsin, we have wonderful sources for fresh spices. Ruth and William Penzey, Sr. opened The Spice House in 1957. Today their children have carried on the family business and Milwaukeans now shop at two locations: the original Spice House on Third Street in Milwaukee and Penzeys Spices in Brookfield. Both The Spice House and Penzeys Spices have mail order catalogs and are on the Internet, www.thespicehouse.com or www.penzeys.com.

 If you want to add more of an herb or a spice to your bread than the amount listed in the recipe, you can (except for cinnamon and garlic). Please check the sections on each to find out why this is so.

Allspice

Allspice is not a combination of all spices. It actually comes from the bay-berry tree in the Caribbean, mostly in Jamaica. The small, round berries vary in size and are dark gray-brown with a rough skin. They have a very delicate, bittersweet flavor that tastes like a mixture of cloves, cinnamon, and a hint of nutmeg. And that explains the name!

Anise

Anise, also called aniseed, is a member of the hemlock family and is grown primarily in the Mediterranean region. The very small anise seed has a surprisingly explosive taste that combines sweetness and a spicy, licorice-like flavor. It has been known as an aid in digestion, a stimulant for a sluggish system, and a cure for flatulence. Don't be concerned, as the small amounts we use to flavor rye breads will not affect the digestive system. To release the full flavor in your bread, crush the seeds before using.

Basil

The warm, pungent aroma and flavor of basil make it one of the best loved of all culinary herbs. You can grow it in your garden, on your windowsill, or buy it fresh in the supermarket. Fresh basil is one of our favorite herbs for pizza and flatbread toppings. We use dried basil in bread doughs.

Caraway

Caraway has grown wild in Europe and Asia since the Stone Age. Today, Holland is the main exporter. The seeds are small, thin, brown, and sweetly spiced, but also have a sharp taste, which livens up rye bread. It is commonly added to German and Austrian foods. Small amounts of Caraway will foster yeast activity. For this purpose use 1 to 1½ teaspoons per 3 cups of flour.

Crushed caraway is in the Beer Rye in Chapter 12 and the Light Rye in Chapter 10.

Cardamom

Cardamom is the most expensive spice after saffron and vanilla, with a strong, powerful, unusual flavor. The price and the flavor may explain why we use it sparingly in our recipes. It is delicate, sweet, and fresh, and is the perfect addition to Scandinavian breads. If time is not important to you, buy cardamom in the pods; then when ready to use, remove the seeds and crush. This method makes a spice that is more aromatic than ready-ground cardamom. Eight crushed seeds equal 1 teaspoon of ground cardamom.

Celery seed

Most celery seed is grown right here in the United States. While celery is harvested in the first year of growth as a vegetable and an herb, it is only in the second year that it develops a flowering stem that produces the spicy seeds.

Do not substitute celery salt for celery seed in bread without decreasing the amount of salt in the recipe. Celery salt obviously has salt added to it; three parts celery seed to one part salt.

Cinnamon

Cinnamon is native to Southeast Asia, India, and China, and is now grown in Sri Lanka, India, Indonesia, and Vietnam. It is the inner bark of an evergreen tree. The bark of the tree is taken from young shoots cut close to the ground once every two years in the rainy season. After the rough outer bark is planed off, these strips are dried, curling into characteristic quills. The fragrance of the cinnamon is strongest when freshly ground.

Cinnamon is a tricky ingredient. Besides being a wonderful, fragrant spice, cinnamon is also a food preservative. And that's what it tries to do in any situation, even in bread dough. Add enough cinnamon to your bread dough and you'll end up preserving the yeast so that it can't ferment. The result will be way too small of a loaf. You can add some to dough (no more than a teaspoon per cup of flour). If you want your bread to be spicier, add small amounts of nutmeg, ginger, and/or cloves. Or, combine sugar and cinnamon and serve with bread or toast. The Babka recipe in Chapter 14 tells you to roll the dough balls in cinnamon sugar before baking.

Cloves

Cloves are grown in southern India, Sri Lanka, Java, Sumatra, Brazil, and the West Indies. They are harvested as unopened flower buds of an evergreen tree and then dried. We use them in sparingly in bread recipes with other spices like nutmeg and cinnamon.

Cloves are available both whole and ground. Unless you plan to use them immediately, it's best to buy them whole. Ground cloves soon lose their freshness and start to taste musty.

Coriander

Coriander is used as both an herb and a spice. The leaves look much like parsley leaves and are becoming increasingly popular in the culinary art in entrees involving lamb, chicken, ham, pork, and smoked meats. Coriander is also used in curries.

Coriander is a bit like orange peel, and excellent in sweet breads.

Dill

Dill is another of those plants that provides both herb and spice for us with their leaves and seeds. We use the seeds and leaves (sold as dill weed) in bread dough. The Onion Dill (Chapter 10) uses dill weed.

Fennel

Maybe it was this spice that inspired someone to write about little girls as "sugar and spice and all things nice." Fennel was hung over doors in the

Middle Ages to ward off evil spirits. In Italy, "to give fennel" meant to flatter someone. We know it's a nice spice. It's delicate, light, and sweet, similar to anise, and in fact can be substituted for anise in a recipe. The plant looks very similar to dill and grows in the same climate as dill. The leaves are herbs; the seeds, spice.

Garlic

Garlic is as ancient as the oldest civilizations. It's written about in the earliest Sanskrit, the Chinese believed it warded off the evil eye, the Egyptian slaves who built the pyramids were fed it, Greek gladiators thought it gave them strength, and those sexy Romans used it for an aphrodisiac. Wonder if that's why garlic is so popular in Italian food?

Garlic bread *sounds* so good. We garlic lovers would like to generously dump garlic into bread dough. But guess what happens when we do that — the bread doesn't rise. Garlic has long been used as a meat tenderizer as it breaks down the fibers in meat. And it does the same thing to dough — breaks down the structure. You can add a *bit* to the dough, as in the Mediterranean Bread (Chapter 10), where a small amount of garlic salt is added. But really, garlic is something you add to the baked product. You can spread it on as generously as you would like; it won't do any damage that way. Unless you're concerned about your breath!

To make a great garlic spread, combine the following ingredients: 2 tablespoons room-temperature butter, 4 tablespoons extra virgin olive oil, 4 cloves minced garlic, a pinch salt, a pinch freshly ground black pepper, and ½ teaspoon oregano. Mash together with a fork until smooth.

A great garlic spread deserves to be on a delicious loaf of bread. Try it on the French bread (Chapter 11). Split a loaf in half lengthwise. Toast it under broiler, crust side up, two to three minutes. Remove from oven, turn over, and spread garlic spread on cut side. Place back under the broiler until lightly toasted.

Ginger

Marco Polo found ginger in China in the thirteenth century. Spice caravans carried ginger from China and India to the Middle East. It was dried after picking so that it could make the long trip. Even today, Chinese cuisine uses fresh ginger, while in the Middle East, dried ginger is used.

Ginger is grown in China, India, America, and the West Indies. The part that is used is the horizontal root known as the rhizome. Many dishes use fresh ginger for flavoring. In bread making, we use ground, dried ginger. Small amounts of ginger (¼ to ½ teaspoon per recipe) actually stimulate yeast activity.

Nutmeg and mace

Nutmeg is the seed of a nutmeg tree, which grows throughout Indonesia and in Grenada. Nutmeg is encapsulated in a fruit resembling an apricot; when you break the flesh open, you discover an outer covering, bright scarlet in color, known as mace. Mace dries to a light brown color. Each fruit produces less mace than nutmeg. Therefore, the price of mace is much higher than the price of nutmeg. We use nutmeg with other spices like cinnamon or cloves. You'll find it in the Hot Cross Buns and Apple Kuchen recipes as well as in the Pineapple Carrot and Pumpkin Quick Breads.

Oregano and marjoram

Marjoram and oregano are both members of the mint family and are frequently mistaken for the other. Marjoram has a more delicate flavor than does oregano. Oregano is used in Mediterranean and Southwest cooking. We use both in breads.

Parsley

Parsley is the best known and most commonly used herb in the United States. It was introduced into this country in the sixteenth century from Europe. The flat-leafed variety was the first known here as Italian or French parsley. The curled leaf variety is most widely grown and has a stronger flavor. The California drying techniques preserve the flavor and color of the leaf. We use parsley in Risotto Bread (Chapter 10) primarily for the color it adds.

Poppy seed

The opium poppy, from which the edible seeds are taken, first grew in Asia Minor and has been widely cultivated in Turkey, Iran, India, and China. The seeds are contained in one large seedpod in the center of the flower. If the unripe seedpod is cut open, opium oozes out. The ripe seeds, however, are harmless; they contain only the poppy seed oil. They better be harmless; we use a whole quarter of a cup in the Lemon Poppy Seed quick bread (Chapter 16), and umm, is it good.

Rosemary

If you have ever looked at fresh rosemary, it will not surprise you to learn that rosemary is an evergreen shrub. Rosemary's leaves appear like small pine needles on long, thin branches. Their fragrance is like pine and mint together. If you are using fresh rosemary in a bread dough, be sure to use kitchen scissors and cut them fairly fine before adding. Dried rosemary retains flavor and color, so it can be substituted for fresh. One half teaspoon dried rosemary is equal to 2 teaspoons of fresh.

Saffron

Saffron is produced from the dried stigmas of the crocus plant. In many countries it is the highest-priced of spices and the highest-prized. It takes about an acre of land and 75,000 flowers to yield one pound of saffron. Each flower blooms for only about one week of the year, during which the stigmas must be handpicked and dried. Saffron is marketed in whole threads or ground into powder. It is advisable to buy threads rather than powder as unscrupulous saffron dealers have been known to dilute saffron by adding the similar-looking safflower, marigold petals, turmeric, or soaking the real threads in oil to add weight. Some like to gently toast them in a metal spoon over low heat before pounding them in a mortar. Our Saffron Bread recipe (Chapter 12) uses only ¼ teaspoon of ground saffron. It is a beautiful golden loaf, with a golden brown crust.

Sesame seed

Sesame seeds are rich in vitamins and minerals and high in fat, thus high in calories. The good news about the fat in sesame seed oil is that it's polyunsaturated — the good kind of fat.

Sesame seeds are greatly enhanced by a preliminary roasting in a skillet pan, over gentle heat, for two to three minutes.

Because of the high oil content in sesame seeds, it is best to store them in the refrigerator — especially in the summer — to prevent rancidity.

Fruits, Vegetables, and Nuts

The following sections describe some of the more common fruit and nut ingredients that can be added to bread.

Orange and lemon zest

Grated lemon and orange peel is also called *zest*. When grating the peels of citrus fruits, remove only the top, colored layer, as the white pith beneath is bitter. You can use a regular grater for making zest or a small handy tool called a *zester,* which will remove the peel from citrus fruits in long strips for garnishing, or fine zest for flavoring, depending on the strokes you use when zesting.

Glenna uses a paring knife to trim thin layers of peel off in small pieces. She puts the strips in a coffee mill to grind into small pieces. She freezes any extra in small plastic bags. That way, when she's making a bread like the Banana Lemon Loaf, which only calls for a teaspoon of grated lemon peel, she can just crumble off 1 teaspoon from the frozen zest. Having zest in the freezer is a time-saver and a convenience.

Dried fruit

There are a variety of dried fruits that taste great in bread. Dried cranberries, a fairly new dried fruit, are especially delicious in bread. We use them in the Cranberry Orange quick bread (Chapter 17) and the Peanut Butter and Jelly bread (Chapter 12). However, many dried fruits (dried apricots, for example) are treated with sulfites to help them retain their bright color when they are dried. Unfortunately, these sulfites inhibit yeast activity. When you are purchasing dried fruit for use in baking bread, be sure to read the label. If at all possible, buy dried fruit that does not list sulfur dioxide as a drying agent. We use mixed dried fruit in the Fall Treasures quick bread because quick breads use baking powder — not yeast — as a leavening agent. But, if you're using dried fruit and yeast together, always check to make sure that the fruit doesn't contain sulfites.

Candied fruit

Cherries and Citrus Fruit Peel are candied in a thick combination of sugar and corn syrup and are used in holiday breads and as garnishes for decorating them. However, because dried fruit is lower in sugar and healthier for us than the candied fruit, we have used it in our recipe for Stollen bread (Chapter 14). For you traditionalists, we do give you the option of using the candied fruit.

If you are tempted to add more dried fruit or candied fruit than is listed in the recipe, you may end up with a dense-textured bread. While yeast do like sugar and they do ferment sugar, giving off gases, and causing the bread to rise, they also have a tendency to gorge themselves if there is too much sugar and then they get sluggish and don't work very hard. (Like people, maybe?) So the old adage, a little is good, a lot is not better holds true for adding sugar to yeast breads.

Almonds

The almond tree is native to western India. Today it is widely grown in the countries that border the Mediterranean Sea. The trees also thrive in California, where commercial groves produce large annual crops of sweet almond nuts.

Sweet almonds have very little fat. Some people like to toast them for salad or garnishes, but use them untoasted as an ingredient in bread. You will find almonds in the Guglehupf recipe (Chapter 14).

Macadamia nuts

Exotic and nutritious nuts from Hawaii, macadamias were the only appropriate nuts to use in the Hawaiian Honey bread (Chapter 14).

Pecans

The pecan tree is a type of hickory that grows naturally in the Mississippi Valley region. Pecan orchards are planted throughout the Southern states as far north as Virginia. Georgia is the leading pecan-growing state.

Pecans are high in fat; sometimes as much as three-fourths of their bulk is fat. But, oh boy, are they delicious if you use them in the Caramel Topping of the Sticky Buns (Chapter 13).

Walnuts

The English walnut tree was brought to the United States from southern Europe. It is grown commercially in California and Oregon. Today, the United States leads the world in the production of walnuts. The thin-shelled nut tastes sweet, and has much nutritive value. It contains both fats and proteins.

The black walnut tree is native to North America and is primarily valued for its wood. It does have a delicious nut, more distinctive in flavor than the English walnut. We prefer the black walnut with its rich flavor for the Black Walnut Coffeecake; you can also use the English walnut.

Dried vegetables

Dehydrating (removing the water) vegetables, intensifies both their flavor and color. They are not commonly used in bread. We do like the color that the sun-dried tomatoes add to the Mediterranean Bread (Chapter 10). Dried onions is another vegetable that we use to bring out a subtle, well-blended onion taste in the Onion Dill Bread and the Risotta Bread (also in Chapter 10).

Bedtime bread

There is a World War II story about the comforting power of bread. (Although we have heard it from different sources, we have no documentation to prove this is absolutely a true tale.) It seems many orphans were gathered up by the Allied Forces, placed in camps, and given excellent care. Yet they had a difficult time sleeping.

Then a psychologist came up with the idea of giving them a piece of bread to hold in their hands while they slept. This proved to be a great solution, as the slice of bread reassured them that they would have food to eat the next day. Feeling secure about the morrow, they were able to have a restful night's sleep.

If your sleep is fitful or you have a hard time falling asleep, try setting up your bread machine with all the ingredients in a delicious morning bread recipe like Whole Wheat Oatmeal (Chapter 11), set the delay timer to have your bread ready to come out of your machine at your wake-up time. Try it. We think you'll find it's a simple answer to a restful night's sleep.

Chapter 7

Measuring 101

. . . .

In This Chapter

▶ Differentiating between liquid and dry measuring cups

▶ Achieving accuracy

▶ Measuring temperature for quality control

▶ Converting from U.S. standard measurements to metric

. . . .

*G*lenna watched her son's girlfriend prepare a meatloaf in her kitchen. When she saw her take a liquid measuring cup to measure the bread crumbs, she said, "Oh, Leah, you probably want to use this cup for dry measurement." She said, "Oh, okay if you think so." Then she poured the bread crumbs in and tapped the cup on the countertop so as to fit more crumbs into the cup. Glenna almost said, "Don't tap dry ingredients down." But she caught herself and thought, "I've eaten her food, it's always tasted delicious, and this is only a meatloaf. Let it go." BUT, if she gets into bread-machine baking, someone will have to teach her all about measuring — for her own good, of course. Because, like cakes and desserts, bread machine recipes are formulas that need exact proportions of ingredients.

It seems so simple; anyone can measure. We've heard it over and over, "I measured to a T and my bread isn't turning out." Or, "Something must be wrong with the recipes. Were they tested before you published them?" Often people will blame their bread machine, and even take it back to the store where they purchased it for an exchange. When Tom was working as a culinary consultant at Bloomingdale's, a customer was on her third bread machine exchange when she happened to see Tom demonstrating measuring techniques and expounding on the complications of inaccurate measuring. Fortunately for her, she took the time to listen to what was being said. Because she didn't realize the importance of proper measuring techniques, she had experienced either a short dumpy loaf, or a loaf that rose nice and high and then fell in the center as soon as the bread machine began to bake. She thought that the thermostat in her machine was off, but the problem was actually in her measuring skills.

You may feel quite confident about your measuring techniques, but if you have even a smidgen of doubt in this area, you will want to review this chapter. It's all about measurements, maybe even some you haven't considered making before, like measuring the temperatures of your liquids or the temperature of completely baked bread. We contrast liquid measuring cups to dry measuring cups and explain their respective uses. We describe how you can improve your accuracy when you measure ingredients and we promote the virtues of using thermometers. We even tell you how you can convert the units of measure in these recipes to the metric equivalent.

Liquid Measuring Cups

Liquid measuring cups, transparent (if glass) or at least translucent (if plastic), make the ingredients visible so that you can measure accurately. The volume measure marks on the side register fractions of a cup and corresponding fluid ounce lines. Sometimes one side of the cup will denote cups and ounces, and the opposite side will show metric measurements of milliliters and deciliters.

Liquid measuring cups (like the ones shown in Figure 7-1) have a pouring spout, extra space at the top to ensure against spilling and come in 1- to 4-cup sizes. We prefer using a 1- or 2-cup size. For measuring bread machine ingredients, you will not measure any amount larger than will fit in a 2-cup size and the larger measuring cups can be cumbersome to use.

Measuring Tools

Figure 7-1:
Measuring
Tools.

A pint's a pound, the world around

This old axiom means one pint of water weighs one pound. Many other ingredients weigh about the same as water, so this conversion works for them as well. For example, one pint of butter weighs about one pound. Using the axiom gives a good guesstimate, but if you use the old saying to help you measure your dry ingredients, you will not be as accurate as you should be — especially for a bread machine. All measurements given in the recipes in this book are in volume and not weight.

Unless you choose to use an eye level shelf in your cupboard, you will measure liquids on "bended knee." At whatever level you choose, place the measuring cup on a solid, level surface. (Do not hold the cup in your hand and attempt to hold it level — it's accuracy you want, and holding the cup in your hand will cause the water to slosh around.) Bring your eye to the same level as the measurement you need. Don't try to look at the measurement line from an angle. Slowly pour the liquid into the measuring cup to the desired level of measurement.

When you empty the liquid measuring cup into the bread pan, use a rubber spatula to clean out all the liquid from the cup, especially when measuring honey, molasses, or oil.

Molasses and honey are so difficult to measure; here's a trick. Measure the oil alternately with the sticky stuff or grease your measuring cup or spoon.

If your butter doesn't come in ¼ pound sticks with measured markings on the packaging, you can still accurately measure it. When you need to measure in teaspoons or tablespoons, let the butter soften to a point that you can press it into the measuring spoon and level with the flat edge of a knife. If, however, you want to measure ¼ cup of butter, fill a liquid measuring cup with very cold water to the ¾ cup level. Carefully spoon pieces of butter into the water until the water reaches the 1-cup mark. Pour off the water; the remaining butter will be exactly ¼ cup.

Dry Measuring Cups

Dry measuring cups come in a group with different sizes, stacked one inside the other. They have a flush rim for leveling. The standard sizes are ¼ cup, ⅓ cup, ½ cup, ⅔ cup, ¾ cup, and 1 cup.

Measuring spoons come in the standard sizes of ⅛ teaspoon, ¼ teaspoon, ½ teaspoon, 1 teaspoon, and 1 tablespoon. Some sets also include 1½ teaspoon and 1 tablespoon plus 1 teaspoon.

To measure flour, use a large spoon or scoop and stir the flour to add air and loosen any compression that naturally occurs during storage. Do not sift. Then, using the spoon or a scoop fill the measuring cup and level off the top with a flat edge (a dinner knife works great), as shown in Figure 7-2.

Accurate Measuring

Figure 7-2:
Measuring
Flour.

Avoid these measuring mishaps when dealing with flour:

✔ Never scoop the flour from the sack or canister with the measuring cup. This packs the flour and changes the measurement.

✔ Never tap the side of the cup to shake it down so that you can get more flour into the measuring cup.

✔ Never measure over the bread pan you are adding the ingredients to. Your hand can shake, or someone can bump you. At any rate, the chance of adding more than the correct amount is great.

Use large containers that are relatively airtight for flour, sugar, salt, and so on. Keep a set of measuring cups or spoons in each. They're inexpensive, and it saves a lot of preparation time (looking for the right size) and clean-up time (they don't have to be washed between each use).

To measure brown sugar, select the correct-size dry measuring cup or spoon and pack the sugar into it all the way to the top. Level off with a flat edge.

Standard measuring equivalents

It comes in handy at times to know the following standard equivalents:

- ✔ 3 teaspoons equal 1 tablespoon
- ✔ 4 tablespoons equal ¼ cup
- ✔ 5 tablespoons + 1 teaspoon equal ⅓ cup
- ✔ Pinch or dash equal less than ⅛ teaspoon
- ✔ ⅓ tablespoon equal 1 teaspoon
- ✔ ½ tablespoon equal 1 ½ teaspoons

- ✔ ⅔ tablespoon equal 2 teaspoons
- ✔ ⅛ cup equal 2 tablespoons
- ✔ ⅜ cup equal ¼ cup + 2 tablespoons
- ✔ ⅝ cup equal ½ cup + 2 tablespoons
- ✔ ⅞ cup equal 1 cup less 2 tablespoons

To measure ⅛ teaspoon, measure ¼ level teaspoon, mark off a half with the point of a knife, and remove.

Kitchen Scales

Some bread machine hobbyists get so enthused that they decide to get technical and want to weigh all their ingredients like professional bakers do. I can assure you that this degree of precision is not necessary to make excellent bread in a bread machine. But a small kitchen scale like the one in Figure 7-3 does come in handy when you are making rolls. It helps to keep them uniform in size. We use 2 ounces as a standard size for rolls. The same holds true when you are making a braid. If all three strands are the same size, the braid will look balanced and even.

Figure 7-3:
A kitchen
scale.

Weight of flour

One cup of flour can weigh from 3¼ ounces to 5½ ounces depending on how it is measured, the blend of wheat, and the weather on the day you measure. Yeah, blame it on the weather; both humidity and temperature affect the weight of flour.

Tearing may be harmful to your dough. To divide dough into portions, use a dough scrapper, a flat edge, or kitchen scissors, and cut the dough. Do not pull or tear dough apart as this damages the dough structure, and your bread may not rise properly.

Kitchen scales are available in three types: spring, balance, and electronic. Spring models are inexpensive, and quick to use, but over time the spring loses its tautness and thus its accuracy. Balance scales are dependably accurate, but they require the adjusting of weights by hand to coincide with desired weight to be measured. Electronic battery-operated scales are very precise.

Be sure to get a scale that weighs in increments no larger than ½ ounce. Glenna uses a small, one-pound spring scale, but if she were replacing it she would purchase — at least — a five pound scale, as she finds that she often wants to weigh heavier foods. Also, get a scale that has a measuring cup and a tray so you can use either.

Thermometers

Some home bakers will tell you they never use a thermometer, but we find thermometers indispensable. When you use a thermometer to check the temperature of liquids before you put them into the bread pan, you take the guesswork out of the process and replace it with a quality-control method. Believe me, it's much better to know for sure than to guess. We suggest liquid temperatures of 75° to 85° for all yeast bread cycles except the one-hour cycle. For the one-hour, 115° to 125° works best.

Do not use an instant-read thermometer to measure the temperature of the inside of your oven. It will melt.

Many bakers tell if their baked bread is done when they tap the bottom of the loaf and hear a certain thud. We compare this to fortune telling: Sometimes it's right on, but not always. You will know for sure that the bread is done if you use an instant-read thermometer to check the internal temperature. A baked loaf of bread should be between 190° and 200°F.

Check your thermometer for accuracy

Place the stem in boiling water. The thermometer should read 212°. If it doesn't, note the difference and allow for that when you use it. Some quality models have a tiny nut on the back side of the dial which can be turned if the thermometer needs adjusting. If you have one that can be adjusted, and your thermometer does not register 212° in boiling water, use pliers to turn the nut until it reads correctly.

If you do not have a thermometer, the second-best liquid temperature is room temperature.

Instant-read thermometers are sold in the housewares section of department stores, at hardware stores, in kitchen-gourmet shops, restaurant-supply houses, and mail-order catalogs. A couple are shown in Figure 7-4.

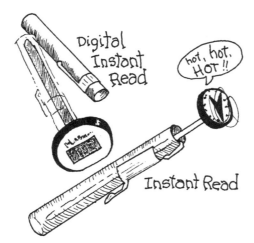

Figure 7-4: Instant-read thermometers.

Converting Measurements from U.S. Standard to Metric

All of the recipes in *Bread Machines For Dummies* use U.S. standard measurements based on teaspoons, tablespoons, and cups. We want you to be able to enjoy these recipes if you use the metric system, so we have included this conversion chart. All measurements given in our bread-machine recipes are volume measurements. If you are measuring in the metric, use milliliters and liters.

Reasonable replacement measures

The following conversion chart is meant only as a guideline. The measurements given are not exact, but have been rounded up or down for easier measuring.

1 teaspoon	5 ml
1 tablespoon	15 ml
¼ cup	60 ml
⅓ cup	75 ml
½ cup	125 ml
⅔ cup	150 ml
¾ cup	175 ml
1 cup	250 ml

Temperature conversions

The recipes in this book use the Fahrenheit system. The following chart can help you make conversions to Celsius.

Fahrenheit	Celsius
80°	40°
100°	50°
200°	100°
300°	150°
325°	160°
350°	180°
375°	190°
400°	200°
425°	220°
450°	230°

Chapter 8

Working with Dough

· ·

In This Chapter

▶ Using the bread machine to make dough

▶ Going beyond a rectangle: Shaping breads

▶ Glazing your bread for effect

▶ Forming rolls

· ·

*M*ost of the time when working with your bread machine, you will simply put your ingredients into the pan, place the pan in your bread machine, select the cycle, and push start. Your machine takes these raw ingredients and what seems like a miracle, turns them into delicious breads fit for casual eating or fine dining.

However, one of the greatest pleasures of owning a bread machine is being able to make an endless variety of hand-shaped breads and rolls. The machine does all the work of mixing and raising the dough. You do the fun part of forming the shape to fit your fancy.

If you mastered Play-Doh as a kid, you can handle yeast dough. While it's true that hand shaping bread dough is quite easy, you may wonder what's going on the first time you try something simple like rolling out a pizza dough. You roll it out and the dough moves right back, almost to the same size it was. The elasticity of the dough seems to be working against your intentions. Relax — the dough that is. You can relax too, because you are going to control that dough, learn how to handle that dough's springiness, and be able to shape it anyway you so desire.

Using the Dough or Manual Setting

Always remember to set the bread machine on the Manual or Dough setting when you plan to hand shape the dough and bake it using a conventional oven. On this setting there is no signal to add fruit or nuts, so if you want them in your dough, you can either put them in at the beginning of the cycle with the other ingredients or near the end of the kneading cycle. If you are concerned that the fruit will be too crushed if you add it early or not evenly distributed if you add it late, then add the fruit (or nuts) by hand after the cycle is complete.

At the end of the dough cycle, some bread machines automatically punch the dough down with a few turns of the kneading blade. If you have a machine that does not do this, all you have to do to accomplish the same thing is select a cycle and press start. Allow the kneading blade to only make a few turns, just enough to punch all the gas bubbles out of the dough, and stop the machine immediately. Of course, you can just dump the dough out onto a lightly floured surface and punch all the air out with your hand, but the machine does such a good job — use it. The punching down process dispels any gas that might cause an irregular texture or unwanted air pockets and it invigorates the yeast in the dough.

Rolling the Dough

The bread machine does a great job of developing elasticity in the dough. You want the dough to be able to stretch, so that as the yeast activity produces gases the dough will expand. But when you're trying to shape the dough first and then have it expand, this dough-spring can be a great frustration.

The first impulse is to put more pressure on the rolling pin and roll harder which, as you probably know, produces little if any difference. The trick is to roll or pat the dough out a bit, then let it set there for a minute or two. The dough will relax and you can roll it a bit further, then let it relax again. Repeat the rolling/hesitation process until the dough is the size you want it. You can use this technique for pizza dough, cinnamon rolls, bread sticks, or any shape that has to be made by first rolling or patting out the dough.

Shaping Breads

Once you have your dough prepared, you probably want your loaf to have a pleasing shape. Here's how you do it:

- **Round loaf:** To shape a round loaf, cup hands around the sides of the dough and rotate in a circular motion on a lightly floured surface until you have formed a ball, as shown in Figure 8-1. Place the dough on a greased cooking sheet; cover, and allow to rise.

- **Log shape:** To form a log shape, roll or pat dough to a 12-x-6-inch rectangle. Starting with the longer side, roll up tightly, pressing the dough with the heel of your hand with each turn. If it is necessary to elongate the loaf or even it out, start with your hands together at the center, and move them apart as you gently roll and stretch the dough, applying pressure as you move. Place the loaf on a cooking sheet that you've greased and covered with corn meal; cover the dough and allow it to rise.

We no longer use a damp towel to cover the rising dough. It would often stick to the dough as it was removed and cause the bread to be misshapen. Now, we use the plastic bags that we've carried our groceries home in. This plastic does not stick to the dough and yet it covers it so that the dough doesn't dry out while it is rising, We cut open the plastic bags so that they will completely cover the shaped dough.

✔ **French bread:** Real French bread, or baguettes, as they are called in France, is thin and long. On a lightly floured surface, roll or pat the dough to a 10-x-6-inch rectangle. Fold the rectangle of dough in half lengthwise. With the side of your hand, form a deep crease down the center of the dough. Fold the dough over the crease, as shown in Figure 8-2. Securely pinch the seams together to form a tight cylinder. Roll the baguette over so that the seam is on the bottom. Quickly rotate the baguette back and forth a few times working your hands from the center out to the ends. This motion will stretch the dough to the desired shape and length and form pointed ends. Be sure to keep the work surface lightly floured so that the dough does not stick to it. Place the dough on a cooking sheet that is greased and covered with cornmeal; cover the dough and allow it to rise.

✔ **Donut shape:** The donut shape begins with a round ball. Form the ball as you would form a round loaf. With your fingers, press down right into the center of the dough until your fingers reach the lightly floured surface. Then use both hands to stretch the donut-shaped loaf so that the hole is between 3-and-4-inches in diameter. Place the dough on a greased baking sheet, in a Bundt pan, or in a tube pan; cover the dough and allow it to rise.

✔ **Crescent shape:** To form a crescent shaped loaf, start with an oval about 1-inch thick. Fold the oval in half lengthwise so that the edges do not meet. Using the heel of your hand, press the top edge to firmly seal it into the dough on the bottom. Curve the dough into a crescent shape. Place it on a greased cooking sheet; cover the dough and allow it to rise.

✔ **Pan loaves:** Roll or pat each loaf into a flat rectangle 1 inch thick, making sure the width is 2 inches shorter than the length of the bread pan. (For example, if your bread pan measures 9-x-5-inches, you would be sure to roll the dough so that it is 7 inches wide.) Starting with the shorter side, roll up tightly, pressing the dough with the heel of your hand into the roll with each turn. Pinch the edges and ends to seal the dough into a loaf. Place in greased bread pans. This procedure is shown in Figure 8-3.

✔ **Braid:** Divide the dough into three parts. On an unfloured surface, roll each third into 12 to 14 inch ropes. Lay all three ropes side by side. Starting at the center, loosely braid towards each end; pinch the ends together and tuck under to seal, as shown in Figure 8-4.

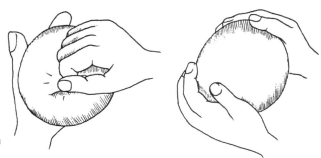

Figure 8-1:
Forming a
round loaf.

Forming a Round Loaf

Figure 8-2:
Forming a
French
bread loaf.

The Cylindrical Loaf

Preparing Dough for a Loaf Pan

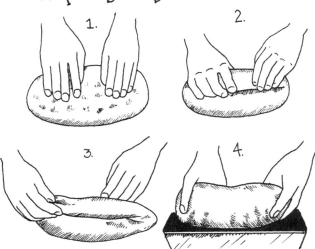

Figure 8-3:
Preparing
dough for a
loaf pan.

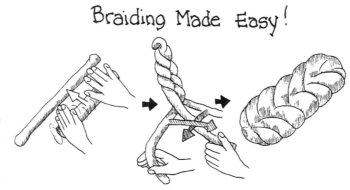

Figure 8-4:
Braiding
dough.

During the first few minutes in the oven, the final expansion of the dough takes place. Because yeast grows quickly when exposed to heat and humidity (which is exactly what happens during the first few minutes in the oven) the volume of the dough increases at an accelerated speed. This is called the *oven spring*. At this time, the loaf will often burst — the network of bread fibers will tear and give a shredded crust on one side of the loaf.

Slashing the Crust

Slashing the top of the dough just before you place it in the oven will give an attractive appearance to the loaf and let you predict the spot where the loaf will expand. You can use this technique to create your own unique, visual style that you apply to all your breads. You could even use your initials, if you too. However, a little bit of know-how is needed.

- ✔ Use a very sharp knife or a razor blade.
- ✔ Cut at a very shallow angle so that you cut under the surface and not down into the loaf, as shown in Figure 8-5.
- ✔ For a long loaf, cut length-wise slashes.
- ✔ For a round loaf, cut cross-wise slashes.

Figure 8-5:
Slashing
dough
before
putting it in
the oven.

Making crust delicious and attractive

What'll you have? Crispy, chewy crusts? Or soft and tender?

If it's soft and tender you like, use milk for the liquid in the recipe and brush the crusts with butter immediately after the bread is baked. (See Chapter 5 for more information on how liquids affect a bread.)

You want crispy and chewy? Here's the secret. Use water for the liquid in the bread dough. Then, after the dough has risen, and just before you're placing it in the hot oven, brush or spray the loaves with cold water. Let the bread bake a couple of minutes and take it out just long enough to brush

it again with cold water. Repeat this two or three times during the first 10 minutes of baking.

How about a glossy look? Combine ¼ cup water and ½ teaspoon cornstarch; bring to a boil and cool. Remove the loaves 5 minutes before the end of their baking-time and brush with the glaze you've created. Return the bread to the oven to finish baking.

For a shiny, golden crust, brush with an egg glaze before baking. To make the glaze, combine 1 slightly beaten egg with 1 tablespoon of milk or water.

Glazing Breads

Glazing a yeast bread adds a special touch. When you glaze, you can add flavor to compliment the flavor in the bread or color for eye appeal. Glazes are thin enough to drizzle over the tops of coffee cakes, rolls, or breads; frostings or icings are thicker, more creamy, and are spread on top of the baked product.

A basic glaze combines 1 cup of powdered sugar, 1 teaspoon of softened butter, and 1 to 2 tablespoons of hot water or milk. You can vary this recipe according to your taste and creativity by adding vanilla, almond extract, rum, brandy, maple flavoring, grated lemon or orange peel, or cocoa. You can also substitute the water or milk with fruit juice: lemon, orange, pineapple, or apple.

Egg glazes are great for making a shiny, golden crust. Combine 1 slightly beaten egg with 1 tablespoon of milk or water. See the sidebar "Making crust delicious and attractive" for other ways to change your crust.

Filling ½ of the eggshell with water is a quick way to measure the tablespoon of water needed for an egg glaze.

Doughs are brushed with an egg glaze after they've risen and when they're ready to pop in the oven. Brush with a soft pastry brush so as not to puncture the dough.

Forming Rolls with Your Dough

If you're making rolls, keep in mind that two ounces of dough makes a standard dinner roll. You should consider using a small kitchen scale as a practical method to divide the dough into equal size rolls. And when you break your dough into rolls, it's better to cut dough into pieces with a dough scraper or kitchen scissors than to tear off pieces. Keep these tips in mind:

- ✔ Three cups of flour makes approximately 12 dinner rolls.

- ✔ A soft dough produces the lightest, most tender rolls. When the dough is firm, it doesn't stretch as easily, so it will be a heavier dense roll.

- ✔ If you are having a problem working with the dough because it seems too sticky, use a little shortening or pan spray on your fingers to make the dough easy to shape.

- ✔ Prevent the dough from drying out while you're working with it by covering it with a piece of plastic. The plastic bags that you carry your groceries home in work wonderfully for covering dough. They keep the moisture in, and the dough doesn't stick to it.

Rolls come in all shapes and sizes. Here's how to form them:

- ✔ **Round rolls and pan rolls:** Use an unfloured work surface. Cup your hand over the piece of dough and rotate in small circles, applying a little pressure with the motion, as shown in Figure 8-6. This is the most common method and forms beautiful, symmetrical balls of dough.

  Some bakers like to roll the dough between their hand to form the ball while others use a pull and tuck method until the top of the ball is completely round and the bottom has the tucked dough.

- ✔ **Cloverleaf rolls:** Divide each piece of dough into three equal parts and shape each into a round ball. Place the three balls in one muffin cup.

- ✔ **Parker House rolls:** On a lightly floured surface, roll the dough out until it is ½-inch thick. Using a biscuit cutter, cut into circles. Brush with melted butter. Make an off-center crease in each circle, as shown in Figure 8-7. Fold the dough so that the top half overlaps slightly. Press edges together. Place 2 to 3 inches apart on greased cookie sheets.

- ✔ **Crescent Rolls:** On a lightly floured surface, roll the dough into a 12-inch circle. Brush with butter. Cut into 12 wedges. Starting with the wide end of the wedge, roll dough toward the point, as shown in Figure 8-8. Place point down, 2 to 3 inches apart on greased cookie sheets; curve to form a crescent shape.

- ✔ **Brioche:** After the dough has been divided into roll-size pieces, cut off ¼ of the dough from each piece. Shape each large and small piece into balls. Place larger ball into a muffin pan cup or a small brioche mold. Make an indentation with your thumb in the top of the larger ball, wet the indentation with egg wash and place the smaller ball in the indentation.

✔ **Knots:** After the dough has been divided into roll size pieces, on an unfloured surface, roll each piece into a 10-inch rope. Tie a loose knot in each rope of dough, stretching the rope gently, if needed.

✔ **Swirls:** After the dough has been divided into roll size pieces, on an unfloured surface, roll each piece into a 10-inch rope. Loosely wrap each rope into a flat coil shape. Gently press the rope end into the side of the coil.

✔ **Rosettes:** After the dough has been divided into roll size pieces, on an unfloured surface, roll each piece into a 12-inch rope. Tie a loose knot, stretching the rope gently, if needed, to leave two long ends. Tuck top end under roll. Bring bottom end up and tuck into center of roll.

Round Rolls

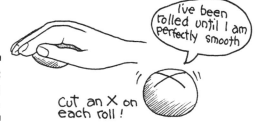

Figure 8-6: Making round rolls.

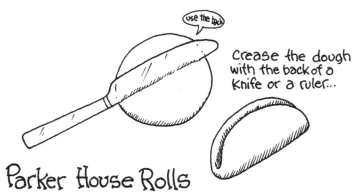

Figure 8-7: Forming Parker House rolls.

Parker House Rolls

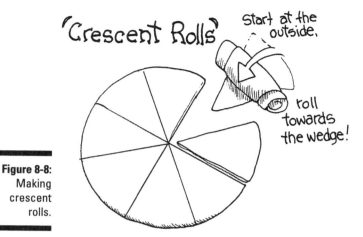

Figure 8-8:
Making
crescent
rolls.

The legacy of Parker House

The Omni Parker House at 60 School Street in Boston, Massachusetts is the longest continuously operating hotel in America. The original house was built in 1704 and by 1808 the mansion was turned into lodgings. Harvey Parker purchased the property in 1833 and turned it into a first-class restaurant. Parker imported a French chef and a German baker in order to maintain a standard of excellence. In 1854 Parker built a hotel adjacent to the restaurant. Those who evaluated it on opening day said it was the grandest building in the city of Boston.

The reputation and influence of the Parker House, especially on culinary matters, spread beyond its walls. Parker House rolls, created by the German baker, as well as his Boston cream pie, have become staples of American cuisine.

Chapter 9

The Rest of the Story

*I*n Chapter 8, we talk about using the Dough cycle on your bread machine to make the dough and how to shape the dough in various ways to prepare it for rising and baking. This chapter shows you what to do with the dough after you've formed it the way you like.

Rising Shaped Dough

There are so many stories about the favorite spots where people rise their dough: under blankets in their beds, on top of their hot-water heater, near a sunny window, beside or on the top of a radiator. And the list goes on. The truth is that yeast will be activated (and rise the dough) just fine if the dough sets right on your kitchen counter. You only need a place that's free from a cool draft.

If you want to hurry it along, you can boil water in your microwave and then set the pan in the microwave. The warm steam will encourage the yeast to work faster. Yeast flourishes in a warm, moist environment. But, if the temperature gets too high, the yeast gets sluggish — just like we do. Also, the dough will develop a yeasty or sour taste if the temperature is too high while it rises.

Knowing when to put your breads, rolls, or coffeecakes in the oven is critical. Dough can rise too much and get too light, so that when you put it in the oven, it may actually fall. It's called *overproofing*. The gluten network overstretches, and when the heat of the oven hits the dough, the honeycomb cells collapse.

It's easy to tell when the dough is ready to go into the oven to bake. Use this simple test: With one finger, gently make an indentation on the side of the loaf or roll. If the dough remains indented, it's ripe for baking. Pop it in the pre-heated oven immediately. Putting dough into the oven when it is ready will assure you a beautiful *oven spring* — that last great rise that happens when the dough is put into the heat of the oven.

Refrigerating Dough

Preliminary planning eases preparation. You can make dough in your bread machine and keep it refrigerated for up to three days. Tom says, "It's like putting your dough down for a nap." With a bread machine, it's simple to make several batches of dough ahead of time. This is a great way to get ready for special occasions. Or let's say you'd planned to make rolls but you're being called away from the task. Put your dough down for a nap and use it later.

Use the Dough cycle on your machine. After the dough is kneaded, hold the Stop/Clear button down to clear the program. (You do not need to have the machine complete the cycle, as the dough will continue to rise in the refrigerator but at a slower pace.) The machine will probably beep to let you know that you've cleared the program and 0:00 may appear on the digital readout.

Don't unplug the bread machine in order to stop the cycle. Use the Stop/Clear button first, and then unplug the machine. This will keep your computer chip in good working order.

Remove the dough and place it in a container that has enough space for the dough to expand and can also be tightly covered. Tom uses self-sealing plastic bags. He forms the dough into a disk shape about an inch thick and places it in the bag. In the disk shape the dough chills at an even rate. A ball will take longer to chill to the center.

Chilling dough slows down the activity of yeast but it does not stop the activity. If you're napping the dough in the refrigerator, check on it after an hour or so. It will have risen, and you'll have to punch it down to remove all the gas bubbles. Punch it down again a couple of hours later. Once the dough is completely cooled, it only needs to be punched down every 24 hours.

If you don't punch down the dough in the first few hours, it may develop a sour taste and an unpleasant odor. If you have to leave and cannot attend to the dough, we suggest you do a fast 10- or 15-minute chill in the freezer to hinder the yeast activity before putting the dough in the refrigerator.

We do not recommend that refrigerator doughs be kept more than three days. Fermentation continues in the refrigerator, and it's possible that undesirable flavors could develop over a period of time longer than three days. Opening and closing the refrigerator door many times a day also helps the dough grow funky. Another reason to use refrigerated dough within three days is that it loses its ability to rise as it gets older.

For easier handling, shape the dough when it's cold, right out of the refrigerator. At this stage, the dough can be rolled as thin or as thick as you desire and shaped as you desire, without the springy quality of freshly mixed and kneaded dough.

Don't forget that it takes longer for cold dough to rise. Use the ripeness test described earlier in the chapter to determine when the dough has risen adequately.

Here's another plan-ahead tip. You can refrigerate dough after it's been shaped. Glenna does this when she's planning a dinner party or when she's having overnight guests who rave about fresh-baked breakfast rolls.

To use the shape-then-refrigerate method, remove the dough from the bread machine and shape it into whatever you're planning to make. Place the bread in or on the appropriate baking pan. Coat some plastic wrap with cooking spray and use it to cover the unbaked item. Place the dough in the freezer for approximately 10 to 15 minutes, for a quick chill. This hinders the yeast development so that you don't need to punch the dough down. Then move the dough to the refrigerator. You can keep the shaped dough refrigerated for up to 24 hours. To bake the dough, remove it from the refrigerator and loosen the plastic wrap. Keep the dough lightly covered while it rises. Test the dough with the ripe test to determine when it's ready to be baked.

Freezing Dough

Organization is your middle name. You like to prepare breads or rolls even further ahead of time than a mere 24 hours — so freeze them.

For individual rolls such as dinner rolls, shape them, place them on a baking sheet or in muffin cups, and freeze them. As soon as they are completely frozen, you transfer them to self-sealing freezer bags. Press out as much air as possible before completely sealing the bag.

Be sure to use freezer weight bags. Other bags are more porous and not thick enough to protect the dough from freezer burn.

Loaves of bread can also be frozen after shaping. After the bread is in a pan, grease the top of the loaf well, and either wrap the pan in freezer-weight aluminum foil or place it in a large, self-sealing bag (pressing out as much air as possible). Freeze for two weeks at the maximum.

To thaw the bread, unwrap the frozen dough, but cover lightly to prevent drying. As the dough thaws and comes to room temperature, it will gradually rise. Be sure to test the dough with the ripe test so that you'll know when to put it in the oven.

Did you ever decide to have a great pizza party, only to change your mind when you realized how much work you'd have to do? Make the dough early, and freeze it in inch-thick disks. On the day of the party, take out the dough and let it thaw. If it thaws too soon and you're not quite ready for it, keep it cold in the refrigerator. This makes preparing pizza a snap. Roll out the dough, use ready-made pizza sauce and your favorite toppings, and bake. Enjoy your pizza and your party.

You don't have to limit freezing unformed dough to pizza crust; you can do this with any dough. After it's completed the Dough/Manual cycle, remove the dough and pat it into a disk shape with a thickness of about an inch. Place it in a self-sealing freezer bag. Pop it in the freezer. It's that simple.

For an even thaw, place the frozen dough in the refrigerator overnight. In the morning, partially unwrap (by opening the freezer bag) and place the dough on the kitchen counter to continue to bring the temperature up. It will take a couple of hours for the dough to return to room temperature. You can shape the dough while it's cool. Be sure to use the ripe test so you will know when it is ready to bake.

Turning Dough into Bread: Baking

You can bake your dough right in your bread machine, or you can use your trusty oven. While the traditional method of baking bread in an oven may seem to give you more control over the finished baked product, the bread machine does a great job. Trusting it to bake to perfection comes with experience. However, when you have shaped a braided bread, rolls, or baguettes, you'll bake them in your conventional oven.

In a bread machine

Ninety-nine percent of the time, the baking time in bread machines will give you a beautiful crust color and great crust thickness. If you feel, for a particular recipe, as if the bread turned out darker than you would prefer, write yourself a note by the recipe to check the baking time. The next time you make it, open the lid about ten minutes before the baking time is complete to see if the bread is done to your satisfaction. If you have any doubt, use an instant-read thermometer as described in Chapter 7. The bread is completely baked if the thermometer reads 190° to 195° when inserted halfway into the loaf.

Perhaps you are consistently experiencing a darker crust than you would like when you use a particular cycle. Many manuals have a chart in them that describes how long each activity in the cycle is. If you have this chart, you will be able to determine if this is the best cycle for you to choose. You can either select a cycle with a shorter baking time or you can check your bread for doneness before the baking time is complete.

If you take your bread out of the machine before the cycle is complete, be sure to hold Stop/Clear until the program has cleared and the machine shuts off. Usually the machine will signal that it's off with a beep, or the digital read-out will register 0:00. To protect your bread machine's computer chip, do not unplug the machine before you've cleared the program. (We've already warned you about this, but we've seen so many bread machines ruined that we thought we'd warn you again.)

We like to take the yeast bread out of the machine and put it on a cooling rack as soon as the baking cycle is complete. The quick breads made with baking powder and baking soda, as well as the gluten-free breads, need a longer time in the pan to firm up their structure. Let them rest approximately ten minutes with the pan on the cooling rack before removing the bread to the rack. If the kneading blade is still in the bread, it can be removed easily while the bread is hot, with minor disruption to the loaf. See the sidebar, "Another use for a crochet hook."

Prevent giving away your kneading blade with your good bread. Get in the habit of *always* removing the kneading blade as soon as you take the bread out of the pan. This will help you keep track of your blade. Very often it's difficult or impossible to get a replacement blade. What good is a bread machine without a kneading blade? It's too small for an end table, and too heavy for a portable cooler.

Another use for a crochet hook

A crochet hook works great to remove a kneading blade from the loaf. Insert it in the hole where the blade fits on the shaft. Gently work the blade out of the loaf. If you do this as soon as you take the bread out of the pan, there is little disruption to the loaf.

Most bread machines have a cooling-down time following the Bake cycle. It's a great feature to use when you're not there to take the bread out of the pan when the baking cycle is complete. If you notice the crust feels damp after the cooling-down time, don't fret. It will be okay as soon as it's exposed, for a short time, to air.

In a conventional oven

Always preheat your oven before you place the unbaked dough into it. A hot oven is what gives your dough that wonderful oven spring.

Too low an oven temperature allows the bread to rise too long before the crust forms. Then the grain is coarse and thick, and the crust is usually very thick. A higher temperature produces a better oven spring, good volume, and a fine grain texture, because the crust sets sooner.

- The temperature most commonly used for baking breads is 375°.
- A very sweet yeast bread or a quick bread is baked at a lower temperature, 350°.
- 400° to 425° is used for breads with low or no sugar, such as French bread.

The baking time for smaller items like dinner rolls or muffins is shorter than it is for breads and coffeecakes, but the oven temperature is the same. The best way to determine if the bread is completely baked is with an instant-read thermometer. If the thermometer reads 190° to 195° when inserted halfway into the loaf, roll, or coffeecake, you're ready to start cooling.

Shiny pans are not always the best baking pans for yeast breads. Often the top of the loaf will brown, but the sides will remain light. To prepare new, shiny pans for baking, wash them thoroughly, and then place them in a 400° oven for several hours. Remove them carefully and cool. Repeat this process two or three times before you use them. The first time you use the pans for actual baking, grease them evenly and thoroughly. Don't wash them when you're done, but wipe them out with a paper towel. The next time you bake with them, it's not necessary to grease the whole pan thoroughly, just the corners. Lightly grease the sides and the bottom.

You may have heard otherwise, but you don't have to lower the temperature of the oven when you're using Pyrex — unless you're baking a very sweet dough with lots of sugar. In this case, lower the oven by 25°.

Parbaking

Here's another plan-ahead trick for dinner rolls.

You can make your own brown-and-serve pan rolls. Bake the rolls in a 275° oven for 50 minutes. Then let set for 30 minutes in pans. Turn the rolls out of the pans; cool on a wire rack to room temperature. Wrap them in freezer weight aluminum foil, and then place in a self-sealing, plastic freezer bag and refrigerate (one week, max) or freeze (one month, max).

It's best to thaw the frozen rolls before you finish baking them. Remove them from the plastic bag, and slightly open the foil. When they are defrosted, bake them in a 450° oven for seven minutes, until golden brown.

Cooling and Slicing

Prevent soggy crust syndrome by cooling your breads on racks, or crosswise on your baking pan. This allows air to circulate around your breads so that evaporating moisture does not condense into your crust.

That bread smells so good, and the gastric juices are flowing. Can you wait 20 minutes more? *The bread actually finishes baking as it cools.* If you tear or cut into a loaf too soon, you will find the center is still doughy. Glenna's boys never could wait. They didn't care if the bread was doughy. You might say they weren't connoisseurs, just aficionados, of fresh bread — with huge appetites.

Thin, serrated knives cut the bread without destroying the crust and the inside texture. Use a back-and-forth sawing motion with a very little pressure on the bread. Let the knife do the work, not your muscle strength. Some people prefer an electric knife. Here again, be sure to let the knife cut the bread without a lot of downward force from your hand. You will notice that when you let the knife cut without you strong-arming you will have more control over the thickness and the evenness of the slices.

Storing Baked Bread

One of the greatest pleasures of home-baked bread is that heavenly aroma during rising and baking. Another is that you know what ingredients go into that bread — no preservatives. Homemade bread, however, has a limited shelf life. Because Glenna's children are now out of the nest, she and John seldom need more than a slice or two at a time. She has a great solution for keeping it fresh for days on end. Freeze it.

Here's how. Slice the completely cooled bread, and then stack the bread back together. Wrap the bread in aluminum foil or plastic wrap to hold it together, with the least amount of air around it. Then place the wrapped loaf in a self-sealing, plastic freezer bag and freeze. When you're ready to serve or eat the bread, you can open the frozen package and pop off just the number of slices you need. Rewrap the remaining part of the loaf and return it to the freezer. The bread slices will thaw in a few minutes at room temperature, or you can microwave them for 10 to 15 seconds on high.

Some people prefer not to slice the bread before freezing. If you don't, it takes about three hours to defrost a solid loaf of bread at room temperature. You can also thaw the loaf in the aluminum foil in a 250° to 300° oven for about 30 to 40 minutes.

Take the time to label the bread with the name of the bread and the date you put it in the freezer. You'll be glad you did when you go to look for what you want in your freezer compartment. It's so easy to have a frozen bread, with no idea how long it's been in the freezer. Actually, it seems like bread will keep fresh forever when wrapped properly and frozen, but still it's a good idea to rotate the stock, so to speak.

All breads freeze well. You don't have to wrap dinner rolls in individual foil, but be sure to use a heavy freezer bag. You can even freeze frosted, iced, or decorated coffeecakes. Place them in the freezer unwrapped until they're frozen. Remove, wrap in freezer foil, place in a large, plastic, self-sealing freezer bag, label, and return to the freezer. The quick freeze sets the icing so that it will not become smeared from the wrapping.

If stale bread is frozen, it will still be stale bread after it's defrosted. If fresh bread is frozen, it will still be fresh bread after defrosting.

Waste Not; Want Not

Ah, ah, ah — you need not throw out that stale bread. It still has many good uses: crumbs for casserole topppings, croutons for salads, cubes for stuffings, crusts for thickening sauces. Or . . . you can feed the woodland animals.

When Glenna was testing breads for this cookbook, she would end up with so many breads that she ended up feeding the squirrels. By the time she was finished she had several families visiting for their handout. Her only concern was they would become dependent on this free lunch and when her project was over, they would starve. They could probably survive on their body fat until they realized they would have to go back to foraging for their food.

Crumbs for casseroles

If you have stale slices of bread, turn them into crumbs. Lay them out on a cookie sheet and place it in a 200° oven for an hour or so until they seem completely dry. If you have a food processor, use it to turn these dry slices of bread into crumbs. Otherwise, place slices in a self-sealing plastic bag; close, pressing out as much air as possible. Use a rolling pin to roll over the outside of the bag to turn the slices into crumbs. Freeze the crumbs in a small freezer bag. They will not stick together and can be used in a moment's notice for breading fish or poultry before frying or adding to ground meat in meat loaf or meatball recipes.

You can get mighty fancy and season the crumbs. Use melted butter to help the crumbs absorb the seasoning. Add your choice of herbs to the melted butter and toss in the bread crumbs. A generic recipe proportion would be ⅓ cup butter to 1 cup of breadcrumbs. Melt the butter with the herbs in a skillet, toss in the crumbs, and stir over medium heat until the crumbs are golden brown and have absorbed the butter.

Top ordinary casseroles with seasoned bread crumbs and you'll think it a gourmet creation. An example would be the standard macaroni and cheese casserole. Topped with seasoned bread crumbs, it looks intriguing and appetizing, and it tastes great. For this casserole, you could season ½ cup bread crumbs with 2 ½ tablespoons of butter, ½ teaspoon of onion powder, and 1 teaspoon of dried parsley.

Croutons for salads

Dress up any salad with your homemade croutons. They are so easy to make, you'll always have them ready to serve.

First, lightly brush slices of bread with olive oil. You can cut your bread into cubes any size you like; lay them out on a cookie sheet and toast in a pre-heated 375° oven for 10 to 15 minutes or until crisp. They are especially good warm on a cold, crisp salad.

Store your croutons in an airtight container in the refrigerator.

Cubes for bread stuffings

If you can slice bread, you can cube it and let it dry out. That's all there is to making bread for stuffings or dressings. After it is cubed and dried, freeze it until you need it. And homemade bread makes wonderful stuffing. For rich delicious stuffings, mix all kinds of bread cubes together (rye, whole wheat, onion dill, challah).

Crusts for thickening

If you have a sauce that is too thin, drop bread crusts into the sauce and let it set for approximately ten minutes so the bread will absorb the sauce. Whisk with a fork or wire whisk. Pronto! Thicker sauce.

Part III
Bread Automatically with the Push of a Button

The 5th Wave   By Rich Tennant

"I'm pretty sure it's pizza dough that gets tossed, not pasta dough."

In this part . . .

Here's the heart and soul of the book. Roll up your sleeves, put on your apron (although you really don't need to since making bread in a machine isn't messy), and get started using these quick and easy recipes for great homemade loaves of bread. We also show you how to use your bread machine to make the dough which you will shape into bakery-like creations to bake in your oven, thus capturing the admiration of your family and friends.

Chapter 10

Basic Breads

A good place to start making bread is with the most basic recipes. The recipes we've selected for this chapter provide you a wide variety of breads. Our guess is that your book will begin to open to these pages as you will use the recipes over and over without tiring of them.

These breads are made primarily with white bread flour and will rise nicely for you into soft-textured breads with chewy, thin crusts. Each recipe is unique. You will be picking many of your favorites from this selection, we're sure.

Good Old American Sandwich Bread

You will love this bread for sandwiches because it doesn't crumble when you cut it and it doesn't fall apart when you laden it with sandwich fillings. The oatmeal makes the bread taste a tad bit sweeter than most breads, without any added sugar. The oatmeal also holds moisture for a soft texture.

Preparation time: *15 minutes*

Approximate cycle time: *2 ½ to 3 hours*

Yield: *1 ½-pound loaf, 12 slices; 2-pound loaf, 16 slices*

1 ½-lb loaf	2-lb loaf
⅔ cup milk	¾ cup milk
⅓ cup water	½ cup water
2 tablespoons vegetable oil or butter	3 tablespoons vegetable oil or butter
1 ½ teaspoon salt	2 teaspoons salt
2 tablespoons sugar	3 tablespoons sugar
2 tablespoons oatmeal	3 tablespoons oatmeal
3 cups bread flour	4 cups bread flour
2 ¼ teaspoons yeast	1 tablespoon yeast

1 Be sure that all the ingredients are at room temperature before you place them in your bread pan in the order listed.

2 Select the Normal or Basic setting and a light to medium crust color and press Start.

3 Open the lid after the machine has kneaded the dough for about five minutes. The dough should be formed into a very soft, sticky ball. If the dough is sticking to the sides or the bottom of the pan, you need to add a bit more bread flour. If the dough is crumbly and not in a ball, or if the ball appears firm, add more water. Your machine still has kneading time and will work the water into your bread dough. Keep checking your dough until you're satisfied that a soft, sticky ball has formed.

4 After the machine has completed the baking cycle, remove the pan from the machine and the bread from the pan to cool on a wire rack. If you cut the bread before it's cooled for about an hour, it will look doughy. The bread has to cool completely to allow the structure to set.

Per serving: Calories 140; Protein 5g; Carbohydrates 26g; Dietary fiber less than 1g; Total fat 2.5g; Saturated fat 0g; Cholesterol 0mg; Sodium 200mg.

Soft White Bread

If you're looking for a bread that's like the soft, white, commercial bread you find in plastic bags in the bread aisle at the grocery store, this is the recipe for you. Kids love it, especially when thick slices are spread with peanut butter and grape jelly.

Preparation time: 10 minutes

Approximate cycle time: 2 ½ to 3 hours

Yield: 1½-pound loaf, 12 slices; 2-pound loaf, 16 slices

1 ½-lb loaf

¾ cup water

1 tablespoon oil or butter

1 cup white cake mix

2 cups bread flour

2 ¼ tablespoons yeast

2-lb loaf

1 cup water

4 teaspoons oil or butter

1 ⅓ cups white cake mix

2 ⅔ cups bread flour

1 tablespoon yeast

1 Be sure that all the ingredients are at room temperature before you place them in your bread pan in the order listed.

2 Select the Normal or Basic setting and a light to medium crust color and press Start.

3 Open the lid after the machine has kneaded the dough for about five minutes. The dough should be formed into a very soft, sticky ball. If the dough is sticking to the sides or the bottom of the pan, you need to add a bit more bread flour. If the dough is crumbly and not in a ball, or if the ball appears firm, add more water. Your machine still has kneading time and will work the water into your bread dough. Keep checking your dough until you're satisfied that a soft, sticky ball has formed.

4 After the machine has completed the baking cycle, remove the pan from the machine and the bread from the pan to cool on a wire rack. If you cut the bread before it's cooled for about an hour, it will look doughy. The bread has to cool completely to allow the structure to set.

Tip: If Soft White Bread becomes a favorite in your household, save time by preparing a few batches of ingredients at a time. Measure the dry ingredients, except the yeast, into self-sealing plastic bags and keep on hand, ready to toss in the bread machine at a moment's notice.

Per serving: Calories 130; Protein 4g; Carbohydrates 23g; Dietary fiber less than 1g; Total fat 2.5g; Saturated fat 0.5g; Cholesterol 0mg; Sodium 85mg.

Milwaukee Beer Bread

Perhaps Milwaukee Beer Bread will not make Milwaukee famous, but you may be when you share it with family and friends. It's definitely a no-fail recipe that you can count on to bring to a potluck supper. Some people think it tastes a bit like sourdough bread.

Preparation time: *10 to 15 minutes*

Approximate cycle time: *2 ½ to 3 hours*

Yield: *1 ½-pound loaf, 12 slices; 2-pound loaf, 16 slices*

1 ½-lb loaf

⅓ cup water

⅔ cup beer

2 tablespoons oil or butter

1 ½ teaspoons salt

2 tablespoons sugar

3 cups bread flour

2 ¼ teaspoons yeast

2-lb loaf

½ cup water

¾ cup beer

3 tablespoons oil or butter

2 teaspoons salt

3 tablespoons sugar

4 cups bread flour

1 tablespoon yeast

1 Be sure that all the ingredients are at room temperature before you place them in your bread pan in the order listed.

2 Select the Normal or Basic setting and a light to medium crust color and press Start.

3 Open the lid after the machine has kneaded the dough for about five minutes. The dough should be formed into a very soft, sticky ball. If the dough is sticking to the sides or the bottom of the pan, you need to add a bit more bread flour. If the dough is crumbly and not in a ball, or if the ball appears firm, add more water. Your machine still has kneading time and will work the water into your bread dough. Keep checking your dough until you're satisfied that a soft, sticky ball has formed.

4 After the machine has completed the baking cycle, remove the pan from the machine and the bread from the pan to cool on a wire rack. If you cut the bread before it's cooled for about an hour, it will look doughy. The bread has to cool completely to allow the structure to set.

Per serving: *Calories 130; Protein 4g; Carbohydrates 25g; Dietary fiber less than 1g; Total fat 1g; Saturated fat 0g; Cholesterol 0mg; Sodium 290mg.*

Buttermilk Farm Bread

Whenever we think of buttermilk in bread, nostalgia sets in and we immediately think of the country kitchens where buttermilk pancakes and buttermilk bread were common food. In the late 1800s and early 1900s, buttermilk was the liquid that remained after cream was churned into butter. Using it was part of a frugal life — waste not, want not. Although today's buttermilk is cultured, it still has the same properties that make bread tender and slightly tangy.

Preparation time: *15 minutes*

Approximate cycle time: *2 ½ to 3 hours*

Yield: *1½-pound loaf, 12 slices; 2-pound loaf, 16 slices*

1 ½-lb loaf	2-lb loaf
¾ cup buttermilk	1 cup buttermilk
¼ cup water	⅓ cup + 1 tablespoon water
2 tablespoons oil or butter	3 tablespoons oil or butter
1 teaspoon salt	1 ½ teaspoons salt
2 tablespoons sugar	3 tablespoons sugar
⅔ cup semolina flour	1 cup semolina flour
2 ⅓ cups bread flour	3 cups bread flour
2 ¼ teaspoons yeast	1 tablespoon yeast

1 Be sure that all the ingredients are at room temperature before you place them in your bread pan in the order listed.

2 Select the Normal or Basic setting and a light to medium crust color and press Start.

3 Open the lid after the machine has kneaded the dough for about five minutes. The dough should be formed into a very soft, sticky ball. If the dough is sticking to the sides or the bottom of the pan, you need to add a bit more bread flour. If the dough is crumbly and not in a ball, or if the ball appears firm, add more water. Your machine still has kneading time and will work the water into your bread dough. Keep checking your dough until you're satisfied that a soft, sticky ball has formed.

4 After the machine has completed the baking cycle, remove the pan from the machine and the bread from the pan to cool on a wire rack. If you cut the bread before it's cooled for about an hour, it will look doughy. The bread has to cool completely to allow the structure to set.

Cooking tip: *If you don't have buttermilk on hand, you may use 1 tablespoon of lemon juice or vinegar to 1 cup of milk as a substitution.*

Per serving: Calories 130; Protein 5g; Carbohydrates 27g; Dietary fiber 1g; Total fat 1g; Saturated fat 0g; Cholesterol 0mg; Sodium 15mg.

Irish Potato Bread

American bread bakers have probably been putting potatoes into bread dough since potatoes were grown in this country. It's thought that the original potatoes for planting came from Ireland, so like soda bread, potato bread is usually credited to the Irish. We like mashed potatoes in bread because the bread crumb is moist and the crust is crisp. This bread rises easily, as the potato water and mashed potatoes help the yeast to ferment and the dough to stretch.

Preparation time: 40 minutes (includes boiling and mashing potatoes and cooling potato water to room temperature)

Approximate cycle time: 2 ½ to 3 hours

Yield: 1 ½-pound loaf, 12 slices; 2-pound loaf, 16 slices

1 ½-lb loaf	2-lb loaf
¼ cup potato water or milk	½ cup potato water or milk
4 teaspoons oil or butter	2 tablespoons oil or butter
1 egg	1 egg
½ cup mashed potatoes	¾ cup mashed potatoes
⅓ cup chopped onions (optional)	½ cup chopped onions (optional)
1 tablespoon sugar	4 teaspoons sugar
¾ teaspoon salt	1 teaspoon salt
2 ⅓ cups bread flour	3 ½ cups bread flour
1 ½ teaspoons yeast	2 ¼ teaspoons yeast

1 Be sure that all the ingredients are at room temperature before you place them in your bread pan in the order listed.

2 Select the Normal or Basic setting and a light to medium crust color and press Start.

3 Open the lid after the machine has kneaded the dough for about five minutes. The dough should be formed into a very soft, sticky ball. If the dough is sticking to the sides or the bottom of the pan, you need to add a bit more bread flour. If the dough is crumbly and not in a ball, or if the ball appears firm, add more water. Your machine still has kneading time and will work the water into your bread dough. Keep checking your dough until you're satisfied that a soft, sticky ball has formed.

4 After the machine has completed the baking cycle, remove the pan from the machine and the bread from the pan to cool on a wire rack. If you cut the bread before it's cooled for about an hour, it will look doughy. The bread has to cool completely to allow the structure to set.

Per serving: Calories 140; Protein 5g; Carbohydrates 26g; Dietary fiber less than 1g; Total fat 2.5g; Saturated fat 0g; Cholesterol 20mg; Sodium 180mg.

Risotto Bread

This is an excellent bread for keeping because the risotto remains moist and the crust doesn't get hard. The combination of Parmesan cheese, onions, and parsley adds mild flavor — delicious. Saffron gives the bread a beautiful color. The extra preparation time allows time to cook and then cool the risotto.

Preparation time: *1 ½ hours*

Approximate cycle time: *2 ½ to 3 hours*

Yield: *1 ½-pound loaf, 12 slices; 2-pound loaf, 16 slices*

1 ½-lb loaf

¾ cup plus 1 tablespoon milk

2 tablespoons vegetable oil

1 tablespoon sugar

⅓ cup Parmesan cheese, grated

¾ cup cooked risotto

4 teaspoons dried parsely

1 tablespoon minced dried onions

6 strands saffron

1 teaspoon salt

3 cups bread flour

1 tablespoon active dry yeast

2-lb loaf

1 cup plus 1 tablespoon milk

3 tablespoons vegetable oil

4 teaspoons sugar

½ cup Parmesan cheese, grated

1 cup cooked risotto

2 tablespoons dried parsely

4 teaspoons minced dried onions

8 strands saffron

1 ½ teaspoons salt

4 cups bread flour

4 teaspoons active dry yeast

1 Be sure that all the ingredients are at room temperature before you place them in your bread pan in the order listed.

2 Select the Normal or Basic setting and a light to medium crust color and press Start.

3 Open the lid after the machine has kneaded the dough for about five minutes. The dough should be formed into a very soft, sticky ball. If the dough is sticking to the sides or the bottom of the pan, you need to add a bit more bread flour. If the dough is crumbly and not in a ball, or if the ball appears firm, add more water. Your machine still has kneading time and will work the water into your bread dough. Keep checking your dough until you're satisfied that a soft, sticky ball has formed.

4 After the machine has completed the baking cycle, remove the pan from the machine and the bread from the pan to cool on a wire rack. If you cut the bread before it's cooled for about an hour, it will look doughy. The bread has to cool completely to allow the structure to set.

Per serving: *Calories 160; Protein 6g; Carbohydrates 28g; Dietary fiber 1g; Total fat 3.5g; Saturated fat 1g; Cholesterol 5mg; Sodium 260mg.*

Hearty White Bread

When you add soy flour and wheat germ you're increasing the nutritional value of the bread. The soy flour is higher in protein and lower in carbohydrates than wheat flour. The wheat germ also provides protein, plus B vitamins and vitamin E. But guess what else? It's delicious.

Preparation time: *15 minutes*

Approximate Cycle time: *2 ½ to 3 hours*

Yield: *1 ½-pound loaf, 12 slices; 2-pound loaf, 16 slices*

1 ½-lb loaf

1 cup water

2 teaspoons canola oil

2 teaspoons honey

1 teaspoons salt

3 tablespoons soy flour

1 tablespoon wheat germ

¼ cup non-fat dry milk

2 ½ cups bread flour

2 ¼ teaspoons active dry yeast

2-lb loaf

1 ¼ cups water

1 tablespoon canola oil

1 tablespoon honey

1 ½ teaspoons salt

¼ cup soy flour

4 teaspoons wheat germ

⅓ cup non-fat dry milk

3 ¼ cups bread flour

1 tablespoon active dry yeast

1 Be sure that all the ingredients are at room temperature before you place them in your bread pan in the order listed.

2 Select the Normal or Basic setting and a light to medium crust color and press Start.

3 Open the lid after the machine has kneaded the dough for about five minutes. The dough should be formed into a very soft, sticky ball. If the dough is sticking to the sides or the bottom of the pan, you need to add a bit more bread flour. If the dough is crumbly and not in a ball, or if the ball appears firm, add more water. Your machine still has kneading time and will work the water into your bread dough. Keep checking your dough until you're satisfied that a soft, sticky ball has formed.

4 After the machine has completed the baking cycle, remove the pan from the machine and the bread from the pan to cool on a wire rack. If you cut the bread before it's cooled for about an hour, it will look doughy. The bread has to cool completely to allow the structure to set.

Per serving: Calories 110; Protein 5g; Carbohydrates 21g; Dietary fiber 1g; Total fat 1g; Saturated fat 0g; Cholesterol 0mg; Sodium 200mg.

Light Rye Bread

The subtle flavor of fennel and caraway makes this an excellent rye bread to serve with an entrée of pork: a roast, spareribs, chops, or steaks. It's also great with corned beef and cabbage. We like using it to make deli-like salami, pastrami, or corned beef sandwiches.

Slice it, cut off the crusts, spread with dilly cream cheese, top with a cucumber — *voilà*, an hors d'oeuvre.

Preparation time: *15 minutes*

Approximate cycle time: *2 ½ to 3 hours*

Yield: *1 ½-pound loaf, 12 slices; 2-pound loaf, 16 slices*

1 ½-lb loaf	2-lb loaf
1 cup water	1 ⅛ cups water
4 teaspoons vegetable oil	2 tablespoons vegetable oil
1 ½ teaspoons salt	2 teaspoons salt
2 tablespoons sugar	3 tablespoons sugar
1 ½ teaspoons fennel seeds	2 teaspoons fennel seeds
1 teaspoon caraway seeds	1 ½ teaspoons caraway seeds
1 ⅓ cups medium rye flour	1 ⅔ cups medium rye flour
2 cups bread flour	2 ⅔ cups bread flour
2 ¼ teaspoons active dry yeast	1 tablespoon active dry yeast

1 Be sure that all the ingredients are at room temperature before you place them in your bread pan in the order listed.

2 Select the Normal or Basic setting and a light to medium crust color and press Start.

3 Open the lid after the machine has kneaded the dough for about five minutes. The dough should be formed into a very soft, sticky ball. If the dough is sticking to the sides or the bottom of the pan, you need to add a bit more bread flour. If the dough is crumbly and not in a ball, or if the ball appears firm, add more water. Your machine still has kneading time and will work the water into your bread dough. Keep checking your dough until you're satisfied that a soft, sticky ball has formed.

4 After the machine has completed the baking cycle, remove the pan from the machine and the bread from the pan to cool on a wire rack. If you cut the bread before it's cooled for about an hour, it will look doughy. The bread has to cool completely to allow the structure to set.

Per serving: *Calories 130; Protein 4g; Carbohydrates 26g; Dietary fiber 2g; Total fat 2g; Saturated fat 0g; Cholesterol 0mg; Sodium 290mg.*

Onion Dill

Here's an old favorite we've adapted to be made in the bread machine. It's a great sopping bread to serve with stews and casseroles.

Preparation time: *15 minutes*

Approximate cycle time: *2 ½ to 3 hours*

Yield: *1½-pound loaf, 12 slices; 2-pound loaf, 16 slices*

1 ½-lb loaf

½ cup plain yogurt

¼ cup water

4 teaspoons vegetable oil

1 egg (extra large)

1 ½ teaspoons salt

2 tablespoons sugar

1 tablespoon dried minced onions

4 teaspoons dill weed

3 cups bread flour

2 ¼ teaspoons active dry yeast

2-lb loaf

¾ cup plain yogurt

½ cup water

2 tablespoons vegetable oil

1 egg (extra large)

2 teaspoons salt

3 tablespoons sugar

4 teaspoons dried minced onions

2 tablespoons dill weed

4 cups bread flour

1 tablespoon active dry yeast

1 Be sure that all the ingredients are at room temperature before you place them in your bread pan in the order listed.

2 Select the Normal or Basic setting and a light to medium crust color and press Start.

3 Open the lid after the machine has kneaded the dough for about five minutes. The dough should be formed into a very soft, sticky ball. If the dough is sticking to the sides or the bottom of the pan, you need to add a bit more bread flour. If the dough is crumbly and not in a ball, or if the ball appears firm, add more water. Your machine still has kneading time and will work the water into your bread dough. Keep checking your dough until you're satisfied that a soft, sticky ball has formed.

4 After the machine has completed the baking cycle, remove the pan from the machine and the bread from the pan to cool on a wire rack. If you cut the bread before it's cooled for about an hour, it will look doughy. The bread has to cool completely to allow the structure to set.

Per serving: *Calories 140; Protein 6g; Carbohydrates 26g; Dietary fiber 1g; Total fat 2g; Saturated fat 0g; Cholesterol 20mg; Sodium 310mg.*

Mediterranean Bread

Here is a basic bread with an Italian flair. Just look at those Italian ingredients — olives and olive oil, garlic, a blend of Italian seasonings, and sun-dried tomatoes. Serve it with any classic American-Italian dish or simply top it with your favorite marinara sauce and pass the salad, please.

Preparation time: *15 minutes*

Approximate cycle time: *2 ½ to 3 hours*

Yield: *1 ½-pound loaf, 12 slices; 2-pound loaf, 16 slices*

1 ½-lb loaf	2-lb loaf
¾ cup water	1 cup + 2 tablespoons water
2 tablespoons olive oil	3 tablespoons olive oil
½ teaspoon salt	¾ teaspoon salt
2 tablespoons sugar	3 tablespoons sugar
½ teaspoon garlic salt	¾ teaspoon garlic salt
1 tablespoon Italian seasonings	4 teaspoons Italian seasonings
4 halves sun-dried tomatoes	6 halves sun-dried tomatoes
15 extra-large, ripe olives, pitted and patted dry	20 extra-large, ripe olives, pitted and patted dry
3 cups bread flour	4 cups bread flour
2 ¼ teaspoons active dry yeast	1 tablespoon active dry yeast

1 Be sure that all the ingredients are at room temperature before you place them in your bread pan in the order listed.

2 Select the Normal or Basic setting and a light to medium crust color and press Start.

3 Open the lid after the machine has kneaded the dough for about five minutes. The dough should be formed into a very soft, sticky ball. If the dough is sticking to the sides or the bottom of the pan, you need to add a bit more bread flour. If the dough is crumbly and not in a ball, or if the ball appears firm, add more water. Your machine still has kneading time and will work the water into your bread dough. Keep checking your dough until you're satisfied that a soft, sticky ball has formed.

4 After the machine has completed the baking cycle, remove the pan from the machine and the bread from the pan to cool on a wire rack. If you cut the bread before it's cooled for about an hour, it will look doughy. The bread has to cool completely to allow the structure to set.

Per serving: Calories 150; Protein 5g; Carbohydrates 26g; Dietary fiber 1g; Total fat 3.5g; Saturated fat 0g; Cholesterol 0mg; Sodium 240mg.

Light Wheat Bread

This is a basic recipe that provides the perfect balance between white and whole-wheat flour. It rises high and is golden in color.

Preparation time: *15 minutes*

Approximate cycle time: *2 ½ to 3 hours*

Yield: *1 ½-pound loaf, 12 slices; 2-pound loaf, 16 slices*

1 ½-lb loaf

3 tablespoons water

½ cup milk

1 egg, extra large

2 tablespoons butter, unsalted

3 tablespoons honey

1 ½ teaspoons

1 cup whole-wheat flour

2 cups bread flour

2 ¼ teaspoons active dry yeast

2-lb loaf

⅓ cup water

⅔ cup milk

1 egg, extra large

3 tablespoons butter, unsalted

¼ cup honey

2 teaspoons salt

1 ⅓ cups whole-wheat flour

2 ⅔ cups bread flour

1 tablespoon active dry yeast

1 Be sure that all the ingredients are at room temperature before you place them in your bread pan in the order listed.

2 Select the Normal or Basic setting and a light to medium crust color and press Start.

3 Open the lid after the machine has kneaded the dough for about five minutes. The dough should be formed into a very soft, sticky ball. If the dough is sticking to the sides or the bottom of the pan, you need to add a bit more bread flour. If the dough is crumbly and not in a ball, or if the ball appears firm, add more water. Your machine still has kneading time and will work the water into your bread dough. Keep checking your dough until you're satisfied that a soft, sticky ball has formed.

4 After the machine has completed the baking cycle, remove the pan from the machine and the bread from the pan to cool on a wire rack. If you cut the bread before cooled about an hour, it will look doughy. It has to cool completely to allow the structure of the bread to set.

Cooking tip: *To give the crust a nice shine and to keep it soft, rub a tablespoon of cold butter over the top and sides of the hot loaf.*

Per serving: *Calories 150; Protein 5g; Carbohydrates 27g; Dietary fiber 2g; Total fat 3g; Saturated fat 1.5g; Cholesterol 25mg; Sodium 210mg.*

Smoked salmon finger sandwich

Here's something you can do with your Onion Dill bread. Remove the crusts from slices of Onion Dill. Lay the slices on a baking sheet and toast under the broiler on one side only. Turn the slices and spread with salmon spread. How do you make salmon spread? Here goes:

3 ounces smoked salmon, shredded

8 ounces cream cheese

2 tablespoons mayonaisse

1 tablespoon lemon juice

1 teaspoon celery salt

1 tablespoon chopped fresh parsley

1 tablespoon chopped fresh dill

1 ½ teaspoons white horseradish

¼ teaspoon white pepper

Combine the ingredients in a food processor and blend until the mixture is even and can be spread easily.

Chapter 11

Hearty and Whole-Grain Breads

In This Chapter
▶ Wheat breads
▶ Other whole-grain breads

*W*ith the heightened interest in wholesome bread, these are the recipes you will find in the small, contemporary bakeries that tout crusty, flavorful bread, with interesting textures and all natural ingredients. They are practical recipes whose goodness match their full-bodied flavors. Each has a distinctive characteristic that will set it apart in your memory. What a repertoire you will have as you select breads from this chapter!

Wheat Breads

Milled from the entire wheat kernel, whole-wheat flour adds flavor, texture, and fiber to bread. Breads made with 100 percent whole-wheat flour are dense, with an earthy flavor. Fortunately, bread machines can handle these heavier doughs effortlessly, with excellent results. When whole-wheat flour is added to white bread flour, the resulting loaves have greater body, while still retaining a light texture. Using cracked wheat, oatmeal, and seeds adds texture to the breads and the necessary fiber for our diet.

100% Whole-Wheat Bread

A bread so delicious, you will wonder if you're truly eating healthy. The egg whites help to make it lighter. The cinnamon and molasses combine to give it just enough seasoning to tantalize the palate.

Preparation time: *15 minutes*

Approximate cycle time: *3 to 4 hours*

Yield: *1 ½-pound loaf, 12 slices; 2-pound loaf, 16 slices*

1 ½-lb loaf	2-lb loaf
¾ cup + 2 tablespoons water	1 cup water
1 egg white, large	2 egg whites, large
3 tablespoons vegetable oil	¼ cup vegetable oil
1 tablespoon molasses	4 teaspoons molasses
1 ½ teaspoons cinnamon	2 teaspoons cinnamon
1 teaspoon salt	1 ½ teaspoons salt
1 tablespoon vital wheat gluten	4 teaspoons vital wheat gluten
3 cups whole-wheat flour	4 cups whole-wheat flour
3 ½ teaspoons active dry yeast	4 ½ teaspoons active dry yeast
½ cup raisins	⅔ cup raisins
½ cup walnuts	⅔ cup walnuts

1 Have all the ingredients at room temperature and place them, except the raisins and walnuts, in the pan in the order listed.

2 Select a Whole Wheat cycle and medium crust color.

3 Add the raisins and the walnuts approximately five minutes before the end of the last kneading. Many machines signal with a beep that it's time to add extras like raisins and nuts.

Per serving: *Calories 200; Protein 6g; Carbohydrates 31g; Dietary fiber 5g; Total fat 7g; Saturated fat 0.5g; Cholesterol 0mg; Sodium 300mg.*

Cracked Wheat Bread

A crunchy texture and a nutty flavor make this bread delicious.

Preparation time: *1 hour*

Approximate cycle time: *2 ½ to 3 ½ hours*

Yield: *1 ½-pound loaf, 12 slices; 2-pound loaf, 16 slices*

1 ½-lb loaf

1 cup + 1 tablespoon water
½ cup cracked wheat
4 teaspoons oil
¾ teaspoon salt
4 teaspoons sugar
2 ¼ cups bread flour
2 ¼ teaspoons active dry yeast

2-lb loaf

1 ⅓ cups water
⅔ cup cracked wheat
2 tablespoons oil
1 teaspoon salt
2 tablespoons sugar
3 cups bread flour
2 ¼ teaspoons active dry yeast

1 Pour the boiling water over the cracked wheat and let it set until it's at room temperature.

2 Have all the other ingredients at room temperature, and place them in the pan in the order listed.

3 Select a Basic White or Normal cycle and medium crust color.

Per serving: *Calories 160; Protein 5g; Carbohydrates 30g; Dietary fiber 2g; Total fat 2.5g; Saturated fat 0g; Cholesterol 0mg; Sodium 290mg.*

Whole-Wheat Oatmeal Bread

What a wholesome bread this is! It's great for toast, and the walnuts make it really special. It can be made as a loaf in your bread machine, baked as a round loaf in your oven, or divided into wonderful dinner rolls.

Preparation time: *15 minutes*

Approximate cycle time: *1 hour and 20 to 30 minutes*

Approximate rising and baking time: *1 ½ hour*

Yield: *1 ½-pound loaf, 12 slices or 12 rolls; 2-pound loaf, 16 slices or 18 rolls*

1 ½-lb loaf	2-lb loaf
1 cup water	1 ¼ cups + 2 tablespoons water
2 tablespoons vegetable oil	3 tablespoons vegetable oil
¼ cup molasses	⅓ cup molasses
1 teaspoon salt	1 ½ teaspoons salt
½ cup oatmeal (dry, not cooked)	⅔ cup oatmeal (dry, not cooked)
1 cup whole-wheat flour	1 ⅓ cups whole-wheat flour
2 cups bread flour	2 ⅔ cups bread flour
2 ¼ teaspoons active dry yeast	1 tablespoon active dry yeast
¾ cup walnuts (coarsely chopped)	1 cup walnuts (coarsely chopped)
1 egg	1 egg
1 tablespoon water	1 tablespoon water
1 tablespoon oatmeal	1 tablespoon oatmeal

1 Have all the ingredients (except the egg, water, and oatmeal used for the topping) at room temperature and place them in the pan in the order listed.

2 Select the dough cycle, and when the cycle is complete, turn the dough onto a lightly floured surface.

3 Punch down to remove air bubbles, and shape the dough into a round loaf or divide it into rolls.

4 Place the loaf or rolls on a greased cookie sheet. (Pan rolls can also be made by placing the balls in a 9- x 12-inch pan.)

5 Cover and let rise in a warm place, until an indentation remains after touching the side of the loaf or roll.

6 With a fork, whisk together 1 egg and 1 tablespoon of water. Brush the egg-wash on top of the loaf. Sprinkle with dry oatmeal.

7 Bake in a preheated 375° oven for 30 to 40 minutes for the loaf, 15 minutes for individual rolls that are on a cookie sheet or in a muffin pan, or 30 to 40 minutes for pan rolls that are in a 9- x 12-inch pan.

Variation: Bake the bread in a bread machine. Lift the lid just before the bread starts to bake (about five minutes before the end of the second rise) and apply the egg-wash and oatmeal. Use a Basic White or Normal cycle.

Per serving: Calories 240; Protein 7g; Carbohydrates 38g; Dietary fiber 3g; Total fat 8g; Saturated fat 0.5g; Cholesterol 0mg; Sodium 300mg.

Seed and Wheat Bread

This recipe makes a hearty bread that's fragrant with cumin and molasses, with added flavor from sunflower nuts and sesame seeds. Enjoy a slice with a bowl of soup and you'll feel satisfied for hours.

Preparation time: 15 minutes

Approximate cycle time: 2 ½ to 3 hours

Yield: 1 ½-pound loaf, 12 slices; 2-pound loaf, 16 slices

1 ½-lb loaf	2-lb loaf
1 ⅓ cups water	1 ½ cups water
3 tablespoons oil	¼ cup oil
¼ cup light molasses	⅓ cup light molasses
1 egg, large	2 eggs, large
1 ½ teaspoons salt	2 teaspoons salt
½ teaspoon cumin	¾ teaspoon cumin
2 tablespoons sesame seeds	3 tablespoons sesame seeds
½ cup sunflower nuts	⅔ cup sunflower nuts
1 cup whole-wheat flour	1 ⅓ cups whole-wheat flour
2 cups bread flour	2 ⅔ cups bread flour
2 ¼ teaspoons active dry yeast	1 tablespoon active dry yeast

1 Have all the ingredients at room temperature and place them in the pan in the order listed.

2 Select a Basic White or Normal cycle and medium crust color.

Per serving: Calories 200; Protein 6g; Carbohydrates 29g; Dietary fiber 3g; Total fat 8g; Saturated fat 1g; Cholesterol 20mg; Sodium 50mg.

Other Hearty Breads

These breads belong in a category all their own. Each one is so unique — crowd pleasers, to say the least. Don't be surprised if you find one at your local pub or restaurant, where they serve it as their signature bread.

French Bread

This wonderful recipe was developed by Don, an owner of a Toastmaster bread machine. He and Glenna worked together to develop a full-flavored French bread with a wonderful, crisp, flaky crust.

This method is very similar to what bakers call the *sponge method*. The first step uses only part of the flour and all of the rest of the ingredients, which makes a batter. By holding this loose dough in the machine for four to eight hours, Don achieved a flavor similar to a mild sourdough and he improved the texture of the bread. Thanks, Don, for letting us share your recipe!

Preparation time: *10 minutes*

Approximate cycle time: *9 hours*

Approximate rising and baking time: *1 hour*

Yield: *12 slices*

1 ⅓ cups water	*1 package yeast*
¾ teaspoon salt	*1 egg white*
4 cups flour	

1 Have all the ingredients at room temperature.

2 Place the water, 2 cups flour, and the yeast in the bread pan.

3 Select the Dough or Manual setting and press Start.

4 Allow the cycle to mix the batter-like dough through the first kneading, and then press Stop.

5 Allow the dough to set in the pan, in the machine, for four to eight hours, and then add the remaining 2 cups of flour and the salt.

6 Select the Dough or Manual setting again, and let the machine continue through the entire cycle.

7 Remove the dough from the machine and divide it in half.

8 Shape each half into a baguette, and place them on a greased cookie sheet that's been floured with cornmeal.

9 Allow the bread to rise until an indentation remains after lightly touching the side of a baguette.

10 Place a 9-x -13-inch pan on the lowest shelf. Add boiling water to 1-inch depth.

11 Brush fully risen loaves with glaze made with 1 tablespoon water and 1 egg white whisked together.

12 With a very sharp knife, make diagonal slashes in the top of the loaf.

13 Carefully remove the hot pan of water from the oven.

14 Bake in a preheated 400° oven for 20 minutes. Cool on racks.

Variation: The bread can also be made in a bread machine, using the French cycle.

Per serving: Calories 120; Protein 5g; Carbohydrates 26g; Dietary fiber 1g; Total fat 0g; Saturated fat 0g; Cholesterol 0mg; Sodium 290mg.

Chili Bread

A terrific snack bread — extraordinarily simple to make. The dough may seem dry as it mixes. Don't add more water; instead, use a rubber spatula to help mix everything together.

Preparation time: *10 minutes*

Approximate cycle time: *2 ½ to 3 hours*

Yield: *12 slices*

15-ounce can canned chili (no beans)	½ cup cornmeal
1 egg	2 ¼ teaspoons active dry yeast
3 ¼ cups bread flour	

1 Have all the ingredients at room temperature and place them in the pan in the order listed.

2 Select a Basic White or Normal cycle and medium crust color.

The two-pound recipe is not given, as it would require a partial can of chili.

Per serving: Calories 180; Protein 8g; Carbohydrates 33g; Dietary fiber 3g; Total fat 3g; Saturated fat 1g; Cholesterol 25mg; Sodium 220mg.

Cheese and Jalapeno Bread

If you like Mexican food, you'll like this bread. The cheddar cheese and jalapeno peppers come together for a south-of-the-border flair. Choose your peppers according to your palate. Some say, the hotter the better!

Preparation time: *20 minutes*

Approximate cycle time: *2 ½ to 3 hours*

Yield: *1 ½-pound loaf, 12 slices; 2-pound loaf, 16 slices*

1 ½-lb loaf	2-lb loaf
¾ cup water	¾ cup + 1 tablespoon water
1 egg	2 eggs
¾ teaspoon salt	1 teaspoon salt
2 tablespoons sugar	3 tablespoons sugar
½ cup cornmeal	¾ cup cornmeal
3 cups bread flour	4 cups bread flour
2 ¼ teaspoons active dry yeast	1 tablespoon active dry yeast
1 cup shredded cheddar cheese	1 ⅓ cups shredded cheddar cheese
2 tablespoons chopped jalapeno peppers	3 tablespoons chopped jalapeno peppers

1 Have all the ingredients at room temperature. Dry canned jalapeno peppers on paper towels.

2 Place the ingredients, except the shredded cheddar cheese and chopped jalapeno peppers, in the pan in the order listed.

3 Select a Basic White or Normal cycle and medium crust color.

4 Add the shredded cheddar cheese and the chopped jalapeno peppers approximately five minutes before the end of the last kneading. Many machines have a beeping signal to tell you when to add extras.

Per serving: *Calories 200; Protein 8g; Carbohydrates 29g; Dietary fiber 1g; Total fat 6g; Saturated fat 2.5g; Cholesterol 30mg; Sodium 380mg.*

Five-Grain Bread

A dense, dark bread made with an interesting blend of grains. The size of this bread may be slightly smaller than others, but it has a wonderful flavor. Plus, it is so nutritious with all the grains and buttermilk.

Preparation time: 20 minutes

Approximate cycle time: 2 ½ to 3 hours

Yield: 1 ½-pound loaf, 12 slices; 2-pound loaf, 16 slices

1 ½-lb loaf	2-lb loaf
2 tablespoons water	2 tablespoons water
1 cup buttermilk	1 ⅓ cups buttermilk
1 tablespoon vegetable oil	4 teaspoons vegetable oil
3 tablespoons dark molasses	¼ cup dark molasses
¼ teaspoon baking soda	¼ teaspoon baking soda
1 teaspoon salt	1 ½ teaspoons salt
¼ cup oat bran	⅓ cup oat bran
¼ cup cornmeal	⅓ cup cornmeal
¼ cup medium rye flour	⅓ cup medium rye flour
¼ cup buckwheat flour	⅓ cup buckwheat flour
½ cup whole-wheat flour	⅔ cup whole-wheat flour
2 cups bread flour	2 ½ cups bread flour
2 ¼ teaspoons active dry yeast	1 tablespoon active dry yeast

1 Have all the ingredients at room temperature and place them in the pan in the order listed.

2 Select a Basic White or Normal cycle and medium crust color.

Per serving: Calories 150; Protein 5g; Carbohydrates 30g; Dietary fiber 2g; Total fat 2g; Saturated fat 0g; Cholesterol 0mg; Sodium 250mg.

Dark Pumpernickel Rye Bread

Warm up on a cold winter's night with this hearty, dark bread and a good bowl of hot soup. The bread is wonderfully rich and has a full-bodied, molasses flavor.

Preparation time: *15 minutes*

Approximate cycle time: *2 ½ to 3 hours*

Yield: *1 ½-pound loaf, 12 slices; 2-pound loaf, 16 slices*

1 ½-lb loaf

1 cup brewed coffee (room temperature)

2 tablespoons vegetable oil

2 tablespoons dark molasses

1 teaspoon salt

1 ½ teaspoons sugar

5 teaspoons cocoa powder

¾ teaspoon onion powder

1 cup medium rye flour

2 cups bread flour

2 ¼ teaspoons active dry yeast

2-lb loaf

1 ⅓ cups brewed coffee (room temperature)

3 tablespoons vegetable oil

3 tablespoons dark molasses

1 ½ teaspoons salt

2 teaspoons sugar

2 tablespoons cocoa powder

1 teaspoon onion powder

1 ⅓ cups medium rye flour

2 ⅔ cups bread flour

1 tablespoon active dry yeast

1 Have all the ingredients at room temperature and place them in the pan in the order listed.

2 Select a Basic White or Normal cycle and medium crust color.

Per serving: *Calories 140; Protein 4g; Carbohydrates 26g; Dietary fiber 2g; Total fat 2.5g; Saturated fat 0g; Cholesterol 0mg; Sodium 250mg.*

Buttermilk Oatmeal Bread

This bread is tender, light, and wholesome. The raisins, sunflower seeds, and sesame seeds add flavor and fiber.

Preparation time: *15 minutes*

Approximate cycle time: *2 ½ to 3 hours*

Yield: *1 ½-pound loaf, 12 slices; 2-pound loaf, 16 slices*

1 ½-lb loaf

¼ cup + 3 tablespoons water

⅔ cup buttermilk

2 tablespoons oil

1 teaspoon salt

2 tablespoons sugar

2 tablespoons sesame seeds

¼ cup raisins

¼ cup sunflower kernels

½ cup oatmeal (dry, uncooked)

3 cups bread flour

2 ¼ teaspoons active dry yeast

2-lb loaf

⅔ cup water

1 cup buttermilk

3 tablespoons oil

1 ½ teaspoons salt

3 tablespoons sugar

3 tablespoons sesame seeds

⅓ cup raisins

⅓ cup sunflower kernels

⅔ cup oatmeal (dry, uncooked)

4 cups bread flour

1 tablespoon active dry yeast

1 Have all the ingredients at room temperature and place them in the pan in the order listed.

2 Select a Basic White or Normal cycle and medium crust color.

Per serving: *Calories 140; Protein 5g; Carbohydrates 25g; Dietary fiber 1g; Total fat 2.5g; Saturated fat 0g; Cholesterol 0mg; Sodium 210mg.*

Chapter 12

Super Fast Cycles

In This Chapter

▶ Breads you can make quite quickly

*T*raditional food scientists said that it couldn't be done — bread in an hour or even less. But when we received the prototypes of these machines, we started to work on the solution and discovered that it is possible. Vital wheat gluten is one *vital* ingredient in this shortened cycle because it helps the dough to stretch easily. Also, the dough must be quite wet to expand quickly. Be sure to use fast-acting yeast or bread-machine yeast. *Do not use active dry yeast* in the short cycles.

Some of the machines begin to heat as soon as you press the Start button so the water temperature can remain at room temperature. Others heated so quickly that we had to use cold water. Yet some machines required a much warmer liquid, 110° to 115°. Be sure to check your bread machine manual to find out the recommended temperature for liquids.

We hesitated to provide recipes for the 1½-pound loaf size because they seem so small. However, we know that some of you want only a small loaf, so we included it. We like the appearance of the 2-pound loaves better. They both taste the same — and that's what counts.

Beer Rye Bread

Beer Rye Bread tastes so close to a sourdough rye that if you were blindfolded, you wouldn't be able to tell the difference.

Preparation time: *15 minutes*

Approximate cycle time: *1 hour*

Yield: *1½-pound loaf, 12 slices; 2-pound loaf, 16 slices*

1½-lb loaf	2-lb loaf
⅓ cup water	½ cup water
⅔ cup dark beer	¾ cup dark beer
1 tablespoon oil	4 teaspoons oil
1 tablespoon molasses	4 teaspoons molasses
1 teaspoon salt	1½ teaspoons salt
2 teaspoons sugar	1 tablespoon sugar
1 tablespoon crushed caraway seeds	4 teaspoons crushed caraway seeds
1 tablespoon vital wheat gluten	4 teaspoons vital wheat gluten
⅔ cup rye flour	1 cup rye flour
2⅓ cups bread flour	3 cups bread flour
1 tablespoon fast-acting yeast	4 teaspoons fast-acting yeast

1 Place all the ingredients in your bread pan in the order listed.

2 Select the Fast cycle.

3 Open the lid after the machine has kneaded the dough for about five minutes. The dough should be formed into a very soft, sticky ball. If the dough is sticking to the sides or bottom of the pan, you need to add a bit more bread flour. If the dough is crumbly — not in a ball or if the ball appears firm — add more water. Your machine still has kneading time and will work the water into your bread dough. Check on your dough until you are satisfied that a soft, sticky ball has formed.

4 After the machine has completed the baking cycle, remove the pan from the machine and transfer the bread from the pan to a wire rack to cool. If you cut the bread before it has cooled for about an hour, it will look doughy. It must cool completely to allow the structure of the bread to set.

Per serving: Calories 130; Protein 5g; Carbohydrates 24g; Dietary fiber 2g; Total fat 1.5g; Saturated fat 0g; Cholesterol 0mg; Sodium 200mg.

Fat-Free Yogurt Bread

If you're on a fat-free diet, this bread's for you. It tastes great plain, with nothing spread on top, or you can use it as a sandwich bread.

Preparation time: 10 minutes

Approximate cycle time: 1 hour

Yield: 1½-pound loaf, 12 slices; 2-pound loaf, 16 slices

1½-lb loaf	2-lb loaf
½ cup yogurt	⅔ cup yogurt
½ cup + 1 tablespoon water	¾ cup water
1 teaspoon salt	1½ teaspoons salt
½ teaspoon baking soda	¾ teaspoon baking soda
2 tablespoons sugar	3 tablespoons sugar
1 tablespoon vital wheat gluten	4 teaspoons vital wheat gluten
3 cups bread flour	4 cups bread flour
1 tablespoon fast-acting yeast	4 teaspoons fast-acting yeast

1 Place all the ingredients in your bread pan in the order listed.

2 Select the Fast cycle.

3 Open the lid after the machine has kneaded the dough for about five minutes. The dough should be formed into a very soft, sticky ball. If the dough is sticking to the sides or bottom of the pan, you need to add a bit more bread flour. If the dough is crumbly — not in a ball or if the ball appears firm — add more water. Your machine still has kneading time and will work the water into your bread dough. Check on your dough until you are satisfied that a soft, sticky ball has formed.

4 After the machine has completed the baking cycle, remove the pan from the machine and transfer the bread from the pan to a wire rack to cool. If you cut the bread before it has cooled for about an hour, it will look doughy. It must cool completely to allow the structure of the bread to set.

Per serving: Calories 120; Protein 5g; Carbohydrates 25g; Dietary fiber 1g; Total fat 0g; Saturated fat 0g; Cholesterol 0mg; Sodium 260mg.

Granola Bread

Honey with granola cereal — that sounds like breakfast. To toast or not to toast, that is the question. Granola Bread tastes great toasted, but it's good fresh out of the machine.

Preparation time: *10 minutes*

Approximate cycle time: *1 hour*

Yield: *1½-pound loaf, 12 slices; 2-pound loaf, 16 slices*

1½-lb loaf	2-lb loaf
⅓ cup water	⅔ cup water
⅔ cup milk	¾ cup milk
3 tablespoons honey	¼ cup honey
1 tablespoon oil	4 teaspoons oil
1 teaspoon salt	1½ teaspoons salt
1 tablespoon vital wheat gluten	4 teaspoons vital wheat gluten
⅓ cup whole-wheat flour	½ cup whole-wheat flour
⅓ cup granola cereal	½ cup granola cereal
2¼ cups bread flour	3 cups bread flour
1 tablespoon fast-acting yeast	4 teaspoons fast-acting yeast

1 Place all the ingredients in your bread pan in the order listed.

2 Select the Fast cycle.

3 Open the lid after the machine has kneaded the dough for about five minutes. The dough should be formed into a very soft, sticky ball. If the dough is sticking to the sides or bottom of the pan, you need to add a bit more bread flour. If the dough is crumbly — not in a ball or if the ball appears firm — add more water. Your machine still has kneading time and will work the water into your bread dough. Check on your dough until you are satisfied that a soft, sticky ball has formed.

4 After the machine has completed the baking cycle, remove the pan from the machine and transfer the bread from the pan to a wire rack to cool. If you cut the bread before it has cooled for about an hour, it will look doughy. It must cool completely to allow the structure of the bread to set.

Per serving: *Calories 140; Protein 5g; Carbohydrates 27g; Dietary fiber 1g; Total fat 2g; Saturated fat 0g; Cholesterol 0mg; Sodium 210mg.*

Muffin Mix Bread

Choose your flavor. Want strawberry bread? Buy a strawberry muffin mix. How about blueberry bread? Blueberry muffin mix to the rescue. We tried this recipe with every kind of muffin mix we could find and it turned out great bread every time.

Preparation time: *10 minutes (maybe 8 minutes — it's quick and easy)*

Approximate cycle time: *1 hour*

Yield: *1½-pound loaf, 12 slices; 2-pound loaf, 16 slices*

1½-lb loaf

1 cup + 2 tablespoons water

1 package (6 to 8 ounces) muffin mix

1 tablespoon vital wheat gluten

2 cups bread flour

1 tablespoon fast-acting yeast

2-lb loaf

1¼ cups + 3 tablespoons water

1 package (6 to 8 ounces) muffin mix

4 teaspoons vital wheat gluten

3 cups bread flour

4 teaspoons fast-acting yeast

1 Place all the ingredients in your bread pan in the order listed.

2 Select the Fast cycle.

3 Open the lid after the machine has kneaded the dough for about five minutes. The dough should be formed into a very soft, sticky ball. If the dough is sticking to the sides or bottom of the pan, you need to add a bit more bread flour. If the dough is crumbly — not in a ball or if the ball appears firm — add more water. Your machine still has kneading time and will work the water into your bread dough. Check on your dough until you are satisfied that a soft, sticky ball has formed.

4 After the machine has completed the baking cycle, remove the pan from the machine and transfer the bread from the pan to a wire rack to cool. If you cut the bread before it has cooled for about an hour, it will look doughy. It must cool completely to allow the structure of the bread to set.

Per serving: *Calories 140; Protein 5g; Carbohydrates 27g; Dietary fiber 1g; Total fat 2g; Saturated fat 0g; Cholesterol 5mg; Sodium 135mg.*

Mushroom Onion Bread

Man cannot live by bread alone. Yes, we agree. Mushroom Onion Bread needs only a bowl of soup to make a complete meal. It's rich, earthy, and good. And it's fat free!

Preparation time: *10 minutes*

Approximate cycle time: *1 hour*

Yield: *1½-pound loaf, 12 slices; 2-pound loaf, 16 slices*

1½-lb loaf

¾ cup + 2 tablespoons water

1 4-ounce can chopped mushrooms, drained

1 teaspoon salt

2 tablespoons sugar

1 tablespoon dried minced onions

¼ teaspoon garlic powder

1 tablespoon vital wheat gluten

3 cups bread flour

1 tablespoon fast-acting yeast

2-lb loaf

1 cup + 3 tablespoons water

1 4-ounce can chopped mushrooms, drained

1½ teaspoons salt

3 tablespoons sugar

4 teaspoons dried minced onions

½ teaspoon garlic powder

4 teaspoons vital wheat gluten

4 cups bread flour

4 teaspoons fast-acting yeast

1 Place all the ingredients in your bread pan in the order listed.

2 Select the Fast cycle.

3 Open the lid after the machine has kneaded the dough for about five minutes. The dough should be formed into a very soft, sticky ball. If the dough is sticking to the sides or bottom of the pan, you need to add a bit more bread flour. If the dough is crumbly — not in a ball or if the ball appears firm — add more water. Your machine still has kneading time and will work the water into your bread dough. Check on your dough until you are satisfied that a soft, sticky ball has formed.

4 After the machine has completed the baking cycle, remove the pan from the machine and transfer the bread from the pan to a wire rack to cool. If you cut the bread before it has cooled for about an hour, it will look doughy. It must cool completely to allow the structure of the bread to set.

Tip: A 4-ounce can of mushrooms equals ¼ cup of solidly packed chopped mushrooms.

Tip: If you're chopping mushrooms in a small food processor, include the canning juices for an efficient chopping process, and then drain the mushrooms well and dry thoroughly on paper towels.

Per serving: Calories 120; Protein 5g; Carbohydrates 25g; Dietary fiber 1g; Total fat 0g; Saturated fat 0g; Cholesterol 0mg; Sodium 210mg.

Peanut Butter and Jelly Bread

Peanut butter and jelly are staples in American homes. Who doesn't remember devouring PB&J sandwiches as a kid? Put the peanut butter and jelly *in* the bread and, mmm, it's good.

Preparation time: *10 minutes*

Approximate cycle time: *1 hour*

Yield: *1½-pound loaf, 12 slices; 2-pound loaf, 16 slices*

1½-lb loaf

¾ cup water

⅓ cup milk

⅓ cup creamy peanut butter

1 egg, extra large

2 tablespoons honey

1 teaspoon salt

½ cup peanut butter chips

½ cup dried fruit

⅓ cup whole-wheat flour

2⅓ cups bread flour

1 tablespoon fast-acting yeast

2-lb loaf

1 cup water

½ cup milk

½ cup creamy peanut butter

1 egg, extra large

3 tablespoons honey

1½ teaspoon salt

⅔ cup peanut butter chips

⅔ cup dried fruit

½ cup whole-wheat flour

3 cups bread flour

4 teaspoons fast-acting yeast

1 Place all the ingredients in your bread pan in the order listed.

2 Select the Fast cycle.

3 Open the lid after the machine has kneaded the dough for about five minutes. The dough should be formed into a very soft, sticky ball. If the dough is sticking to the sides or bottom of the pan, you need to add a bit more bread flour. If the dough is crumbly — not in a ball or if the ball appears firm — add more water. Your machine still has kneading time and will work the water into your bread dough. Check on your dough until you are satisfied that a soft, sticky ball has formed.

4 After the machine has completed the baking cycle, remove the pan from the machine and transfer the bread from the pan to a wire rack to cool. If you cut the bread before it has cooled for about an hour, it will look doughy. It must cool completely to allow the structure of the bread to set.

Per serving: Calories 210; Protein 8g; Carbohydrates 31g; Dietary fiber 3g; Total fat 6g; Saturated fat 2g; Cholesterol 20mg; Sodium 260mg.

Potato Bread

Use potatoes to create a rich, soft-textured bread, the kind that mothers used to make. At first, we thought that you would use leftover mashed potatoes for this bread. But then we thought that maybe you don't mash potatoes, or if you do, you don't have any on hand. In that case, you'll need to boil some potatoes. A 6-ounce potato will yield approximately ¾ cup mashed; an 8-ounce potato will yield about 1 cup. If you do boil the potatoes just for this bread, use the cooled potato water as the water ingredient in this recipe.

Preparation time: *10 minutes*

Approximate cycle time: *1 hour*

Yield: *1½-pound loaf, 12 slices; 2-pound loaf, 16 slices*

1½-lb loaf

¾ cup mashed potatoes

¾ cup + 1 tablespoon water

4 teaspoons oil

1 tablespoon sugar

1 teaspoon salt

1 tablespoon vital wheat gluten

3 cups bread flour

1 tablespoon fast-acting yeast

2-lb loaf

1 cup mashed potatoes

1 cup + 2 tablespoons water

2 tablespoons oil

4 teaspoons sugar

1¼ teaspoons salt

4 teaspoons vital wheat gluten

4 cups bread flour

4 teaspoons fast-acting yeast

1 Place all the ingredients in your bread pan in the order listed.

2 Select the Fast cycle.

3 Open the lid after the machine has kneaded the dough for about five minutes. The dough should be formed into a very soft, sticky ball. If the dough is sticking to the sides or bottom of the pan, you need to add a bit more bread flour. If the dough is crumbly — not in a ball or if the ball appears firm — add more water. Your machine still has kneading time and will work the water into your bread dough. Check on your dough until you are satisfied that a soft, sticky ball has formed.

4 After the machine has completed the baking cycle, remove the pan from the machine and transfer the bread from the pan to a wire rack to cool. If you cut the bread before it has cooled for about an hour, it will look doughy. It must cool completely to allow the structure of the bread to set.

Per serving: *Calories 140; Protein 5g; Carbohydrates 26g; Dietary fiber 1g; Total fat 2g; Saturated fat 0g; Cholesterol 0mg; Sodium 230mg.*

Pumpkin Pie Bread

You've heard the saying "easy as pie." This delicious bread is made by using pumpkin pie mix, and it's as easy as pie to make. Believe it or not, we could not include a 2-pound size for Pumpkin Pie Bread because it would overflow the pan. It has a great flavor and a moist, tender texture.

Preparation time: *10 minutes*

Approximate cycle time: *1 hour*

Yield: *1½-pound loaf, 12 slices*

1 cup pumpkin pie mix	*½ cup toasted chopped pecans*
2 eggs, large	*1 tablespoon vital wheat gluten*
4 teaspoons butter	*3 cups bread flour*
¼ cup oatmeal	*1 tablespoon fast-acting yeast*
⅓ cup raisins	

1 Place all the ingredients in your bread pan in the order listed.

2 Select the Fast cycle.

3 Open the lid after the machine has kneaded the dough for about five minutes. The dough should be formed into a very soft, sticky ball. If the dough is sticking to the sides or bottom of the pan, you need to add a bit more bread flour. If the dough is crumbly — not in a ball or if the ball appears firm — add more water. Your machine still has kneading time and will work the water into your bread dough. Check on your dough until you are satisfied that a soft, sticky ball has formed.

4 After the machine has completed the baking cycle, remove the pan from the machine and transfer the bread from the pan to a wire rack to cool. If you cut the bread before it has cooled for about an hour, it will look doughy. It must cool completely to allow the structure of the bread to set.

Per serving: *Calories 200; Protein 7g; Carbohydrates 33g; Dietary fiber 2g; Total fat 6g; Saturated fat 1.5g; Cholesterol 45mg; Sodium 45mg.*

Saffron Bread

Tom is most familiar with Saffron Bread from Sweden. We adapted one of his recipes to use on the Fast cycle. Although saffron brings a golden color and its own distinct flavor to the bread, and a little saffron is good, too much saffron gives a medicinal flavor. Use only as directed.

Preparation time: *10 minutes*

Approximate cycle time: *1 hour*

Yield: *1½-pound loaf, 12 slices; 2-pound loaf, 16 slices*

1½-lb loaf

⅔ cup milk

2 eggs, large

4 teaspoons butter

1 teaspoon salt

2 tablespoons sugar

¼ teaspoon saffron

1 tablespoon vital wheat gluten

3 cups bread flour

1 tablespoon fast-acting yeast

2-lb loaf

¾ cup milk

3 eggs, large

2 tablespoons butter

1½ teaspoons salt

3 tablespoons sugar

¼ teaspoon saffron

4 teaspoons vital wheat gluten

4 cups bread flour

4 teaspoons fast-acting yeast

1 Place all the ingredients in your bread pan in the order listed.

2 Select the Fast cycle.

3 Open the lid after the machine has kneaded the dough for about five minutes. The dough should be formed into a very soft, sticky ball. If the dough is sticking to the sides or bottom of the pan, you need to add a bit more bread flour. If the dough is crumbly — not in a ball or if the ball appears firm — add more water. Your machine still has kneading time and will work the water into your bread dough. Check on your dough until you are satisfied that a soft, sticky ball has formed.

4 After the machine has completed the baking cycle, remove the pan from the machine and transfer the bread from the pan to a wire rack to cool. If you cut the bread before it has cooled for about an hour, it will look doughy. It must cool completely to allow the structure of the bread to set.

Tip: Crush slightly less than ½ teaspoon saffron threads to make ¼ teaspoon powdered saffron.

Per serving: *Calories 140; Protein 6g; Carbohydrates 25g; Dietary fiber 1g; Total fat 2.5g; Saturated fat 1g; Cholesterol 45mg; Sodium 210mg.*

Spaghetti Bread

This is a wonderful sopping bread. Try it with beef stew. You won't want to eat stew without Spaghetti Bread ever again. You'll spend longer making the stew than the bread.

Preparation time: 10 minutes (depending on how long it takes you to open a can)

Approximate cycle time: 1 hour

Yield: 1½-pound loaf, 12 slices; 2-pound loaf, 16 slices

1½-lb loaf

1⅓ cups spaghetti sauce

2 tablespoons vegetable oil

1 tablespoon vital wheat gluten

3 cups bread flour

1 tablespoon fast-acting yeast

2-lb loaf

1¾ cups spaghetti sauce

3 tablespoons vegetable oil

4 teaspoons vital wheat gluten

4 cups bread flour

4 teaspoons fast-acting yeast

1 Place all the ingredients in your bread pan in the order listed.

2 Select a fast cycle.

3 Open the lid after the machine has kneaded the dough for about five minutes. For this recipe, the dough should be soft and sticky, cleaning the side of the pan but not the bottom. If the dough is crumbly — not in a ball or if the ball appears firm — add more water. Your machine still has kneading time and will work the water into your bread dough. Check on your dough until you are satisfied that a soft, sticky ball has formed.

4 After the machine has completed the baking cycle, remove the pan from the machine and transfer the bread from the pan to a wire rack to cool. If you cut the bread before it has cooled for about an hour, it will look doughy. It must cool completely to allow the structure of the bread to set.

Per serving: *Calories 150; Protein 5g; Carbohydrates 25g; Dietary fiber 2g; Total fat 3.5g; Saturated fat 0g; Cholesterol 0mg; Sodium 150mg.*

Chapter 13

Celebrate the Seasons

- -

- -

*I*n this chapter, we give you some great seasonal recipes — one for every month of the year, in fact. We hope you don't mind that all these recipes cater to those with a sweet tooth.

Before You Begin

You need to become accustomed to using the Basic Danish Dough before trying the recipes in this chapter. It's the kind of dough that you'll want to use when you are making dinner rolls, coffee cakes, and sweet rolls. Maybe you will be in a fine restaurant or a bakery and find an idea from their specialty breads. Chances are pretty good that you'll be able to copy the idea using this versatile dough. This dough is easy to prepare in your bread machine and easy to work with. Best of all, it can be made, refrigerated, and used up to three days later.

Basic Danish Dough

Preparation time: 10 minutes

Approximate cycle time: 20 minutes

Yield: Approximately 12 rolls or 1½-pound bread

2 eggs, large	1½ teaspoons salt
½ cup milk	3 cups bread flour
4 tablespoons unsalted butter, softened	2¼ teaspoons active dry yeast
¼ cup sugar	

1 Have all ingredients at room temperature.

2 Place in the bread machine.

3 Select the Dough or Manual setting.

4 When the kneading is complete, stop the machine. You do not want the dough to rise in the machine.

5 Remove the dough, and place it in a lightly oiled bowl or a large self-sealing plastic bag.

6 Refrigerate for at least eight hours.

7 Punch the dough down approximately one hour after you put it in the refrigerator; repeat again in about two hours. When the dough has completely chilled, it will continue to rise very slowly. If you are keeping it longer than eight hours, punch it down at least once a day, and maybe twice.

Per serving: Calories 170; Protein 6g; Carbohydrates 27g; Dietary fiber less than 1g; Total fat 5g; Saturated fat 3g; Cholesterol 50mg; Sodium 310mg.

The Seasonal Recipes

After you've mastered the Basic Danish Dough, you can try the rest of the recipes in this chapter.

Cooks sometimes talk about putting "love" in their recipes, especially when referring to the kinds of comfort foods that families often share. The recipes in this chapter certainly fall in the category of comfort food. After all, what's more comforting than warm cinnamon buns or applesauce donuts? Maybe that love people refer to is actually something as simple as sugar (and the desire to make sweet treats for one's loved ones, of course).

So a word of caution: With everything from elephant ears to coffee cake on the following pages, if you have a sweet tooth, you'll have a hard time resisting the concoctions in this chapter. Even if sweets aren't on your list of favorite things, we're sure that you'll find these recipes delicious.

January — Frosted Cinnamon Buns

Tom likes to start off the new year on a sweet note with these delicious sticky buns. Because most of us like to sleep in on the first day of the new year, you can do as he does and prepare the dough the day before, chilling in the refrigerator for at least eight hours. Remove the dough before going to bed and let it rise, still covered, in an unlit oven during the night. Simply punch the dough down when you get up, shape it, and let it rise for a second time as the oven preheats. Then wait and watch as the rest of the family gets lifted out of bed by the rich aroma of cinnamon and spice.

Preparation time: 20 minutes

Approximate rising time: 2 hours

Baking time: 25 to 30 minutes

Yield: Approximately 12 rolls

Use 1 recipe Basic Danish Dough

Add 1½ teaspoon grated lemon peel

2 tablespoons unsalted butter, softened (do not add this to the dough)

1 Pat or roll dough into a flat rectangle.

2 Roll out the dough to approximately a 17-x-13-inch rectangle (about ¼-inch thick).

3 Spread the unsalted butter to within 1 inch of the edges of the dough.

4 Sprinkle the dough with the filling (see the following recipe).

5 Beginning with the short side, roll the dough into a 13-inch-long log.

6 Cut the log into 12 buns.

7 Place the buns in either two greased 9-inch cake pans or a greased 9-x-13-inch pan.

8 Cover and let rise for approximately two hours or until indentation remains when lightly touched.

9 Bake in a preheated oven at 350° for 25 to 30 minutes.

10 Cool the buns on a wire rack for 15 minutes, and then add frosting (see the following recipe).

When the buns are rising in the pan, you can tell that they are ready to pop in the oven by lightly pushing one finger into the side of one roll to make a slight indentation. If the indentation remains, the rolls are oven ready. If the dough moves back out, you need to let them rise more.

Variation: *In place of the melted butter, you can brush the dough with 1 slightly beaten egg, mixed with 1 tablespoon of water. Some bakers think the egg adds to the tenderness of the dough.*

Filling

½ cup finely chopped walnuts

⅓ cup granulated sugar

¼ cup packed light brown sugar

1½ teaspoons ground cinnamon

1 cup golden raisins

1 Mix the filling ingredients together.

Frosting

1 ounce cream cheese, room temperature

1¼ cups confectionery sugar, sifted

1½ tablespoons orange juice

¼ teaspoon vanilla

1 While the buns bake, beat the frosting ingredients in a medium bowl with an electric beater until smooth.

2 Spoon the glaze evenly over the warm buns.

Per serving: *Calories 300; Protein 7g; Carbohydrates 51g; Dietary fiber 2g; Total fat 9g; Saturated fat 3.5g; Cholesterol 55mg; Sodium 320mg.*

February — Glazed Cherry Heart

Here's a Valentine from the kitchen. Some bakers express their love with cookies and cakes, but you can use this idea for a special coffee cake. We added the dried sweet cherries because they are red, they taste good, and — one more reason — George Washington cut down his father's cherry tree, remember? He did not tell a lie, and neither will we. The almond extract, nutmeg, and cardamom blended into the dough make this an extraordinary coffee cake.

Preparation time: 30 minutes

Approximate rising time: 2 hours

Baking time: 20 to 25 minutes

Yield: 1 cake

Use 1 recipe Basic Danish Dough
Add the following:
½ teaspoon almond extract

¼ teaspoon ground nutmeg
½ teaspoon ground cardamom

Glaze

1 egg, extra large
1 teaspoon sugar

1 teaspoon water

Filling

½ cup dark brown sugar
¾ cup ground walnuts or pecans

1½ teaspoons ground cinnamon
⅔ cup dried sweet cherries

1 On a lightly floured surface, roll the dough into a 12-x-18-inch rectangle (about ½-inch thick).

2 Wisk together the glaze ingredients with a fork.

3 Brush the dough with half the glaze mixture.

4 Combine the filling ingredients and sprinkle the filling over the dough.

5 Starting with wide side, roll the dough tightly and pinch the seams and ends.

6 Place the dough on a greased baking sheet, seam side up.

7 Fold the roll in half (on top of itself), sealing the ends together.

8 With scissors, cut from the folded end down to the center of the roll to within 1 inch of the other end.

9 Make a heart by turning the cut halves out with the cut side up.

10 Cover and let rise for about two hours or until an indentation remains after lightly touching side of the dough.

11 Brush the remaining glaze on the dough heart.

12 Bake in a preheated oven at 350° for 20 to 25 minutes, or until golden brown.

Variation: Grated orange peel can be substituted for the almond extract. Grated nutmeg or ground cinnamon can be substituted for the cardamom.

Per serving: Calories 230; Protein 8g; Carbohydrates 34g; Dietary fiber 2g; Total fat 8g; Saturated fat 3g; Cholesterol 50mg; Sodium 310mg.

March — Hot Cross Buns

Hot Cross Buns were sold in the streets of London on Good Friday. You probably already know that and didn't know you knew. Remember the nursery rhyme, "One-a-penny, two-a-penny, hot cross buns," from the beckoning chant of the peddler?

From the bakeries of England to your home, we present to you the American version of Hot Cross Buns for a traditional Easter morning breakfast.

Preparation time: 30 minutes

Approximate rising time: 2 hours

Baking time: 10 to 12 minutes

Yield: 12 buns

Use 1 recipe Basic Danish Dough	*¼ teaspoon ground cloves*
Add the following:	*⅛ teaspoon grated nutmeg*
1½ teaspoon grated lemon peel	*⅓ cup raisins or currants*

Frosting

1 cup confectioners sugar	*3 tablespoons milk*
½ teaspoon vanilla extract	

Glaze

1 extra large egg white	*1 teaspoon water*

1 On a lightly floured work surface, cut the dough into three equal parts and then cut each part into four pieces. (Lightly sprinkle the dough with flour if it is too sticky to handle.)

2 Shape each piece into a smooth ball.

3 Place balls on a lightly greased 13-x-9-x-1-inch baking pan, with sides barely touching.

4 Cover and let rise until an indentation remains after lightly touching the side of one bun, approximately two hours.

5 Beat together the glaze ingredients with a fork and brush on buns.

6 Bake in a preheated oven at 375° for 10 to 12 minutes, or until lightly golden.

7 Mix together the frosting ingredients and set aside.

8 Remove the buns from the oven and cool on a wire rack.

9 When the buns are cool, pipe a cross of frosting on each bun.

You can form the dough pieces into balls in several different ways. Any method takes practice to perfect. Here are three ways:

- *You can hold the ball in one hand and with the other hand, pinch a small section between your thumb and first two fingers. Gently stretch out the dough, pulling it down toward the center of the bottom of the ball. Turn the ball, and continue until you have rounded the top and tucked in the bottom.*

- *You can roll the dough into a ball between the palms of both hands like you would if you have a chunk of modeling clay.*

- *You can place the ball of dough on the work surface, cup your hand over the dough, and rotate the ball with your hand.*

Per serving: *Calories 220; Protein 6g; Carbohydrates 39g; Dietary fiber 1g; Total fat 5g; Saturated fat 3g; Cholesterol 50mg; Sodium 320mg.*

April — Greek Easter Bread

The distinction of a Greek Easter Bread is anise. The Basic Danish Dough is so tender that it can become an ethnic bread simply with the addition of aniseed (also called anise).

Greek Easter Bread was made with red colored raw eggs implanted in the top of the dough and baked with the bread. However, we are aware now that this is not a good idea because of food safety. The eggs need to be refrigerated as soon as the bread is cooled, and the refrigerator is not a good place for keeping the bread fresh.

Therefore, for health safety, we suggest that when you present the bread at the table, you place hard-boiled eggs (that you've dyed red) in the center of the braid circle.

Preparation time: 30 minutes

Approximate rising time: 2 hours

Baking time: 25 to 30 minutes

Yield: 1 loaf

Use 1 recipe Basic Danish Dough   *Add 1 teaspoon aniseed*

Glaze

1 egg, extra large   *1 teaspoon water*

1 On a lightly floured board, divide the dough into three equal sections.

2 Roll each section into an 18-inch rope.

3 Lay the three ropes side by side.

4 Braid ropes from center to ends.

5 Form the braid into a circle, weaving the ends together.

6 With your hands in the center of the circle, gently pull the braid outward so that you create a space in the middle of the braided circle. Place a small, greased, oven-proof bowl in center to maintain shape.

7 Cover and allow to rise until an indentation remains after lightly touching the side of the braid, approximately two hours.

8 Whisk together the glaze ingredients with a fork and brush the glaze on the braid.

9 Bake in a preheated oven at 375° for 25 to 30 minutes.

10 Remove the bread from the oven, and cool on a rack.

Per serving: Calories 180; Protein 7g; Carbohydrates 27g; Dietary fiber less than 1g; Total fat 6g; Saturated fat 3g; Cholesterol 75mg; Sodium 320mg.

May — Baked Applesauce Spice Donuts

When Glenna made these for her teenage sons and their friends, she could never make enough. Boys absolutely love these donuts. Come to think of it, they sometimes had their girlfriends along, who ate their fair share as well. Glenna used to make donuts and fry them, but with fat being on the "watch it" list, she tried this method and it works fine.

Preparation time: 30 minutes

Approximate rising time: 2 hours

Baking time: 12 to 15 minutes

Yield: 12 donuts, 12 holes, and some dough scraps (bake them too for the kitchen crew)

Use 1 Basic Danish Dough

Substitute 2 eggs with ½ cup unsweetened applesauce

Add 2 teaspoons ground cinnamon

Topping

3 tablespoon melted butter for brushing on warm donuts

½ cup granulated sugar

½ teaspoon ground cinnamon

1 Pat the dough into a circle, about ½-inch thick.

2 Using a donut cutter, cut out donuts and holes, rerolling the dough as necessary.

3 Place on two well-greased baking pans.

4 Let rise until an indentation remains after lightly touching the side of a donut, approximately two hours.

5 Bake in a preheated oven at 400° for 12 to 15 minutes.

6 Cool on a rack.

7 Brush all sides of warm donuts with melted butter.

8 Combine the sugar and cinnamon for the topping, and sprinkle on the warm buttered donuts.

If you do not have a donut cutter, you can use two different sizes of biscuit cutters. You can also cut the dough into strips and twist the strips for an interesting effect.

Per serving: Calories 230; Protein 6g; Carbohydrates 37g; Dietary fiber 1g; Total fat 8g; Saturated fat 4.5g; Cholesterol 60mg; Sodium 310mg.

June — Sandwich Tea Rolls

Entertaining friends and family in June with graduation open houses, bridal showers, wedding receptions, and/or membership appreciation events can be time-consuming. You can make these sandwich tea rolls in steps and yet have them fresh for your special occasion. They are quite attractive and will dress up any tea sandwich you plan to have.

Preparation time: 20 minutes

Approximate rising time: 2 hours

Baking time: 10 to 12 minutes

Yield: Approximately 24 tea rolls

Use 1 recipe Basic Danish Dough   *Add 1½ teaspoons grated lemon peel*

1 Make the dough and refrigerate or freeze it.

2 When you know that you'll have a block of time, plan to have the dough thawed and at room temperature.

3 To make rolls with an equal amount of dough in each roll, use a small kitchen scale to make the rolls into 1-ounce pieces. If you do not have a scale, divide the dough in half, and then half again and again. You should have eight equal pieces. Divide each of these pieces into thirds, and you will have 24 rolls.

4 Shape the dough into rolls (see the directions for Hot Cross Buns in this chapter).

5 Place the rolls 2 inches apart on greased cookie sheets.

6 Cover and let rise until an indentation remains after lightly touching side of one roll, approximately two hours.

7 Bake in a preheated oven at 375° for 10 to 12 minutes, or until lightly golden.

8 Remove the rolls from the oven, and cool on wire racks.

The baked rolls may be frozen until the day you serve them.

Thaw the rolls and place them in a brown paper grocery bag. Run the bag under the water faucet to wet, not soak, the entire bag.

Place the bag in the oven at 300° for approximately ten minutes until the bag is dry. The rolls will be as warm and fresh as if they were coming out of the oven for the first time.

Per serving: *Calories 170; Protein 6g; Carbohydrates 27g; Dietary fiber less than 1g; Total fat 5g; Saturated fat 3g; Cholesterol 50mg; Sodium 310mg.*

July — Red, White, and Blue Danish

Whether you're patriotic enough to make these for the morning of the Fourth of July or just decide to make them for the morning of the fourth of December, your family and friends will appreciate a wonderful treat with little effort on your part. These danish rolls are quick and easy to form, fill, and frost.

Preparation time: 20 minutes

Approximate rising time: 2 hours

Baking time: 12 to 15 minutes

Yield: 12 rolls

Use 1 recipe Basic Danish Dough

Filling

Strawberry and blueberry pie filling

Icing

1½ cups confectioners sugar, sifted
3 tablespoons water

½ teaspoon vanilla extract

1 On a lightly floured work surface, divide the dough into four sections, and then divide each section into three pieces.

2 Roll each piece into a 16-inch-long rope.

3 Loosely coil each rope, tucking the end under the coil.

4 Place on lightly greased baking pans 2 inches apart.

5 Cover and let rise until an indentation remains after lightly touching the side of one roll, approximately two hours.

6 Form a 2-inch-wide well in the center of each danish by gently pressing down with your fingertips.

7 Barely fill the well with the desired filling. (If you overfill, the filling will run out onto the pan during baking.)

8 Bake in a preheated oven at 400° for 12 to 15 minutes, or until golden brown.

9 Remove the danish from the baking sheet and cool on wire racks.

10 Combine ingredients for icing and lightly frost the danish while they are slightly warm.

Per serving: Calories 240; Protein 6g; Carbohydrates 44g; Dietary fiber 1g; Total fat 5g; Saturated fat 3g; Cholesterol 50mg; Sodium 320mg.

August — Peach Pizza

If you are fortunate enough to live in a state like Michigan, Ohio, or Georgia where home-grown peaches are sold at roadside fruit stands, you will love this recipe. The rest of us will have to trust our luck at finding trucked-in peaches with good flavor or use canned peaches to enjoy Peach Pizza.

Preparation time: 20 minutes

Approximate rising time: 1 to 2 hours

Baking time: 25 to 30 minutes

Yield: 2 12-inch pizzas

Use 1 recipe Basic Danish Dough

Topping

8 large ripe peaches, peeled and sliced into eighths

8 ounces of cream cheese, softened to room temperature

½ cup sugar

2 teaspoons cornstarch

1 teaspoon ground cinnamon

½ teaspoon grated nutmeg

1 On a lightly floured board, divide the dough into two sections.

2 Roll or pat each section into a 12-inch circle on an ungreased pizza pan.

3 Spread each circle with 4 ounces of softened cream cheese.

4 Place peaches in a concentric circle on top of dough, overlapping slightly.

5 Combine sugar, ground cinnamon, and grated nutmeg, and sprinkle over the peaches.

6 Lightly cover and let rise until an indentation remains when lightly touched, approximately 1 to 2 hours.

7 Bake in a preheated oven at 375° for 25 to 30 minutes.

Per serving: Calories 300; Protein 8g; Carbohydrates 43g; Dietary fiber 2g; Total fat 12g; Saturated fat 7g; Cholesterol 75mg; Sodium 370mg.

September — Apple Kuchen

Kuchen is a yeast coffee cake. What better way to showcase fresh fall apples than on a base of soft but not too sweet cake? Perhaps slightly warm from the oven? Maybe with a scoop of ice cream?

Preparation time: 20 minutes

Approximate rising time: 2 hours

Baking time: 25 to 30 minutes

Yield: 2 9-inch cakes

Use 1 recipe Basic Danish Dough

6 Granny Smith, Macintosh, or other tart baking apples, peeled, cored, and cubed

2 tablespoons unsalted butter, melted

Topping

⅓ cup unsalted butter, softened

⅔ cup all-purpose flour

⅓ cup dark brown sugar, packed

4 teaspoons granulated white sugar

2 teaspoons ground cinnamon

¼ teaspoon grated or ground nutmeg

Dusting

¼ cup confectionery sugar

1 On a lightly floured work surface, divide the dough into two parts.

2 Pat each half into a greased 9-inch round cake pan, forming a narrow rim around the edge.

3 Spread with softened butter.

4 Arrange the apples evenly over the dough.

5 Combine the remaining topping ingredients and sprinkle over the apples.

6 Cover and let rise until an indentation remains after lightly pushing in with a finger on the rim of the kuchen, approximately two hours.

7 Bake in a preheated oven at 350° for 25 to 30 minutes until the edges are golden brown.

8 Cool on a wire rack.

9 Generously dust the cooled kuchen with powdered sugar.

Per serving: Calories 330; Protein 7g; Carbohydrates 50g; Dietary fiber 2g; Total fat 12g; Saturated fat 7g; Cholesterol 70mg; Sodium 320mg.

October — Elephant Ears

Calling all kids — we have your favorite snack! You can even make them yourself. And they have cinnamon and chocolate! Yum. They are so good. You could use them for a party. You could even decorate them to look like jack-o'-lanterns for Halloween.

Preparation time: 30 minutes

Approximate rising time: 2 hours

Baking time: 15 to 18 minutes

Yield: 1 cake

Use 1 recipe Basic Danish Dough

Add 2 squares (1 ounce each) semisweet chocolate, melted but not hot

2 tablespoons melted butter (do not add this to the dough)

Filling

⅓ cup sugar

1 teaspoon cinnamon

Topping

2 tablespoons melted butter (do not add this to other topping ingredients)

½ cup sugar

½ cup finely chopped pecans or walnuts

1 teaspoon cinnamon

1 On a lightly floured surface, roll the dough to a 12-inch square.

2 Brush the dough with melted butter.

3 Sprinkle filling over dough.

4 Roll the dough tightly.

5 Pinch the edge to seal.

6 Cut the dough into 12 slices.

7 Place on greased cookie sheets 3 to 4 inches apart.

8 Flatten each slice to a 4-inch circle.

9 Cover and let rise until an indentation remains after lightly pushing in with a finger on side of one roll (about two hours).

10 Prepare topping by combining sugar, nuts, and cinnamon.

11 Cover each roll with waxed paper.

12 With a rolling pin, flatten each roll to ⅛-inch thick.

13 Brush the rolls with melted butter.

14 Sprinkle the topping over the rolls and re-cover each roll with waxed paper.

15 With a rolling pin, roll the topping into the rolls.

16 Bake in a preheated oven at 400° for 15 to 18 minutes until rolls are crisp around the edges.

17 Cool on wire racks.

Per serving: Calories 310; Protein 7g; Carbohydrates 44g; Dietary fiber 1g; Total fat 14g; Saturated fat 7g; Cholesterol 65mg; Sodium 310mg.

Chicken salad spread

A simple chicken salad served in a tea roll (see the June recipe) with a few small lettuce leaves is elegant and appeals to everyone's palate.

> 2 cups finely diced chicken
>
> 1 cup finely chopped celery
>
> 2 tablespoons chopped pickles
>
> 1 teaspoon seasoned salt
>
> 1 teaspoon poultry seasoning
>
> ⅓ cup mayonnaise or salad dressing
>
> 3 tablespoons plain yogurt

1 Combine ingredients and refrigerate.

2 Fill sandwiches just before serving.

Canned boneless chicken eliminates the time-consuming cooking and chopping steps, and comes precooked in chunk or shredded form as white, dark, or mixed meat. It is packed in broth, sauce, or water, with both salted and low-salt varieties available to suit most any flavor. We usually choose shredded, mixed white and dark meat in water for fillings and spreads.

November — Pumpkin 'n Spice Dinner Rolls

These delicately spiced pumpkin rolls are filled with flavors of the fall: ginger, nutmeg, cinnamon, walnuts, dried cranberries, and dark raisins.

Preparation time: 30 minutes

Approximate rising time: 2 hours

Baking time: 15 to 20 minutes

Yield: 12 to 18 dinner rolls

Use 1 recipe Basic Danish Dough (but eliminate one egg when you make the dough)

Add the following:

1½ teaspoons grated lemon peel

½ cup canned pumpkin

¼ teaspoon ground ginger

¼ teaspoon ground nutmeg

¼ teaspoon ground cinnamon

½ cup finely chopped walnuts

¼ cup dried cranberries

¼ cup dark raisins

Making Parker House rolls

1 Divide dough in half and then each half into three equal sections. Separate each section into three equal parts to make 18 rolls.

2 Flatten each part into a 2½-inch slightly oval shape.

3 Make a crease in the dough, slightly off the middle.

4 Fold the smaller side over the larger side.

5 Press the edges together.

6 Place rolls 2 to 3 inches apart on greased cookie sheets.

7 Cover and let rise until an indentation remains after lightly pushing in with a finger on side of one roll (about two hours).

8 Bake rolls in a preheated oven at 375° for 12 to 15 minutes.

Making Cloverleaf rolls

1 Grease the cups of a muffin pan.

2 Divide dough in half and then half again. Separate each section into three equal parts to make 12 rolls.

3 Divide dough for each roll into thirds.

4 Shape each third into a smooth ball (see the cooking tip for shaping dough balls in Chapter 8).

5 Place three balls in each muffin cup.

6 Cover and let rise until an indentation remains after lightly pushing in with a finger on side of one roll (about two hours).

7 Bake rolls in a preheated oven at 375° for 15 to 20 minutes.

Variation: *You can brush warm rolls with melted butter for a softer crust.*

Per serving: *Calories 220; Protein 7g; Carbohydrates 33g; Dietary fiber 2g; Total fat 8g; Saturated fat 3g; Cholesterol 50mg; Sodium 310mg.*

December — Saint Lucia Crown

In Sweden, this double-tiered braided coffee cake, which looks like a crown, is served with hot coffee at dawn on St. Lucia's Day, December 13, to signal the opening of the Christmas season. Even if you're not Scandinavian, this "crown" makes a beautiful centerpiece for holiday brunches or buffets.

Preparation time: 30 minutes

Approximate rising time: 2 hours

Baking time: 20 to 25 minutes

Yield: 12 dinner rolls

Use 1 recipe Basic Danish Dough

Add the following:

1½ teaspoons grated lemon peel

½ teaspoon saffron threads powdered to ¼ teaspoon

3 tablespoons chopped candied citron

3 tablespoons chopped almonds

Glaze

1 egg, large

1 teaspoon water

Icing and decorations

1 cup sifted confectionery sugar

2 tablespoons hot water

½ teaspoon vanilla extract

Candied cherries

1 Cut off one-third of the dough and set aside.

2 Divide the remaining dough into three equal parts.

3 On a lightly floured surface, roll each third to a 24-inch rope.

4 Loosely braid from center to ends and shape the braid into a circle, weaving the ends into each other.

5 Place the braids on a large, greased cookie sheet, 3 to 4 inches apart.

6 Make a smaller braided wreath with the remaining third of dough.

7 Cover and let rise until an indentation remains after lightly pushing in with a finger on side of one braid (about two hours).

8 Whisk together the glaze ingredients with a fork, and brush on braided wreaths.

9 Bake at 350° for 25 minutes for large wreath, 20 minutes for small wreath, or until wreaths are golden brown.

10 Remove from cookie sheets and cool.

11 Combine icing ingredients (confectionery sugar, hot water, and vanilla extract).

12 Make holes for 16 candles in the small wreath.

13 Place the small wreath on the large wreath.

14 Drizzle with icing.

15 Decorate with candied cherries and candles.

Per serving: Calories 240; Protein 7g; Carbohydrates 39g; Dietary fiber 1g; Total fat 7g; Saturated fat 3g; Cholesterol 75mg; Sodium 320mg.

Festival of Light on St. Lucia's Day

The Christmas season in Sweden begins on December 13 to celebrate the return of more hours of daylight to the dark Sweden winter. This day begins when an appointed daughter plays the role of St. Lucia, a young Christian girl martyred in the year 304 in Syracuse, Italy.

The daughter rises early in the morning, puts on a long white dress, sometimes with a crimson sash and stockings. On her head, she wears a crown of evergreen leaves, topped with seven lighted candles. In this costume, she goes through the house serving hot coffee and special holiday breads to her family before they get out of bed.

Chapter 14

Breads Extraordinaire

. . . .

In This Chapter

▶ Great breads for special occasions

. . . .

*F*or ages, bakers and homemakers have prepared breads for holidays and special occasions. Each generation has revised, adapted,
converted, and changed recipes for contemporary
time. We, too, have synchronized the aged recipes
in this chapter to our modern bread machine use.

Babka

Russians and Poles make a rich coffee cake called Babka, pronounced *bob-kah,* which translates in English as "grandmother." Some think the name is significant because the bread is generally made in a fluted pan that resembles a grandmother's skirt. We think it was probably made by the grandma and when she presented the bread, those who were about to eat it sighed, "Oh, grandma," in anxious anticipation of the rich treat they were about to have.

Preparation time: Approximately 4 hours

Yield: 24 slices

½ cup milk

⅓ cup water

2 large eggs

½ cup butter

½ cup sugar

1 teaspoon salt

4 cups all-purpose flour

2 packages active dry yeast (4½ teaspoons)

Topping

¾ cup sugar

1 tablespoon cinnamon

Fresh grated orange peel from one orange

1 Be sure that all ingredients are at room temperature before you place them in your bread pan in the order listed.

2 Select the Dough or Manual setting, and press the Start button.

3 After the machine has completed the cycle, remove the dough and place it on a lightly floured work surface.

4 Divide dough into four equal sections, and then divide each section into four parts. You end up with 16 pieces.

5 Roll each piece into a ball.

6 Roll each ball in cinnamon/orange topping.

7 Place balls in greased and floured 10-inch fluted tube or Bundt© pan.

8 Cover and let rise until an indentation remains after lightly touching the side of the dough (about 1 to 1½ hours).

9 Bake in preheated 350° oven for 40 to 45 minutes or until Babka is gold brown.

10 Cool in pan on rack for ten minutes.

11 Remove from pan and cool on rack.

Tip: *Some people like to sprinkle Babka with confectionery sugar before serving.*

Per serving: *Calories 160; Protein 3g; Carbohydrates 27g; Dietary fiber less than 1g; Total fat 4.5g; Saturated fat 2.5g; Cholesterol 30mg; Sodium 110mg.*

Challah

Challah is a traditional egg bread served in Jewish homes with their Sabbath and special holiday meals. It is different from other egg breads because it has no milk products.

Preparation time: Approximately 3 hours

Yield: 12 slices

½ cup water	1½ teaspoons salt
2 large eggs	2 tablespoons sugar
1 egg yolk	3 cups bread flour
2 tablespoons oil	1 package (2¼ teaspoons active dry yeast)

1 Whisk together the 2 large eggs and 1 egg yolk. Reserve 2 tablespoons to brush on risen loaf just before baking. The remaining egg mixture is part of the dough and is added to the pan with the other ingredients.

2 Be sure that all ingredients are at room temperature before you place them in your bread pan in the order listed.

3 Select the Dough or Manual setting, and press the Start button.

4 After the machine has completed the cycle, remove the dough and place it on a lightly floured work surface.

5 Punch the dough down to remove the air bubbles.

6 Divide the dough into three equal pieces.

7 Roll each piece into a 16-inch-long rope.

8 On a greased cookie sheet, loosely braid the ropes from center to ends.

9 Pinch the ends and tuck under to seal.

10 Cover and let rise until an indentation remains after lightly touching side of the dough (about 30 to 40 minutes).

11 Brush with the reserved egg mixture.

12 Bake in a preheated 400° oven for 25 to 30 minutes, or until golden brown.

13 Remove from the cookie sheet and cool on a rack.

Variation: *You may sprinkle poppy seeds or sesame seeds after brushing loaf with egg wash.*

Per serving: Calories 150; Protein 6g; Carbohydrates 25g; Dietary fiber less than 1g; Total fat 3.5g; Saturated fat 0.5g; Cholesterol 60mg; Sodium 310mg.

Black Walnut Bubble Coffee Cake

This very special coffee cake, with a delightful black walnut flavor, is attractive and rich enough to serve as dessert or at a coffee party.

Preparation time: About 3 hours, 40 minutes

Yield: 24 slices

½ cup milk	2 large eggs
¼ cup water	1 teaspoon salt
3 tablespoons honey	4 cups all-purpose flour
¼ cup butter	1 tablespoon active dry yeast

Filling

1½ cups packed brown sugar	2 tablespoons honey
⅓ cup evaporated milk	½ teaspoon black walnut flavor
⅓ cup butter	½ cup chopped black walnuts

1 Be sure that all ingredients are at room temperature before you place them in your bread pan in the order listed.

2 Select the Dough or Manual setting, and press the Start button.

3 While your bread machine is kneading the dough and letting it rise, prepare the filling. Combine the brown sugar, milk, butter, and honey, and cook over low heat until the sugar has dissolved and the butter has melted. Set aside to cool. Stir in the black walnut flavor after the sauce cools.

4 After the machine has completed the cycle, remove the dough and place it on a lightly floured work surface.

5 Roll or pat the dough to a 9-inch square.

6 Cut the dough into nine 1-inch strips, and then cut the strips into 1-inch squares.

7 Pour one-third of the filling into a well-greased 12-cup Bundt pan.

8 Sprinkle with half of the black walnuts.

9 Place half of the dough pieces in the pan.

10 Pour one-third of the filling over dough.

11 Sprinkle with the remaining black walnuts.

12 Place the remaining pieces of dough in pan.

13 Pour the remaining filling on top.

14 Cover and let rise until an indentation remains after lightly touching the top of the dough (about 30 to 40 minutes).

15 Bake in a preheated 350° oven for 35 to 40 minutes.

16 Invert the pan onto a cooling rack that has been placed on aluminum foil.

17 Remove from pan and cool on rack.

Per serving: Calories 150; Protein 3g; Carbohydrates 20g; Dietary fiber less than 1g; Total fat 7g; Saturated fat 3.5g; Cholesterol 35mg; Sodium 310mg.

French toast

Challah makes the best French toast, so Tom has provided his favorite recipe. Tom tells of the time when his daughter Christina was young and had a sleepover party. He established himself in the little girls' estimation as a great dad and a great cook when he served them French toast sandwiches. He spread each slice of bread with jam and sprinkled sliced almonds on half of the slices before putting together. He then dipped each sandwich into the egg mixture.

Glenna has never made the French toast sandwich, but has used single slices of Challah for French toast, with fabulous results. People have different ways of preparing French toast. They have a different proportion of eggs to milk and different ideas about how much egg/milk mixture they like soaked into the bread before they fry it. If you haven't made French toast before, here is a basic guiding recipe to get you started. We're sure you'll soon be making it your own special way.

4 eggs

¼ cup milk

¼ teaspoon cinnamon

½ teaspoon vanilla

1 Whisk the ingredients together.

2 Dip each bread slice into the egg mixture.

3 Fry toast pieces in a large greased skillet over medium to low heat until golden brown.

4 Use a spatula to turn and brown the other side.

5 Serve hot with maple syrup, fruit spread, or sprinkled with powdered sugar.

Guglehupf

Guglehupf (goo-gl-hoopf) is said to have originated in Alsace Lorraine. However, you'll hear many similar names for this bread — gugelhupf, suglehuph, kugelhuph, kugelhoff, kougloff — and you can find many places that claim its origin. It is a rich, sweet bread traditionally flavored with lemon rind, almonds, and raisins. This specialty bread is quite classy when baked in its own special pan, a Guglehupf mold, a near replica of the ceramic, domed mold. However, if you do not have one, you can use a Bundt pan or tube pan.

Preparation time: Approximately 3½ hours

Yield: 20 servings

⅓ cup milk

3 eggs

½ cup butter

½ cup sugar

1 teaspoon salt

4 cups bread flour

1 teaspoon grated orange peel

1 teaspoon grated lemon peel

½ cup golden raisins

½ cup slivered almonds

1 tablespoon active dry yeast

1 Be sure that all ingredients are at room temperature before you place them in your bread pan in the order listed.

2 Select the Dough or Manual setting, and press the Start button. After the machine has completed the cycle, remove the dough and place it on a lightly floured work surface.

3 Form the dough into a 20-inch-long rope.

4 Lay the rope in a greased 10-cup Guglehupf pan, pinching ends into each other with your finger. Pat the dough so that it is of an even thickness all around the pan.

5 Cover the dough and let it rise in a warm place for one to two hours, or until an indentation remains after lightly touching the dough.

6 Bake in a preheated 350° oven for 45 to 55 minutes, or until medium golden brown.

7 Remove the bread from the pan, and cool on a wire rack.

Tip: *It looks sharp when blanched whole almonds are placed in the top peaks of the mold before the dough is put into it.*

Variation: *Some people like to glaze this with a simple powdered sugar glaze. You can also sprinkle liberally with powdered sugar.*

Variation: *Because we have a beautiful Guglehupf mold and we like this dough so much, we were inspired to make a few of our own variations to the Guglehupf collection.*

Per serving: *Calories 190; Protein 6g; Carbohydrates 27g; Dietary fiber 1g; Total fat 7g; Saturated fat 3.5g; Cholesterol 50mg; Sodium 130mg.*

Cheesy Guglehupf

Use the basic Guglehupf recipe, but omit the raisins and almonds.

Cheese Filling

1 pound dry cottage cheese

1 egg

5 tablespoons sugar

1 teaspoon lemon zest

1 teaspoon lemon juice

¼ cup flour

⅛ teaspoon cinnamon

⅛ teaspoon nutmeg

⅛ teaspoon ginger

1 Place all ingredients in a blender or food processor bowl, and mix until well blended.

2 Pat or roll the dough into a 10-x -20-inch rectangle.

3 Spread the cheese filling to cover the dough about 1 inch from the edge.

4 Starting with the longer side, roll the dough into a log shape and pinch seams to seal.

5 Place the seam side of the roll toward the center of a 10-inch Guglehupf pan, working the ends into each other and sealing with your fingers.

6 Cover and let rise in a warm place for one to two hours, or until an indentation remains after lightly touching the dough.

7 Bake in a preheated 350° oven for 45 to 55 minutes, or until medium golden brown.

8 Shield with aluminum foil after 35 minutes to keep the top from getting too brown.

9 Remove the bread from the pan, and cool on a wire rack.

Per serving: *Calories 230; Protein 10g; Carbohydrates 32g; Dietary fiber 1g; Total fat 8g; Saturated fat 3.5g; Cholesterol 65mg; Sodium 140mg.*

Ham and Olive Stuffed Guglehupf

Use the basic Guglehupf recipe, but omit the raisins and almonds.

Ham and Olive Filling

1 cup thinly sliced baked ham, cut into small pieces

1 cup sliced ripe olives

1 Pat or roll dough into a 10-x -20-inch rectangle.

2 Sprinkle ½-cup baked ham and ½-cup sliced olives on the center third of the dough, lengthwise.

3 Fold one-third of the dough over the filling.

4 Sprinkle the remaining baked ham and sliced olives on top of the folded layer.

5 Fold the remaining third of the dough over the other layers. Pinch seams to seal.

6 Place the seam side of the roll toward the center of a 10-inch Guglehupf pan, working the ends into each other and sealing with your fingers.

7 Cover and let rise in a warm place for one to two hours, or until an indentation remains after lightly touching the dough.

8 Bake in a preheated 350° oven for 50 to 60 minutes, or until medium golden brown.

9 Shield with aluminum foil after 35 minutes to keep the top from getting too brown.

10 Remove the bread from the pan, and cool on a wire rack. Allow the bread to cool completely before slicing.

Tip: *To store, cover tightly with plastic wrap and refrigerate.*

Per serving: *Calories 170; Protein 6g; Carbohydrates 24g; Dietary fiber less than 1g; Total fat 6g; Saturated fat 3.5g; Cholesterol 55mg; Sodium 290mg.*

Chocolate Craisin Guglehupf

Use the basic Guglehupf recipe, but omit the raisins and almonds.

Chocolate Craisin Filling

1 6-ounce package semisweet chocolate chips

½ cup dried cranberries or craisins

1 cup finely chopped walnuts

½ teaspoon cinnamon

1 Pat or roll the dough into a 10-x -20-inch rectangle.

2 Spread half the filling on the center third of the dough, lengthwise.

3 Fold one third of the dough over the filling.

4 Spread the remaining filling on top of the folded layer.

5 Fold the remaining third of the dough over the other layers.

6 Place the seam side of the roll toward the center of a 10-inch greased Guglehupf pan, working the ends into each other and sealing with your fingers.

7 Cover and let rise in a warm place for one to two hours, or until an indentation remains after lightly touching the dough.

8 Bake in a preheated 350° oven for 45 to 55 minutes, or until medium golden brown.

9 If the top is getting too brown, shield with aluminum foil after 40 minutes.

10 Remove the bread from the pan, and cool on a wire rack. Allow the bread to cool completely before slicing.

Per serving: Calories 250; Protein 6g; Carbohydrates 32g; Dietary fiber 2g; Total fat 12g; Saturated fat 5g; Cholesterol 50mg; Sodium 130mg.

Apricot Bittersweet Chocolate Guglehupf

Use the basic Guglehupf recipe, but omit the raisins and almonds.

Apricot Bittersweet Chocolate Filling

½ cup packed light brown sugar

1 cup chopped bittersweet chocolate

1 cup finely chopped dried apricots

2 teaspoons instant coffee crystals

2 tablespoons butter at room temperature

1 Mix all filling ingredients together.

2 Pat or roll the dough into a 10-x -20-inch rectangle.

3 Sprinkle the filling over the dough, covering it to about 1 inch from edge.

4 Starting with the longer side, roll the dough into a log shape.

5 Place the seam side of the roll toward the center of a 10-inch greased Guglehupf pan, working the ends into each other and sealing with your fingers.

6 Cover and let rise in a warm place for one to two hours, or until an indentation remains after lightly touching the dough.

7 Bake in a preheated 350° oven for 45 to 55 minutes, or until medium golden brown.

8 Shield with aluminum foil after 35 minutes to keep the top from getting too brown.

9 Remove the bread from the pan, and cool on a wire rack.

Per serving: Calories 260; Protein 6g; Carbohydrates 42g; Dietary fiber 1g; Total fat 9g; Saturated fat 5g; Cholesterol 55mg; Sodium 135mg.

Panettone

This bread filled with anise, candied fruit, and raisins is an Italian favorite. Panettone means "little loaf." It is often associated with the Christmas holiday in the U.S., but in Italy it is served year-round. The flavor improves with age when the bread is wrapped tightly after it has completely cooled.

Preparation time: Approximately 3½ hours

Yield: 24 servings

½ cup milk	1½ teaspoons anise seeds
½ cup water	4½ cups all-purpose flour
2 large eggs	4½ teaspoons active dry yeast
¼ cup butter	½ cup raisins
¾ teaspoon vanilla	½ cup chopped nuts
1 teaspoon salt	⅓ cup chopped candied fruit
½ cup sugar	

1 Be sure that all ingredients are at room temperature before you place them in your bread pan in the order listed.

2 Select the Dough or Manual setting, and press the Start button.

3 After the machine has completed the cycle, remove the dough and place it on a lightly floured work surface.

4 Divide the dough in half.

5 Shape each half into a round loaf.

6 Place on a large, greased cookie sheet.

7 Cover and let rise until an indentation remains after lightly touching dough (approximately 30 to 45 minutes).

8 Combine 1 egg and 1 tablespoon water, and brush on risen loaves.

9 Bake in a preheated oven at 350° for 30 to 35 minutes until golden brown or until thermometer reads 190°.

10 Remove the bread from the cookie sheet.

11 Cool on a wire rack.

Per serving: *Calories 160; Protein 4g; Carbohydrates 27g; Dietary fiber 1g; Total fat 4.5g; Saturated fat 1.5g; Cholesterol 25mg; Sodium 110mg.*

Hawaiian Honey Bread

When John and Glenna were celebrating their 36th wedding anniversary in Hawaii, they tasted this delicious bread for the first time. Returning home, Glenna discovered Hawaiian Honey Bread was already popular in some sections of the mainland U.S. You can probably find as many variations of Hawaiian Honey as you can find bakers to make it, but we believe that this recipe will give you a real "island treat."

Preparation time: 3 hours, 20 minutes

Yield: 12 slices

1½-pound loaf	2-pound loaf
⅔ cup pineapple juice	¾ cup pineapple juice
large egg	2 large eggs
3 tablespoons vegetable oil	¼ cup vegetable oil
2 drops yellow food coloring	2 drops yellow food coloring
3 tablespoons honey	¼ cup honey
1 teaspoon salt	1½ teaspoons salt
¼ teaspoon baking soda	¼ teaspoon baking soda
3 tablespoons dry milk	¼ cup dry milk
3 cups bread flour	4 cups bread flour
2¼ teaspoons active dry yeast	1 tablespoon active dry yeast
¼ cup macadamia nuts, coarsely chopped	⅔ cup macadamia nuts, coarsely chopped

1 Be sure that all ingredients are room temperature before you place them in your bread pan in the order listed. Reserve the macadamia nuts until the machine signals that about five minutes remain before the end of the second kneading.

2 Select a sweet bread setting and a light to medium crust color.

3 Start the machine.

4 You will want to do a quality check on the dough early in the cycle. Open the lid after the machine has kneaded the dough for about five minutes. The dough should be a soft tacky ball so that the dough can stretch easily during the rising time. If the dough is still sticking to the sides or bottom of the pan, you need to add a bit more bread flour. If the dough is crumbly and not in a ball, or if the ball is hard and not tacky, you should add more water. Your bread machine still has plenty of kneading time left to work the water into your bread dough. Keep checking your dough until you are satisfied with the ball that it has formed.

5 Add the macadamia nuts at the machine's signal, or five minutes before the end of the second kneading.

If the nuts do not easily work into the dough, your dough is too stiff and will not rise adequately. Add a teaspoon or so more water.

6 After the machine has completed the baking cycle, remove the pan from the machine and transfer the bread from the pan on a wire rack to cool. If you cut the bread before it has cooled for about an hour, it will look doughy. It must cool completely to allow the structure of the bread to set.

To complete Hawaiian Honey Bread in your oven:

1 Select the dough cycle.

Most machines do not have a signal with the dough cycle to add nuts or fruit. Also, most machines have only one kneading time with the dough cycle. So you can either add the macadamia nuts with the other ingredients or be careful to watch your kneading time and add them five minutes before it is done.

2 When the cycle is complete, turn the dough onto a lightly floured surface and shape it into a round loaf.

3 Place the dough in a greased 8-inch or 9-inch pie or cake pan.

4 Cover and let rise in a warm place until an indentation remains after lightly touching the side of the dough (approximately 20 to 30 minutes).

5 Combine 1 egg and 1 tablespoon of water and brush this mixture on the dough.

6 Bake at 375° for 25 to 30 minutes until golden brown, or until thermometer registers 190°.

7 Remove the bread from the pan, and cool on a rack.

Per serving: *Calories 180; Protein 5g; Carbohydrates 29g; Dietary fiber 1g; Total fat 5g; Saturated fat 0.5g; Cholesterol 20mg; Sodium 230mg.*

Kolache

The Kolache (koh-lotch-eh) has always been so much a part of the Czech and Slovak cultures. They serve Kolaches at every type of celebration or special occassion: weddings, funerals, holidays. One common sampler found in Czech kitchens is *Bez práce nejsou kolá_e* ("Without work, there are no kolacky"). Kolache, sometimes spelled Kolachy, means "several small fruit-filled goodies that you can hold in your hand."

Preparation time: Approximately 3 hours

Yield: 18 Kolache

¾ cup milk	1 teaspoon salt
¼ cup water	¼ cup sugar
¼ cup butter	4 cups all-purpose flour
1 egg	2¼ teaspoons active dry yeast

1 Be sure that all ingredients are at room temperature before you place them in your bread pan in the order listed.

2 Select the Dough or Manual setting, and press the Start button.

3 After the machine has completed the cycle, remove the dough and place it on a lightly floured work surface.

4 Divide the dough in half.

5 Roll each half into a 12-inch square.

6 Cut each 12-inch square into nine 4-inch squares.

7 Spoon 1 tablespoon of a filling into the center of each square. (See the recipes that follow for the fillings.)

8 Fold one corner of the dough square into the center.

9 Moisten the top of the folded dough with water.

10 Fold the opposite corner over and seal.

11 Place on greased cookie sheets.

12 Cover and let rise until an indentation remains after touching the dough (about 15 minutes).

13 Bake in a preheated oven at 375° for 12 to 15 minutes, or until golden brown.

14 Brush the tops of the Kolache with melted butter.

15 Remove from cookie sheets.

16 Serve warm or cold.

Prune Orange Filling

1 pound dried prunes

3 tablespoons sugar

½ teaspoon cinnamon

½ teaspoon ground cloves

3 tablespoons of grated orange rind

1 teaspoon lemon juice

1 In a small saucepan, cover the prunes with water and cook until soft.

2 Allow the prunes to cool before removing seeds.

3 Purée the prunes in a blender.

4 In a small bowl, blend the prunes with the remaining ingredients.

Cottage Cheese Filling

2 cups dry curd cottage cheese

2 slightly beaten eggs

½ cup sugar

¼ teaspoon salt

¼ teaspoon vanilla

¼ teaspoon cinnamon

1 tablespoon butter

1 In a small bowl, blend all ingredients together.

Apricot Filling

1 cup dried apricots

⅓ cup packed brown sugar

½ teaspoon cinnamon

1 In a small saucepan, cover the apricot halves with water.

2 Cook over medium heat until the water is absorbed and the apricots are tender.

3 Purée the apricots in a blender.

4 In a small bowl, blend the apricots with brown sugar and cinnamon.

Per serving: Calories 130; Protein 3g; Carbohydrates 22g; Dietary fiber less than 1g; Total fat 3.5g; Saturated fat 2g; Cholesterol 20mg; Sodium 140mg.

Sour Cream Nut Rolls

These little rolls are delicate treats. Tom often includes them with his buffet meals. They add a wonderful touch to any food gathering.

Preparation time: Approximately 3 hours

Yield: 48 rolls

⅔ cup sour cream	3 tablespoons water
4 egg yolks	¼ cup sugar
⅔ cup soft butter	4 cups flour

1 Be sure that all ingredients are at room temperature before you place them in your bread pan in the order listed.

2 Select the Dough or Manual setting, and press the Start button.

3 After the machine has completed the cycle, remove the dough and place it on a lightly floured work surface.

4 Divide the dough into four equal parts.

5 Roll each part into a nine-inch circle.

6 Cut into eight pie-shaped wedges.

7 Spread each wedge lightly with a nut filling (see the following recipe).

8 Starting at the wide end, roll each wedge toward the point.

9 Place rolls point side down on a greased cookie sheet.

10 Cover and let rise until an indentation remains after touching the side of a roll (about one hour).

11 Bake in a preheated oven at 350° for 12 to 15 minutes.

Nut Filling

3 egg whites	1 cup ground walnuts
¼ cup sugar	½ teaspoon vanilla or almond extract
dash salt	

1 Beat the egg whites until stiff.

2 Combine the sugar, salt, and walnuts.

3 Fold the mixture into the egg whites.

Per serving: *Calories 130; Protein 3g; Carbohydrates 11g; Dietary fiber less than 1g; Total fat 9g; Saturated fat 3.5g; Cholesterol 40mg; Sodium 15mg.*

Sticky Buns

Now this is an American favorite if ever there was one. Glenna made these one time when our family-at-large had rented several cabins on a lake. Wow, were they a hit! She wished she'd brought enough ingredients to make them for a treat every morning. Back then, she had to make a mess and use elbow grease to produce these rolls.

Now with a bread machine, it's a quick and easy task. And you should see what great fun it is to make these buns with Tom. We were licking our fingers and smacking our lips over these simple to make Sticky Buns.

Preparation time: 2 hours, 20 minutes

Yield: 12 buns

⅓ cup milk	1 teaspoon salt
¼ cup water	3 tablespoons sugar
1 egg	3 cups all-purpose flour
2 tablespoons butter	1 package active dry yeast

1 Be sure that all ingredients are at room temperature before you place them in your bread pan in the order listed.

2 Select the Dough or Manual setting, and press the Start button.

Caramel Topping

⅓ cup butter	½ cup chopped nuts
⅓ cup brown sugar	

1 Combine all ingredients and divide the topping evenly into 12 greased muffin cups.

2 After the machine has completed the cycle, remove the dough and place it on a lightly floured work surface.

3 Divide dough into four equal parts, and then divide each part into three pieces.

4 Shape each piece into a smooth ball.

5 Place balls in muffin cups.

6 Cover and let rise until an indentation remains after lightly touching a bun (about 20 minutes).

7 Bake in a preheated oven at 375° for 10 to 12 minutes until golden brown.

8 Remove from oven.

9 Cover the muffin pan with foil and invert onto cooling rack.

10 Allow the buns to set for one minute before removing muffin pan.

Per serving: Calories 260; Protein 5g; Carbohydrates 34g; Dietary fiber 1g; Total fat 11g; Saturated fat 5g; Cholesterol 40mg; Sodium 210mg.

Stollen

Stollen is a traditional German Christmas bread chock-full of candied fruit and nuts for the holidays. We have updated it with dried fruits, and we like it even better than with the candied cherries and citron. Of course, you get to decide how you like it best — candied fruit or dried fruit. Stollen is simple to make and is an excellent bread to give as a holiday gift.

Preparation time: Approximately 3 hours

Yield: 18 to 20 slices

⅔ cup milk	3¼ cups bread flour
2 eggs	1 tablespoon active dry yeast
2 tablespoons butter	⅓ cup dried fruit bits
2 teaspoons salt	Grated peel from 1 large orange
¼ cup sugar	½ cup pecan pieces

1 Be sure that all ingredients are at room temperature before you place them in your bread pan in the order listed.

2 Select the Dough or Manual setting, and press the Start button.

3 After the machine has completed the cycle, remove the dough and place it on a lightly floured work surface.

4 Roll or pat the dough into a 14-x -8-inch oval.

5 Spread the dough with 1 tablespoon softened butter.

6 Fold in half lengthwise and curve the dough into a crescent shape.

7 Press the folded edge firmly to partially seal.

8 Place on a greased cookie sheet.

9 Cover and let rise until an indentation remains when touched.

10 Bake in a preheated oven at 350° for 25 to 30 minutes.

11 Remove the stollen from the cookie sheet and cool.

12 Drizzle with Powdered Sugar Glaze, and garnish with additional fruit and nuts.

Variation: *If you wish to use the candied fruit in place of the dried fruit bits, you may. We suggest the following proportions:*

⅓ cup chopped candied cherries	3 tablespoons raisins
3 tablespoons chopped citron	

Powdered Sugar Glaze

1 cup powdered sugar
½ teaspoon vanilla

3 to 4 teaspoons water

1 In a small mixing bowl, combine ingredients and mix until smooth.

Per serving: *Calories 130; Protein 4g; Carbohydrates 23g; Dietary fiber 2g; Total fat 4g; Saturated fat 0g; Cholesterol 0mg; Sodium 125mg.*

Sweet Bread Twist

This recipe uses a simple shaping procedure and makes a fancy presentation. It's a dramatic show for any table. The flavor is slightly sweet and the texture is fine and soft.

Preparation time: Approximately 3½ hours

Yield: 18 to 20 slices

1 cup milk
2 large eggs
4 tablespoons butter
1½ teaspoons salt
⅓ cup sugar

¼ teaspoon nutmeg
4 cups bread flour
½ cup golden raisins
1 tablespoon active dry yeast

1 Be sure that all ingredients are at room temperature before you place them in your bread pan in the order listed.

2 Select the Dough or Manual setting, and press the Start button. After the machine has completed the cycle, remove the dough and place it on a lightly floured work surface.

3 Roll the entire dough into a 36-inch-long rope.

4 Fold the rope in half, and twist it a couple of times.

5 Place the dough on a greased cookie sheet.

6 Cover and let rise until an indentation remains after touching side of the dough (about one hour).

7 Brush with an egg wash (1 egg whisked together with 1 tablespoon of water).

8 Bake in a preheated oven at 350° for about 45 minutes.

Per serving: *Calories 140; Protein 4g; Carbohydrates 25g; Dietary fiber less than 1g; Total fat 3g; Saturated fat 2g; Cholesterol 30mg; Sodium 190mg.*

Tea Ring

The Swedish Tea Ring is easy to make and very attractive. This is the special treat that Glenna makes for holiday giving. In fact, friends have come to count on receiving a warm wreath delivered on Christmas Eve. Glenna bakes them ahead and keeps them wrapped in aluminum foil and frozen. Then she allows them to thaw on Christmas Eve day. While she and her family are at the Christmas Eve church service, she places them in a warm oven.

Upon returning home, she unwraps the aluminum foil enough to drizzle Powdered Sugar Glaze over each one, and then loosely folds the foil back over the wreath. She wraps the rings in big bath towels to keep them warm during the delivery time. Members of her family love to help with the deliveries just to hear the oohs and aahs.

Preparation time: 3½ hours

Yield: 18 to 20 slices

½ cup milk	¼ cup sugar
¼ cup water	3 cups bread flour
1 egg	2¼ teaspoon active dry yeast
2 tablespoons butter	
1 teaspoon salt	

1 Be sure that all ingredients are at room temperature before you place them in your bread pan in the order listed.

2 Select the Dough or Manual setting, and press the Start button.

3 After the machine has completed the cycle, remove the dough and place it on a lightly floured work surface.

4 Roll the dough into a 15-x -12-inch rectangle.

5 Brush with an egg wash (1 egg slightly beaten with 1 tablespoon water).

6 Spread with the filling of your choice. (See the recipes following for our ideas.)

7 Starting with the longer side, roll up the dough tightly and pinch the edges to seal.

8 Form a ring, work the ends together, and pinch to seal.

9 Place the ring, seam side down, on a greased cookie sheet.

10 With scissors, make cuts 1 inch apart along the outside edge to within 1 inch of the center of the ring.

11 Turn each slice on its side.

12 Cover and let rise in a warm place until an indentation remains after lightly touching the side of ring.

13 Bake in a preheated oven at 350° for 25 to 30 minutes.

Cinnamon Filling

½ cup sugar

2 teaspoons cinnamon

Variation: *To the basic cinnamon filling, you may add ½ cup finely chopped nuts or ½ cup raisins, or both. Glenna often slices apples and places them on top of the cinnamon filling before rolling up the dough.*

Variation: *Using brown sugar in place of white sugar and adding ½ teaspoon maple flavoring makes an interesting filling. In place of the egg wash, you could brush the dough with maple syrup before baking.*

Cranberry Date Filling

¼ cup sugar

¼ cup corn syrup

⅓ cup water

1 cup fresh cranberries

½ cup whole dates, chopped

¼ cup chopped nuts

2 teaspoons lemon juice

1 In medium saucepan, boil the sugar, corn syrup, and water for five minutes.

2 Add cranberries, cover, and cook for four minutes, stirring occasionally.

3 Add chopped dates, and cook for one minute.

4 Remove from heat, and stir in nuts and lemon juice.

5 Cool completely before placing on the dough.

Per serving: *Calories 110; Protein 3g; Carbohydrates 21g; Dietary fiber less than 1g; Total fat 1.5g; Saturated fat 1g; Cholesterol 15mg; Sodium 125mg.*

Chapter 15

Bread Bowls, Bread Sticks, Pizzas, and Other Special Treats

. . . .

In This Chapter

▶ Using bread bowls to dress up your soups and salads

▶ Making traditional bread sticks, and trying some new variations

▶ Creating great homemade pizzas

. . . .

Making Bread Bowls and Salads to Put in Them

Call us copycats, that's okay. Why reinvent the wheel? We had salad in a bread bowl and thought, "Aha, this would be simple to do." And it is. We use a basic, no-fat, low-sugar bread recipe to create salad bowls. You can also use these bowls for soup.

The first recipe in this section shows you how to make the bread bowls. As a bonus, we throw in some of our favorite salad recipes. We wouldn't want you to have bread bowls with nothing to put in them.

Bread Bowls

Glenna likes to bake the dough in a ball shape and then hollow out the baked bread, forming a bowl. Tom prefers to shape the dough before cooking so that the bread bowls are ready for filling when they come out of the oven (and have cooled a bit). It's chic to serve your soup or salad in an edible bowl, and either method works.

Preparation time: *Approximately 3 hours*

Yield: *3 bowls*

1 ¼ cups water	3 tablespoons white cornmeal
1 teaspoon salt	3 ½ cups bread flour
1 ½ teaspoons sugar	2 ¼ teaspoons active dry yeast

1 Be sure that all the ingredients are at room temperature before you place them in your bread pan in the order listed. Select the Dough or Manual setting and press Start.

2 After the machine has completed the cycle, remove the dough onto a lightly floured work surface.

Glenna's method:

3 Divide and shape into three round balls and place the balls on a greased cookie sheet covered with cornmeal.

4 Cover and let rise until an indentation remains after touching.

5 Bake in a preheated 425° oven for 20 to 30 minutes. Spray or brush the loaf with cold water several times during the first ten minutes of baking for a crisper crust.

7 Remove from cookie sheet and cool.

8 Cut a thin slice off the top and then hollow out the inside, leaving half-inch sides. Place the bowls in a 300° oven for ten minutes to dry the inside and prevent premature soaking from the salads or soups.

Tom's method: Follow Steps 1 and 2 above, and then do the following:

3 Divide the dough into four equal parts and roll or pat each part into a circle ¼-inch thick.

4 Lay the dough over the outside of well-greased ovenproof bowls, place the bowls upside-down on a cookie sheet, cover, and let rise for only 15 minutes.

5 Bake in a preheated 425° oven for approximately 20 minutes. Allow the bread to remain on the ovenproof bowls for at least ten minutes before inverting them onto a cooking rack.

Per serving: Calories 480; Protein 19g; Carbohydrates 105g; Dietary fiber 5g; Total fat 0g; Saturated fat 0g; Cholesterol 0mg; Sodium 790mg.

Large Bread Bowl

Form the dough into one large salad bowl for family-style dining. A large bread bowl also makes a beautiful and impressive presentation on a buffet table for picnics or pitch-ins.

Preparation time: *3 hours*

Yield: *1 bread bowl*

1 Shape the dough into one round loaf and place it on a greased cookie sheet covered with cornmeal.

2 Cover and let rise until an indentation remains after touching (approximately 30 minutes).

3 Bake in a preheated 425° oven for 30 to 35 minutes. Spray or brush the loaf with cold water several times during the first ten minutes of baking for a crisper crust.

4 Remove the bread from the cookie sheet and cool (approximately one hour).

5 Cut a thin slice off the top, and then hollow out the inside, leaving half-inch sides.

6 Place the bowl in a 300° oven for ten minutes to dry the inside and prevent premature soaking from the salad or soup.

7 Spread the inside of the bread bowl with a thin layer of mayonnaise to prevent the bread from absorbing moisture from the salad or drying out. Then line the bowl with lettuce leaves.

Per serving: *Calories 480; Protein 19g; Carbohydrates 105g; Dietary fiber 5g; Total fat 0g; Saturated fat 0g; Cholesterol 0mg; Sodium 790mg.*

Glenna's Toss Salad

Glenna's everyday Toss Salad looks special served in a large bread bowl or small bread bowls. If the cucumber is really fresh, do not peel it. Make breaks in the skin by drawing a fork down the length of the cucumber before cutting it into chunks. You can use the Italian dressing recipe below or your favorite bottled dressing.

Preparation time: *20 minutes*

Yield: *6 servings*

1 head of leaf lettuce

1 red onion, sliced thin, or an equal amount of chopped green salad onions

1 fresh cucumber, chunked

5 radishes, sliced thin

Toss together and divide into bread bowls.

Italian Dressing

½ teaspoon crushed basil leaves (use fresh basil if you have it)

½ teaspoon crushed oregano leaves (use fresh oregano if you have it)

¾ teaspoon salt

¼ teaspoon garlic powder

2 tablespoons balsamic vinegar

¼ cup extra-virgin olive oil

1 hard-cooked egg

1 Shake or rapidly whisk all the dressing ingredients together.

2 Pour the dressing over the salad in the bread bowls.

3 Slice the hard-cooked egg and use it as a garnish.

Per serving: *Calories 110; Protein 2g; Carbohydrates 4g; Dietary fiber less than 1g; Total fat 10g; Saturated fat 1.5g; Cholesterol 35mg; Sodium 15mg.*

Taco Salad

If your family likes quesadillas, empanadas, or tacos from Mexican cuisine, this salad will be a hit with them. Serving it in a salad bowl makes it quite practical (a one dish meal).

Preparation time: *30 minutes*

Yield: *6 servings*

1 pound lean ground beef

½ cup chopped onions

1 package taco seasoning mix

¾ cup water

4 cups shredded lettuce

1 ½ cups chopped tomatoes

½ cup chopped red or green pepper (optional)

1 cup grated cheddar cheese

Taco sauce and sour cream (optional)

1 Brown the ground beef and onions over medium heat in a 10-inch frying pan until the meat has lost its pink color and the onions are soft.

Although it isn't necessary, we drain the fat off the browned ground beef before adding the taco seasoning mix and water by dumping the mixture into a colander or wire strainer that has been placed over a shallow pan or dish to catch the drippings. We return the meat and onions to the frying pan before continuing to the next step.

2 Stir the taco seasoning mix and water into the ground beef and onion mixture; simmer for 25 minutes.

3 Toss together with shredded lettuce and tomatoes and, if desired, the chopped peppers.

4 Place in bowls, top with the cheddar cheese, and pass the taco sauce and sour cream, if desired.

Variation: *You can also make bread bowls especially for taco salad by adding 1 cup of crushed corn chips and 2 teaspoons of finely chopped onion to the dough. The corn chips may absorb too much water and cause the dough to be somewhat dry. Check the dough consistency as it is kneading.*

Per serving: *Calories 250; Protein 21g; Carbohydrates 11g; Dietary fiber 2g; Total fat 13g; Saturated fat 7g; Cholesterol 45mg; Sodium 730mg.*

Spanish Salad

Since Tom married his Spanish sweetheart many years ago, he returns to Spain every summer. This is a common recipe in the household of his in-laws.

Preparation time: *30 minutes*

Yield: *6 servings*

5 ounces ham, cubed	*1 medium onion, sliced*
5 ounces cheddar cheese, cubed	*½ cup cooked corn*
3 hard-boiled eggs, quartered	*1 cup sliced celery*
½ cup whole black olives	*1 cup cherry tomatoes*

1 Put aside a few olives, four egg quarters, and four or five cherry tomatoes.

2 Toss the remaining salad ingredients together.

Dressing

¾ cup extra-virgin olive oil	*¼ teaspoon salt*
4 tablespoons vinegar	*⅛ teaspoon black pepper*
1 clove garlic, pressed	

1 Whisk together the ingredients and add the dressing to the salad.

2 Place the salad in a large bread bowl and garnish with the reserved olives, egg quarters, and cherry tomatoes.

Per serving: Calories 420; Protein 15g; Carbohydrates 12g; Dietary fiber 2g; Total fat 35g; Saturated fat 6g; Cholesterol 140mg; Sodium 640mg.

Great Food for Kids: Bread Sticks and Corn Dogs

We don't know anyone who doesn't like bread sticks. They make great appetizers, and they're quite portable. And kids love 'em too. This section has recipes for a couple of variations on the classic bread stick, and an easy corn dog recipe as well.

Bread Sticks

Bread sticks are like soft pretzels; they're great for snacking and go well with soup or salad. You can serve them warm or cold.

Preparation time: *Approximately 3 hours*

Yield: *24 sticks*

1 cup water	*2 ¼ teaspoons active dry yeast*
2 tablespoons vegetable oil	*1 egg white*
2 teaspoons salt	*1 tablespoon water*
1 tablespoon sugar	*3 to 4 tablespoons of poppy or sesame seeds (optional)*
3 cups all-purpose flour	

1 Be sure that all the ingredients are at room temperature before you place them in the bread pan in the order listed.

2 Select the Dough or Manual setting and press Start.

3 After the machine has completed the cycle, remove the dough onto a lightly floured work surface and divide into four parts. Then divide each fourth into six pieces.

4 Roll each piece into an 8-inch rope, place the ropes on a greased cookie sheet, and brush with egg white glaze (1 egg white whisked together with 1 tablespoon water). Sprinkle with poppy or sesame seeds, if desired.

5 Cover and let rise in a warm place for about ten minutes.

6 Bake in a preheated 400° oven for 15 to 20 minutes until the breadsticks are a deep, golden brown. Remove them from the cookie sheet and place on a cooling rack.

Per serving: *Calories 80; Protein 2g; Carbohydrates 13g; Dietary fiber less than 1g; Total fat 1.5g; Saturated fat 0g; Cholesterol 0mg; Sodium 200mg.*

Cheesy Bread Sticks with Prosciutto

These fabulous sticks are small enough to make elegant hors d'oeuvres.

Preparation time: *Approximately 3½ hours*

Yield: *30 bread sticks*

½ cup milk

½ cup water

1 large egg

2 tablespoons oil

1 cup shredded sharp cheddar cheese

⅓ cup dry vegetable soup mix (without noodles or meat)

½ teaspoon salt

2 tablespoons sugar

3⅔ cups bread flour

2¼ teaspoons active dry yeast

Cream cheese or Robiola (a creamy, mild cheese from Italy)

1 pound thinly sliced prosciutto or Virginia ham

1 Be sure that all the ingredients are at room temperature before you place them in your bread pan in the order listed.

2 Select the Dough or Manual setting and press Start.

3 After the machine has completed the cycle, remove the dough onto a lightly floured work surface and divide it into thirds. Divide each third in half (you should have six dough pieces now). Then divide each piece into 5 equal balls so that you have 30 pieces total.

4 Roll the balls into short logs and place them on lightly greased cookie sheets. Cover and let rise for about 15 minutes.

5 Bake in a preheated oven at 350° for 15 minutes. Cool the bread sticks on racks.

6 Spread cream cheese or Robiola cheese on the sticks and wrap prosciutto around them.

Per serving: *Calories 60; Protein 4g; Carbohydrates 2g; Dietary fiber 0g; Total fat 4g; Saturated fat 1.5g; Cholesterol 20mg; Sodium 200mg.*

Cheese Corn Dogs

The ol' pigs in a blanket are still popular with kids of all ages. We've developed a good, textured bread for the wieners by adding cheddar cheese and cornmeal to the dough.

Preparation time: *Approximately 3 hours*

Yield: *10 corn dogs*

1 cup water

1 egg

½ cup shredded sharp cheddar cheese

1 tablespoon sugar

1 teaspoon salt

2 tablespoons cornmeal

3 ¼ cups all-purpose flour

2 ¼ teaspoons active dry yeast

10 wieners

1 Be sure that all the ingredients are at room temperature before you place them (all except the wieners) in your bread pan in the order listed.

2 Select the Dough or Manual setting and press Start.

3 After the machine has completed the cycle, remove the dough onto a lightly floured work surface and divide it in half.

4 Roll each half into a circle ¼-inch thick. Cut the circles into five wedges. Beginning with wide edge of the wedge, roll the dough around a wiener.

5 Place the corn dogs on a greased cookie sheet. Cover and let rise for approximately 15 minutes.

6 Bake in a preheated oven at 375° for 15 to 20 minutes.

Variation: *You can slit the wieners lengthwise and insert a strip of cheddar cheese into the slit before wrapping the wiener with dough.*

Tip: *Corn dogs brushed with mustard butter are delicious. To make mustard butter, melt ½ stick of butter and combine the butter with 1 tablespoon of prepared mustard.*

Per serving: *Calories 380; Protein 13g; Carbohydrates 36g; Dietary fiber 1g; Total fat 20g; Saturated fat 8g; Cholesterol 65mg; Sodium 860mg*

Pizza

Pizza is the second most popular fast food in the United States, behind hamburgers. Making pizza dough is the second most popular use of bread machines, behind making white bread.

Given pizza's popularity, *Bread Machines For Dummies* wouldn't be complete without some pizza recipes. We give you a basic dough recipe and then add variations so that you can give your family and friends a real taste treat with homemade pizzas. Of course, you can treat yourself with these pizzas, too!

Pizza

The traditional toppings for pizza always include pizza sauce and mozzarella cheese, with any combination of the following: crumbled sausage, thinly sliced pepperoni, sliced mushrooms, chopped green pepper, chopped onion, anchovies, black olives, and diced tomatoes.

Preparation time: *1 hour*

Yield: *2 pizzas or 10 to 12 servings*

1 cup water	*3 cups bread flour*
2 tablespoons olive oil	*2¼ teaspoons active dry yeast*
1 teaspoon salt	*Your favorite toppings*

1 Be sure that all the ingredients are at room temperature before you place them (except the toppings) in your bread pan in the order listed.

2 Select the Dough or Manual setting and press Start.

3 After the machine has completed the kneading cycle, press Stop or Clear and remove the dough onto a lightly floured work surface. For pizza dough, the machine does not have to go through the entire rising cycle.

4 Let the dough rest for 15 minutes.

5 Divide the dough into 2 parts and roll or pat each part into a 12-inch circle. Press each into a generously greased, 12-inch round pizza pan sprinkled with cornmeal.

6 Prebake the crust for 10 to 12 minutes in a preheated 400° oven until the edge of the dough begins to turn golden brown. Add the desired toppings and bake for an additional 15 minutes.

The amount of sauce and number and amount of toppings is your creation. The following are only approximations to give you an idea of where to begin the construction of your signature pizza. Each 12-inch pizza crust will hold approximately ¾ cup of prepared pizza sauce and 8 ounces of grated cheese.

Mozzarella cheese is the most common on pizza and you can buy it already grated for a price comparable to the same amount of cheese in a whole block. We like the combination of six or eight cheeses, grated together in a package. They make a smooth topping with a full-bodied flavor.

Variation: *To make a deep-dish pizza, roll the dough into one 16-inch round crust (for a 14-inch round pan) or a 15- x 11-inch rectangle (for a 9-x-12 or 10-x-13 baking pan).*

Variation: *To make a whole-wheat pizza crust, either substitute whole-wheat flour for ½ of the white flour or use whole-wheat blended flour.*

Tip: *For a more Italian flavor in the crust, add 1 teaspoon dried Italian herbs and ¼ cup grated Parmesan or Romano cheese.*

Per serving: Calories 120; Protein 4g; Carbohydrates 22g; Dietary fiber less than 1g; Total fat 2.5g; Saturated fat 0g; Cholesterol 0mg; Sodium 200mg.

Spanish Pizza

Thanks to Tom, here's another recipe from Spain. After you try Spanish Pizza, you will be glad we included it. The toppings are unusual for those of us who only think of pizza as the American tomato-and-cheese pizza we are accustomed to eating.

Use the crust from the basic pizza recipe and top with the following ingredients.

1 cup pesto

16 to 20 sliced black olives

Two 8-ounce jars artichokes, drained and chopped

1 cup chopped tomato

½ cup chopped red or yellow pepper

2 cups shredded mozzarella cheese

Pesto sauce looks like a green paste. We find it in the produce department packaged in a heavy, plastic, transparent tube.

Pesto sauce is a snap to make if you have a food processor. But it takes a lot of fresh basil — like two cups of it (loosely packed). Put the basil in the food processor with pine nuts (about ½ cup), peeled garlic cloves (two or three depending on how much you like garlic) and ½ cup grated Parmesan cheese. Start the machine and slowly pour approximately ½ cup of extra virgin olive oil through the feeding tube. We say approximately ½ cup because it may take more or less depending on the consistency of the sauce. It should be thick, not runny. After you have it out of the food processor, start tasting and adding salt and pepper to suit yourself.

Per serving: Calories 300; Protein 13g; Carbohydrates 27g; Dietary fiber 3g; Total fat 16g; Saturated fat 5g; Cholesterol 20mg; Sodium 510mg

White Pizza

Use the basic pizza crust with the variation that includes Italian herbs and cheese in the dough, and top with the following ingredients.

2 cups ricotta cheese (one 15-ounce container)

½ cup shredded mozzarella cheese

¼ cup grated fontina cheese

¼ cup grated provolone cheese

2 tablespoons grated Parmesan cheese

2 tablespoons minced Italian (flat leaf) parsley

Per serving: Calories 220; Protein 12g; Carbohydrates 25g; Dietary fiber 1g; Total fat 8g; Saturated fat 4g; Cholesterol 20mg; Sodium 360mg

Pizza Sticks

Glenna made these pizza sticks for the Milwaukee Chapter of the American Institute of Wine and Food Membership Appreciation Event. Members followed her around to get another. They make wonderful appetizers.

Preparation time: *Approximately 2 hours*

Yield: *16 sticks*

1 Make the dough from the basic pizza recipe and roll into a 16- x 12-inch rectangle.

2 With a dough scraper, sharp knife, or kitchen scissors, cut the rectangle into 12 4-inch squares.

3 Spoon 1 tablespoon of pizza sauce into the center of each square and then sprinkle with shredded mozzarella cheese.

4 Fold the square in half and seal the edges by pressing with your fingers and then with a fork. Brush the tops with egg wash (1 egg whisked with 1 tablespoon water).

5 Bake in a preheated 400° oven for 12 to 15 minutes. Serve warm.

Per serving: Calories 110; Protein 5g; Carbohydrates 18g; Dietary fiber less than 1g; Total fat 3g; Saturated fat 1g; Cholesterol 5mg; Sodium 220mg.

Focaccia

This popular, flat, crusty Italian bread is traditionally served warm and broken into pieces to eat with soup, salads, and barbecued meals — or any meal, for that matter. It normally has a light topping. You can use your imagination for the toppings; they are as varied as the people who create them. We'll give you some suggestions, and then you're on your own.

Focaccia

Suggested toppings include two thinly sliced fresh or jarred roasted peppers, sun-dried tomatoes, thinly sliced fresh red onions, sliced olives, green pepper slices, sesame seeds, and sautéed onions with sugar and salt.

Preparation time: *Approximately 3 hours*

Yield: *10 to 12 servings*

1 cup water	4 teaspoons sugar
2 tablespoons olive oil	3 cups flour
1 teaspoon salt	2 1/4 teaspoons active dry yeast

1 Be sure that all the ingredients are at room temperature before you place them in your bread pan in the order listed.

2 Select the Dough or Manual setting and press Start.

3 After the machine has completed the cycle, remove the dough onto a lightly floured work surface and shape it into a ball. Place on a greased cookie sheet and flatten to a 10-inch circle.

4 Give your Focaccia a unique appearance: With a table knife, cut a circle in the dough about 1 inch from the edge, cutting almost through to the cookie sheet; with a fork, prick all over the center section.

5 Arrange the selected toppings in the center section and drizzle with olive oil over the entire Focaccia. Sprinkle with Italian seasonings, salt, and pepper to suit your taste. Cover and let rise for approximately 15 minutes.

6 Bake in a preheated 375° oven for 25 to 30 minutes.

Per serving: Calories 140; Protein 4g; Carbohydrates 26g; Dietary fiber 1g; Total fat 2.5g; Saturated fat 0g; Cholesterol 0mg; Sodium 200mg.

Chapter 16

Quick Breads

. . . .

In This Chapter

▶ Using fruits in your quick breads

▶ Adding yummy vegetables to quick breads

▶ Making sweet quick breads

. . . .

*P*lanning a buffet table? Place quick breads beside trays of fruit or vegetables to present a complete picture.

Taking a spot of tea? Try a slice of quick bread to satisfy your palate.

Making hors d'oeurves? Serve a variety of quick breads cut in squares, diamonds, and circles.

Having overnight guests? Quick breads are great for breakfast.

But what, exactly, is a quick bread? Food scientists labeled quick breads as such, not only because one could mix them together in a few minutes, but also because there is no rising time required. Mix baking powder and/or baking soda with liquid and heat: You see an immediate reaction. With a bread machine the preparation time is about the same as putting together the ingredients for yeast breads but the cycle is much shorter. There is a short mixing time and then the machine immediately bakes the bread.

Quick breads can be sweet or savory so you can use them as a dessert or a meal accompaniment. They are moister and more crumbly than yeast breads so they do not hold together well for sandwich ingredients such as sliced meat or egg salad. If you'd like to have them for toast, you will want to toast them flat under your oven broiler rather than upright in a toaster.

Do not remove the quick bread from the pan immediately after taking the pan out of the machine. Allow about ten minutes for the bread to firm up so that it does not fall apart when you slide it out of the pan.

Apple Bread

Here is a blue-ribbon winner. We served it at a reception next to sharp cheddar cheese. The platters were empty long before the event was over.

Preparation time: *20 minutes*

Approximate cycle time: *1 hour and 20 minutes*

Yield: *16 slices, 32 servings*

1 cup granulated sugar	*½ teaspoon baking soda*
1 cup sour cream	*2 cups all-purpose flour*
2 large eggs	*1 ½ cups chopped, peeled, tart apples (Granny Smith apples are plenty tart and excellent for baking)*
2 teaspoons vanilla	
½ teaspoon salt	*1 cup pecan pieces*
2 teaspoons baking powder	

1 Place the ingredients in the pan in the order listed.

2 Select Quick or Cake setting and start your bread machine.

3 Keep the lid open and use a rubber spatula around the edges to be sure that the dry ingredients get completely moistened during the mixing time.

4 When the cycle is complete, remove the pan from the machine but do not take the bread out of the pan for ten minutes.

5 Remove the bread from the pan and allow it to completely cool before slicing.

If you want to make Apple Bread into Apple Mufffins, stop the bread machine after it has mixed the dough. Fill greased muffin cups ⅔ full (you can also use muffin paper liners). Bake in preheated 400° oven for approximately 20 minutes. The batter is enough for 12 muffins. If you have any empty muffin cups, fill them with water so the pan doesn't over-heat and cause the other muffins to burn.

Per serving: *Calories 110; Protein 2g; Carbohydrates 15g; Dietary fiber less than 1g; Total fat 4.5g; Saturated fat 1.5g; Cholesterol 20mg; Sodium 60mg.*

Banana Lemon Loaf

Kids of all ages love banana nut bread. We've added lemon juice to bring out the banana flavor, which intensifies as the bread ages. However, with the great taste and texture of this bread, don't count on it aging.

Preparation time: *15 minutes*

Approximate cycle time: *1 hour and 20 minutes*

Yield: *16 slices, 32 servings*

1 cup very ripe mashed bananas

2 large eggs

2 tablespoons lemon juice (about 1 squeezed lemon)

½ cup vegetable oil

1 tablespoon baking powder

½ teaspoon salt

1 cup sugar

2 cups all-purpose flour

1 cup chopped walnuts

1 teaspoon grated lemon peel

1 Place the ingredients in the pan in the order listed.

2 Select Quick or Cake setting and start your bread machine.

3 Keep the lid open and use a rubber spatula around the edges to be sure that the dry ingredients get completely moistened during the mixing time.

4 When the cycle is complete, remove the pan from the machine but do not take the bread out of the pan for ten minutes.

5 Remove the bread from the pan and allow it to completely cool before slicing.

If you have bananas that are getting too ripe to eat, but you don't yet want to bake with them, freeze the bananas in their skin. No extra work, just toss them in the freezer. When it's time to bake, you have those very ripe bananas on hand. Lay them in a dish to thaw; peel them with a small paring knife when they are still frosty frozen.

To accurately measure ripe bananas, place (mashed) in a dry measuring cup and level off the top.

Per serving: *Calories 120; Protein 2g; Carbohydrates 15g; Dietary fiber less than 1g; Total fat 6g; Saturated fat 0.5g; Cholesterol 15mg; Sodium 125mg.*

Cheddar Cheese Corn Bread

With the cream-style corn enhancing the wonderful corn flavor of the cornmeal and the cheddar cheese making it moist, you will love this version of corn bread. It tastes so good. Serve it with soup or salad. It's also wonderful toasted and accompanying bacon and eggs.

Preparation time: *15 minutes*

Approximate cycle time: *1 hour and 20 minutes*

Yield: *16 slices, 32 servings*

8½-ounce can cream-style corn

1 large egg

2 tablespoons salad oil

½ cup shredded cheddar cheese

2 tablespoons sugar

1 tablespoon baking powder

½ teaspoon salt

1 ½ cups all-purpose flour

1 cup cornmeal

1 Place the ingredients in the pan in the order listed.

2 Select Quick or Cake setting and start your bread machine.

3 Keep the lid open and use a rubber spatula around the edges to be sure that the dry ingredients get completely moistened during the mixing time.

4 When the cycle is complete, remove the pan from the machine but do not take the bread out of the pan for ten minutes.

5 Remove the bread from the pan and allow it to completely cool before slicing.

Tip: *Purchase the cheddar cheese already grated. Keep grated cheese frozen. It breaks apart fairly easily when you knock it against the counter a couple of times.*

Per serving: *Calories 60; Protein 2g; Carbohydrates 10g; Dietary fiber less than 1g; Total fat 2g; Saturated fat 0.5g; Cholesterol 10mg; Sodium 115mg.*

The mystery of the too-small bread

At one point while writing this chapter, we had a problem when we were testing the Cheddar Cheese Corn Bread recipe. The loaves were coming out small and dense. Then, we happened to think about the age of our baking powder. Oops. It was old. We used new baking powder. Bingo! Back to good volume and good texture.

Lemon Poppy Seed Bread

Lemon Poppy Seed Bread is wonderful when it's served just barely cool enough to cut. However, if you want to intensify the delicate flavor of this tea bread, wrap it in foil (after it has completely cooled) and refrigerate for 12 hours or longer. It will slice well. Definitely a palate pleaser.

Preparation time: *15 minutes*

Approximate cycle time: *1 hour and 20 minutes*

Yield: *16 slices, 32 servings*

2 tablespoons lemon juice	½ teaspoon salt
1 teaspoon vanilla	1 teaspoon baking soda
2 tablespoons vegetable oil	1 tablespoon grated lemon peel
2 large eggs	¼ cup poppy seeds
⅔ cup applesauce	2 cups all-purpose flour
1 cup sugar	

1 Place the ingredients in the pan in the order listed.

2 Select Quick or Cake setting and start your bread machine.

3 Keep the lid open and use a rubber spatula around the edges to be sure that the dry ingredients get completely moistened during the mixing time.

4 When the cycle is complete, remove the pan from the machine but do not take the bread out of the pan for ten minutes.

5 Remove the bread from the pan and allow it to completely cool before slicing.

Tip: Save any extra grated lemon peel in a small, plastic freezer bag. Press out any excess air from the bag before sealing. Store in the freezer for future use. It will thaw very quickly when you need it.

Per serving: *Calories 70; Protein 2g; Carbohydrates 13g; Dietary fiber 0g; Total fat 1.5g; Saturated fat 0g; Cholesterol 15mg; Sodium 60mg.*

Mushroom-Cheese Bread

The blend of vegetables with cheese makes this a wholesome bread. A great accompaniment with soup or salad, or toast it and serve with scrambled eggs.

Preparation time: *20 minutes*

Approximate cycle time: *1 hour and 20 minutes*

Yield: *16 slices, 32 servings*

¼ cup buttermilk	*1 cup sharp cheddar cheese*
2 large eggs	*½ teaspoon salt*
¼ cup vegetable oil	*2 teaspoons baking powder*
¼ cup diced green pepper	*½ teaspoon baking soda*
¼ cup diced red pepper	*⅛ teaspoon garlic salt*
¼ cup minced onions	*2 cups all-purpose flour*
1 4-ounce can chopped, drained mushrooms	

1 Place the ingredients in the pan in the order listed.

2 Select Quick or Cake setting and start your bread machine.

3 Keep the lid open and use a rubber spatula around the edges to be sure that the dry ingredients get completely moistened during the mixing time.

4 When the cycle is complete, remove the pan from the machine but do not take the bread out of the pan for ten minutes.

5 Remove the bread from the pan and allow it to completely cool before slicing.

After draining the mushrooms, pat out extra moisture between paper towels.

Tip: *Here is a good application for dry buttermilk powder. If you do not have fresh buttermilk on hand, use ¼ cup water and 1 tablespoon of dry buttermilk powder.*

Tip: *If you have green or red pepper left over, dice it, freeze on a flat surface (a cookie sheet or cake pan works) and then place in a small freezer bag. Push out the extra air before closing the bag. Store frozen.*

Per serving: Calories 60; Protein 29g; Carbohydrates 7g; Dietary fiber 0g; Total fat 3.5g; Saturated fat 1g; Cholesterol 20mg; Sodium 130mg.

Orange Date Bread

Ummm, you'll smack your lips when you taste this one. It's a taste treat par excellence. Serve with fruit for a light dessert.

Preparation time: *20 minutes*

Approximate cycle time: *1 hour and 20 minutes*

Yield: *16 slices, 32 servings*

½ cup orange juice	1 ½ teaspoons baking powder
½ cup water	1 teaspoon baking soda
1 cup finely chopped dates	2 cups all-purpose flour
1 teaspoon vanilla	½ cup chopped nuts
2 tablespoons vegetable oil	2 tablespoons grated orange rind
¾ cup sugar	

1 Place the ingredients in the pan in the order listed.

2 Select Quick or Cake setting and start your bread machine.

3 Keep the lid open and use a rubber spatula around the edges to be sure that the dry ingredients get completely moistened during the mixing time.

4 When the cycle is complete, remove the pan from the machine but do not take the bread out of the pan for ten minutes.

5 Remove the bread from the pan and allow it to completely cool before slicing.

Save any extra grated orange peel in a small, plastic freezer bag. Press out any excess air from the bag before sealing. Store in the freezer for future use. It will thaw very quickly when you need it.

Per serving: Calories 80; Protein 1g; Carbohydrates 14g; Dietary fiber less than 1g; Total fat 2g; Saturated fat 0g; Cholesterol 0mg; Sodium 25mg.

Pineapple Carrot Bread

Cinnamon, nutmeg, and allspice blend into this bread to spice it up — delicious.

Preparation time: *20 minutes*

Approximate cycle time: *1 hour and 20 minutes*

Yield: *16 slices, 32 servings*

½ cup crushed pineapple, drained

½ cup raisins

½ cup finely grated carrots

1 tablespoon molasses

½ cup applesauce

¾ cup light-brown sugar

¼ teaspoon allspice

¼ teaspoon nutmeg

½ teaspoon cinnamon

½ teaspoon salt

2 teaspoons baking powder

½ teaspoon baking soda

2 ½ cups all-purpose flour

1 Place the ingredients in the pan in the order listed.

2 Select Quick or Cake setting and start your bread machine.

3 Keep the lid open and use a rubber spatula around the edges to be sure that the dry ingredients get completely moistened during the mixing time.

4 When the cycle is complete, remove the pan from the machine but do not take the bread out of the pan for ten minutes.

5 Remove the bread from the pan and allow it to completely cool before slicing.

Per serving: Calories 70; Protein 1g; Carbohydrates 16g; Dietary fiber less than 1g; Total fat 0g; Saturated fat 0g; Cholesterol 0mg; Sodium 90mg.

Pumpkin Bread

A delicate bread that is a perfect accompaniment for a chicken or turkey salad entrée or as a light dessert. You can choose which nuts to use; walnuts are good, pecans are even better.

Preparation time: *15 minutes*

Approximate cycle time: *1 hour and 20 minutes*

Yield: *16 slices, 32 servings*

¾ cup canned pumpkin	1 teaspoon cinnamon
3 tablespoons oil	¼ teaspoon nutmeg
1 large egg	2 cups all-purpose flour
½ cup sugar	½ cup raisins
1 teaspoon baking powder	¼ cup coarsely chopped nuts
¼ teaspoon baking soda	

1 Place the ingredients in the pan in the order listed.

2 Select Quick or Cake setting and start your bread machine.

3 Keep the lid open and use a rubber spatula around the edges to be sure that the dry ingredients get completely moistened during the mixing time.

4 When the cycle is complete, remove the pan from the machine but do not take the bread out of the pan for ten minutes.

5 Remove the bread from the pan and allow it to completely cool before slicing.

Warning: *Coarsely chopped nuts show up in the bread. If you chop them too fine you will wonder where they are.*

Tip: *Grated carrots may be purchased at the salad bar in the grocery store. You can buy the amount you need — no waste.*

Warning: *Raisins plumped for baking disintegrate when the bread machine mixes. Sun-dried raisins used directly from the package will remain intact.*

Per serving: *Calories 70; Protein 1g; Carbohydrates 12g; Dietary fiber less than 1g; Total fat 2g; Saturated fat 0g; Cholesterol 10mg; Sodium 40mg.*

Soda Bread

Virginia Riositti, our mutual friend, contributed this recipe. We think it is one of the best soda bread recipes we have tasted.

Preparation time: *10 minutes*

Approximate cycle time: *1 hour and 20 minutes*

Yield: *16 slices, 32 servings*

2 cups buttermilk	1 teaspoon soda
½ cup sugar	4 cups all-purpose flour
1 ½ teaspoons salt	½ cup raisins

1 Place the ingredients in the pan in the order listed.

2 Select Quick or Cake setting and start your bread machine.

3 Keep the lid open and use a rubber spatula around the edges to be sure that the dry ingredients get completely moistened during the mixing time.

4 When the cycle is complete, remove the pan from the machine but do not take the bread out of the pan for ten minutes.

5 Remove the bread from the pan and allow it to completely cool before slicing.

Per serving: *Calories 80; Protein 2g; Carbohydrates 18g; Dietary fiber less than 1g; Total fat 0g; Saturated fat 0g; Cholesterol 0mg; Sodium 170mg.*

Toasted Coconut Bread

It's teatime: Make it elegant! Slice this bread and cut the slices into quarters. It's a dandy!

Preparation time: *20 minutes*

Approximate cycle time: *1 hour and 20 minutes*

Yield: *16 slices, 64 servings*

1 cup milk	1 teaspoon salt
1 large egg	1 tablespoon baking powder
4 teaspoons oil	1 cup flaked sweetened coconut, lightly toasted
1 teaspoon vanilla	2 teaspoons grated orange peel
¾ cup sugar	2 cups all-purpose flour

1 Place the ingredients in the pan in the order listed.

2 Select Quick or Cake setting and start your bread machine.

3 Keep the lid open and use a rubber spatula around the edges to be sure that the dry ingredients get completely moistened during the mixing time.

4 When the cycle is complete, remove the pan from the machine but do not take the bread out of the pan for ten minutes.

5 Remove the bread from the pan and allow it to completely cool before slicing.

To toast the coconut, spread it on a jellyroll pan and place the pan under a broiler. Do not take your eyes off the coconut while it is broiling. The sugar in the coconut browns very quickly.

Tip: *Save any extra grated orange peel in a small, plastic freezer bag. Press out any excess air from the bag before sealing. Store in the freezer for future use. It will thaw very quickly when you need it.*

Per serving: *Calories 70; Protein 1g; Carbohydrates 12g; Dietary fiber 0g; Total fat 1.5g; Saturated fat 1g; Cholesterol 10mg; Sodium 130mg.*

Zucchini Bread

This version of Zucchini Bread works great in a bread machine. We've cut back on the amount of sugar that other recipes may call for and enhanced the flavor with maple flavoring. Our taste-testers raved about how good it is. The loaves dome so beautifully, you could take it with pride to any potluck dinner or bake sale.

Zucchini Bread is a great keeper. It stores well and tastes even better as it ages.

Preparation time: *20 minutes*

Approximate cycle time: *1 hour and 20 minutes*

Yield: *16 slices, 32 servings*

2 eggs, large	1 teaspoon baking soda
½ cup vegetable oil	1½ teaspoons baking powder
2 teaspoons maple flavoring, or 2 teaspoons maple syrup	1 teaspoon cinnamon
	⅓ cup uncooked dry oatmeal
¾ cup white sugar	2 cups all-purpose flour
1½ cups grated fresh zucchini	½ cup coarsely chopped nuts
1 teaspoon salt	

1 Place the ingredients in the pan in the order listed.

2 Select Quick or Cake setting and start your bread machine.

3 Keep the lid open and use a rubber spatula around the edges to be sure that the dry ingredients get completely moistened during the mixing time.

4 When the cycle is complete, remove the pan from the machine but do not take the bread out of the pan for ten minutes.

5 Remove the bread from the pan and allow it to completely cool before slicing.

Per serving: Calories 100; Protein 1g; Carbohydrates 12g; Dietary fiber 0g; Total fat 5g; Saturated fat 0g; Cholesterol 10mg; Sodium 130mg.

Chapter 17

Betty's Quick Breads

In This Chapter

▶ Making your own quick bread mix

▶ Using the mix to create wonderful breads

Recipes in This Chapter

▶ Betty's Base Bread Mix
▶ Apple Date Bread
▶ Carrot Raisin Bread
▶ Cranberry Orange Bread
▶ Chocolate Chunk Bread
▶ Corn Bacon Bread
▶ Fall Treasures Bread
▶ Oatmeal Walnut Bread
▶ Multi-Grain Bread
▶ Pumpkin Raisin Bread

*B*etty McLaughlin prepared these recipes — originally for school food-service programs. Fortunately for us, Betty not only has a formula for mixing 25 pounds of the base mix, but she also has a recipe for the 1-pound size. Just a bit of tweaking and voilà — a quick-bread mix that's perfect for bread machines.

The Foundation: Betty's Bread Mix

Using a mix saves you time. Instead of getting all the various ingredients out, measuring them, and then cleaning up all your measuring cups and spoons, you only have to measure the appropriate amount of the mix, add your other ingredients, and you're done. Of course, you do have to take some time, initially, to create the basic mix.

Betty's Base Bread Mix

This recipe is the basis for all the other recipes in this chapter. It includes each of the basic elements found in a good loaf of bread-machine bread (except the liquid). We give you some suggestions for how to use the mix in the other recipes in the chapter, but we also encourage you to experiment.

Preparation time: 20 minutes

Approximate cycle time: 1½ hours

Yield: 3 quick breads

6 cups all-purpose flour	⅓ cup dry milk
1 ½ cups sugar	¼ cup baking powder
4 ½ teaspoons salt	3 teaspoons baking soda

1 Thoroughly blend all the ingredients in a large bowl with a wire whisk or place in a large, self-sealing plastic bag and rotate the bag to mix the ingredients together.

2 Store in an airtight container or large, self-sealing plastic bag. Use within three months.

Here's how you use the base bread mix for the rest of the recipes in this chapter:

1 Place the wet ingredients for the specific recipe in the bread machine pan.

2 Add the prepared mix and the other dry ingredients, such as dried fruit, chocolate pieces, or nuts, to the pan and place the pan in the bread machine.

3 Select the Quick or Cake setting and start the machine.

4 Do not close the lid during the start of the mixing time. Instead, help the ingredients mix together by using a rubber spatula. Be certain that all the dry ingredients become moist.

5 When the cycle is complete, test the bread to be sure it's done. Some people trust a toothpick inserted into the center of the loaf. If the toothpick comes out clean, the loaf is done. A more accurate method is to use an instant-read thermometer. Bread is thoroughly baked when a thermometer inserted into the middle of the loaf reads 190° to 200°.

6 If the bread is not completely baked and your machine has a Bake setting, select Bake and continue to bake an additional 10 to 15 minutes. If your machine does not have a Bake setting, you can complete the baking in your oven at 400°. Do not worry about pre-heating. Turn the oven on and immediately put in the pan containing the bread.

7 When the bread is completely baked, let it sit in the pan for ten minutes. During this time, the structure of the dough will settle, so that when you do take the bread out of the pan it won't fall apart. Also, bread slides out of the pan much easier after it's cooled for ten minutes. Finish cooling on a rack.

If your machine doesn't have a Quick or Cake setting, but does have a Dough and a Bake setting, you can still make quick breads. Mix the ingredients for three to five minutes on the Dough setting. When the dry ingredients are completely moistened, hold Stop until the digital display reads 0:00. Then select the Bake setting and start the machine.

Recipes Based on Betty's Base Bread Mix

For the following recipes, all you have to do is follow the instructions in the preceding section. By making the mix, you've already done half the work. Couldn't be easier!

Apple Date Bread

Tart apples and sweet dates — what a combination. We love this bread with nothing added, but when we place a dish of cream cheese beside it on a buffet table, both the Apple Date Bread and the cream cheese disappear. It's also great as a dessert with a scoop of vanilla ice cream on the top. Maybe a tad bit of carmel on the ice cream?

Preparation time: *20 minutes*

Approximate cycle time: *1½ hours*

Yield: *16 slices, 32 servings*

1 cup apple juice

¼ cup vegetable oil

1 large egg

1 ⅓ cups Betty's Base Bread Mix

¾ cup all-purpose flour

¼ cup whole-wheat flour

¼ cup sugar

½ cup finely chopped apples

¼ cup chopped dates

1 Follow the directions under Betty's Basic Bread Mix, earlier in this chapter.

You may use any fresh apple, but we prefer the tartness of the Granny Smith variety.

Variation: *If you like a drier bread, use diced, dried apples.*

Per serving: *Calories 70; Protein 1g; Carbohydrates 11g; Dietary fiber 0g; Total fat 2g; Saturated fat 0g; Cholesterol 10mg; Sodium 110mg.*

Carrot Raisin Bread

For an afternoon snack or a light dessert, spread cream cheese on a slice of this bread and serve it with a dish of peaches.

Preparation time: *15 minutes*

Approximate cycle time: *1½ hours*

Yield: *16 slices, 32 servings*

¾ cup water

¼ cup orange juice

¼ cup vegetable oil

¼ cup honey

1 large egg

¼ cup crushed pineapple, drained

⅔ cup grated carrots

¼ cup raisins

1 ⅓ cups Betty's Base Bread Mix

½ cup whole-wheat flour

½ cup all-purpose flour

½ teaspoon ground cinnamon

⅛ teaspoon ground cloves

1 Follow the directions under Betty's Basic Bread Mix, earlier in this chapter.

Per serving: *Calories 70; Protein 1g; Carbohydrates 11g; Dietary fiber less than 1g; Total fat 2g; Saturated fat 0g; Cholesterol 10mg; Sodium 110mg.*

Cranberry Orange Bread

Make Cranberry Orange Bread as a holiday gift for your special friends. This bread gets better with age, so make it a ahead of time to have it ready for serving or giving during the holiday season. Freezing is the best way to store the bread. After it is completely cool, wrap it tightly in aluminum foil, and place the loaf in a freezer bag. If you are giving it as a gift, the aluminum foil makes a perfect wrapping paper — add a red ribbon and bow. What a presentation for a holiday gift!

If you plan to serve the Cranberry Orange Bread, cut the bread into slices before freezing. The slices can be easily popped apart for quick thawing.

Preparation time: *15 minutes*

Approximate cycle time: *1½ hours*

Yield: *16 slices, 32 servings*

¾ cup water	1 cup all-purpose flour
¼ cup orange juice	¼ cup sugar
¼ cup vegetable oil	1 cup dried cranberries
1 large egg	1 tablespoon grated orange rind
1 ⅓ cups Betty's Base Bread Mix	

1 Follow the directions under Betty's Basic Bread Mix, earlier in this chapter.

Per serving: Calories 70; Protein 1g; Carbohydrates 12g; Dietary fiber less than 1g; Total fat 2g; Saturated fat 0g; Cholesterol 10mg; Sodium 110mg.

Chocolate Chunk Bread

You will satisfy any chocolate lovers you know with this quick bread. It also makes wonderful muffins. Either way you prepare this recipe, we can guarantee you that it will quickly disappear.

Preparation time: *15 minutes*

Approximate cycle time: *1½ hours*

Yield: *16 slices, 32 servings, or 12 muffins*

¾ cup water

¼ cup orange juice

¼ cup vegetable oil

1 large egg

1 ⅓ cups Betty's Base Bread Mix

1 cup all-purpose flour

¼ cup sugar

1 tablespoon grated orange rind

¾ cup (4 ounces) chocolate chunks

1 Follow the directions under Betty's Basic Bread Mix, earlier in this chapter.

Variation: *You may substitute ¾ cup chocolate chunks with ¾ cup chocolate chips or ⅔ cup mini chocolate chips.*

Tip: *If you would like to make Chocolate Chunk Muffins, stop the bread machine after it has mixed the dough. Fill greased muffin cups ⅔ full. (You can also use muffin paper liners.) Bake in a preheated 400° oven for approximately 20 minutes. The batter makes 12 muffins. If you have any empty muffin cups, fill them with water so the pan doesn't overheat and cause the other muffins to burn.*

Per serving: *Calories 80; Protein 1g; Carbohydrates 12g; Dietary fiber 0g; Total fat 3g; Saturated fat 1g; Cholesterol 10mg; Sodium 110mg.*

Corn Bacon Bread

Here is good old-fashioned corn bread at its finest. The bacon drippings and the crumbled bacon enhance the flavor to make it lip smackin' good. Give this to a Southern boy and he'll think he's in heaven.

Preparation time: 10 minutes

Approximate cycle time: 1½ hours

Yield: 16 slices, 32 servings

1 cup buttermilk

3 tablespoons vegetable oil

1 tablespoon bacon drippings

1 large egg

1 ⅓ cups Betty's Base Bread Mix

1 cup yellow cornmeal

2 tablespoons crumbled, cooked bacon

1 Follow the directions under Betty's Basic Bread Mix, earlier in this chapter.

Tip: The next time you cook bacon, save the grease in a small container in the refrigerator. Save a couple of strips of bacon and place them in a small freezer bag. When you're ready to make Corn Bacon Bread, you'll have the bacon and the drippings on hand.

Per serving: Calories 230; Protein 1g; Carbohydrates 8g; Dietary fiber 0g; Total fat 22g; Saturated fat 1.5g; Cholesterol 10mg; Sodium 125mg.

Fall Treasures Bread

Dried fruit morsels make this bread sweet and moist. A very versatile quick bread that goes with everything. Perfect for an after-school snack.

Preparation time: *15 minutes*

Approximate cycle time: *1¹⁄₂ hours*

Yield: *16 slices, 32 servings, or 12 muffins*

1 cup apple juice	1 cup all-purpose flour
¹⁄₄ cup vegetable oil	¹⁄₄ cup sugar
1 large egg	¹⁄₂ teaspoon ground nutmeg
1 teaspoon vanilla	¹⁄₂ cup dried fruit, chopped
1 ¹⁄₃ cups Betty's Base Bread Mix	¹⁄₄ cup chopped nuts

1 Follow the directions under Betty's Basic Bread Mix, earlier in this chapter.

Per serving: *Calories 80; Protein 1g; Carbohydrates 12g; Dietary fiber less than 1g; Total fat 3g; Saturated fat 0g; Cholesterol 10mg; Sodium 110mg.*

Oatmeal Walnut Bread

If you haven't got the time to make a yeast bread, but you need a hearty bread quickly, here's an easy one. Chances are you have all the ingredients on your pantry shelf.

Preparation time: *15 minutes*

Approximate cycle time: *1½ hours*

Yield: *16 slices, 32 servings, or 12 muffins*

1 cup buttermilk	¾ cup whole-wheat flour
¼ cup vegetable oil	¼ cup dry oatmeal
1 large egg	½ cup brown sugar
1 ⅓ cups Betty's Base Bread Mix	⅓ cups chopped walnuts

1 Follow the directions under Betty's Basic Bread Mix, earlier in this chapter.

Tip: When we say dry oatmeal, you can use old-fashioned rolled or quick-cooking oats.

Tip: You can substitute dry buttermilk powder for buttermilk. You do not have to reconstitute the powder in water first. Replace the 1 cup of buttermilk with 1 cup of water and measure ¼ cup dry buttermilk powder in with the dry ingredients.

Per serving: Calories 80; Protein 2g; Carbohydrates 11g; Dietary fiber less than 1g; Total fat 3g; Saturated fat 0g; Cholesterol 10mg; Sodium 120mg.

Multi-Grain Bread

You can increase fiber in your diet with this healthy quick bread. It's good for you and it tastes delicious.

Preparation time: 15 minutes

Approximate cycle time: 1½ hours

Yield: 16 slices, 32 servings, or 12 muffins

¾ cup water

¼ cup orange juice

¼ cup vegetable oil

1 large egg

1 ⅓ cups Betty's Base Bread Mix

¾ cup whole-wheat flour

¼ cup dry oatmeal

¼ cup corn meal

2 tablespoons 7-grain cereal

1 Follow the directions under Betty's Basic Bread Mix, earlier in this chapter.

If you like nuts in your quick breads, you may add ½ cup coarsely-chopped nuts to any quick bread recipe without changing any other ingredient amount.

Seven-grain cereal may not be something you usually have on your pantry shelf. You can buy a box and divide it into small amounts, stored frozen in small freezer bags. Be sure to get as much air as possible out of the bag before closing it.

Per serving: Calories 60; Protein 1g; Carbohydrates 9g; Dietary fiber less than 1g; Total fat 2g; Saturated fat 0g; Cholesterol 0mg; Sodium 105mg.

Pumpkin Raisin Bread

Here's a fall bread that's ideal for school or church bake sales. Everyone seems to like a good pumpkin bread, and this is one of the best.

Preparation time: *15 minutes*

Approximate cycle time: *1½ hours*

Yield: *16 slices, 32 servings*

¾ cup apple juice

½ cup mashed pumpkin

¼ cup vegetable oil

1 large egg

1 ⅓ cups Betty's Base Bread Mix

½ cup all-purpose flour

½ cup whole-wheat flour

¼ cup brown sugar, packed

1 teaspoon pumpkin pie spice

½ cup raisins

1 Follow the directions under Betty's Basic Bread Mix, earlier in this chapter.

If you use canned pumpkin, you will have some left over. You can freeze it for later use. If you think you'll be using it to make more pumpkin bread, measure out the pumpkin in ½ cup amounts and freeze it; you'll have the exact amount you need the next time you make this bread.

Per serving: Calories 70; Protein 1g; Carbohydrates 12g; Dietary fiber less than 1g; Total fat 2g; Saturated fat 0g; Cholesterol 10mg; Sodium 110mg.

Chapter 18

Breads for Alternative Diets

Maybe you're one of the many people who have discovered that the bread you've always had in your diet is causing you distress. Your doctor or dietician says, "No more wheat bread." Sounds simple, until you begin a diet without it. Pretty soon you're craving bread, and even cheating and sneaking some into your diet, only to wish that you hadn't.

If you know that your body simply can't tolerate wheat-based bread, you'll appreciate your bread machine even more than you used to. Thanks to the bread machine, you can have breads made with flours other than wheat, oats, barley, and rye. Of course, these gluten-free breads feel and taste different than traditional, wheat-flour breads, but they are quite good and they're good for you. Try a few of them, even if you're able to eat traditional bread. You may be surprised at how good they are.

Wheat flour is the only kind of flour that contains protein that becomes gluten when wet, is elastic when kneaded, and forms the honeycomb structure in breads. In preparing recipes without wheat, we used xanthan gum as a bonding agent because it also becomes elastic and stretches to form the structure of the dough in gluten-free breads. While many of the gluten-free flours are available in the dietetic health food section of your supermarket, you probably will have to purchase xanthan gum at a health food store or through a mail-order catalog. (See Chapter 3 for a mail-order source.)

We've provided a well-rounded variety of breads so that you can have a sandwich, a great piece of toast, a pizza, a sweet bread with your coffee or tea, and a spelt (mock whole wheat). Some of you may not be able to use the spelt recipe because spelt is a distant cousin of wheat. However, many people are discovering that spelt is okay for them, even when wheat isn't.

For more information on alternative flours, see Chapter 3.

Making Gluten-Free Bread: General Tips

Before you begin making gluten-free bread, we suggest that you read the following list of cooking tips to avoid any unnecessary problems:

- ✔ To bring cold eggs to room temperature, place them in a bowl of very warm water for several minutes. This method is safer than having eggs sit out for an extended period of time.

- ✔ The easiest way to thoroughly blend the dry ingredients is to place all of them into a gallon-size, self-sealing plastic bag, seal, rotate, and shake. Some people like to mix the dry ingredients using a wire whisk in a bowl.

- ✔ You can prepare several bread mixes at one time by measuring the dry ingredients into the self-sealing bag and storing in your freezer for future use. Do not mix the yeast into the mixture, although you can freeze yeast. We place one unopened package of active dry yeast in each bag of mix. Bring the mix to room temperature before using. Open the yeast and add to the mix before pouring it into the liquid ingredients.

- ✔ Open the lid of the machine while the dough is mixing. After five minutes of mixing, the dough consistency should look similar to a pancake batter. You should see a swirl forming that slightly cones in the middle. If the dough is too thin and does not swirl with a cone, add more flour; if it's too thick, add water.

✔ If your bread machine has two kneading times, be sure to open the lid of the machine when the second kneading begins. You may have to use your rubber spatula to push the top of the dough down to mix with the lower portion that is churning around with the kneading blade.

✔ Some people prefer to remove the kneading blade from the machine after the first kneading. This prevents the machine from kneading twice and there is less disruption to the dough with just the small shaft leaving a hole. If you do this, be sure to thoroughly clean the shaft inside the pan after use.

✔ To test your bread for doneness, insert a toothpick in the center. If it comes out clean, the bread is done.

✔ There is some inconsistency in the labeling of potato starch and potato flour. Be sure you buy potato starch and not potato flour. Potato starch looks and feels like cornstarch. Potato flour looks more like coarse, white, wheat flour.

Gluten-Free Bread Recipes

All gluten-free recipes in this chapter are written for a 1 ½ pound loaf. Larger loaves do not hold their shape well and do not bake through without a prolonged baking time, resulting in a thick, hard crust.

Delicious, grilled ham-and-cheese sandwiches

Put the Gluten-Free White Bread to good use by making one of our favorite sandwiches: grilled ham-and-cheese.

Toast the bread slices before making the sandwich. Spread mustard on one piece, then add the cheese of your choice and a slice of ham, and top with the other slice of bread. Melt a pat of butter in a frying pan on medium-low heat and place the sandwich in the pan to brown the bread and melt the cheese. Flip the sandwich to brown the opposite side.

Gluten-Free White Bread

If you've never made gluten-free bread, we suggest that you begin with this white bread. It's a very basic bread, and when you get used to eating gluten-free bread, you will find that this will be your standard recipe.

Actually, we don't need to eat gluten-free bread and we find that we really like this one. It's quite versatile and can be used for a meal accompaniment, a sandwich, or toast.

Preparation time: *20 minutes*

Approximate cycle time: *2½ to 3 hours*

Yield: *12 to 16 slices*

Wet Ingredients

3 large eggs

1 ½ cups water

3 tablespoons pure maple syrup

3 tablespoons vegetable oil

Dry Ingredients

2 ¼ cups white rice flour

½ cup potato starch

½ cup tapioca flour

½ cup dry milk powder

1 tablespoon xanthan gum

1 teaspoon salt

2 ¼ teaspoons active dry yeast

1 Be sure that all the ingredients are at room temperature.

2 Combine the wet ingredients and pour them into the bread machine pan.

3 Measure the dry ingredients, including the yeast, and mix well to blend, and then place them in the pan.

4 Place the pan in the bread machine.

5 Select the Normal, White, or Basic cycle and press Start.

Tip: If your machine is programmable, use a 20-minute knead time, a 70-minute rise time, and a 60-minute bake time.

If your machine has a Bake cycle, begin by using the Dough cycle. When it ends, select the Bake cycle. If the bread is not done at the end of the baking time, reset the Bake cycle and continue baking the bread until it is done. (Use the toothpick test to determine whether or not the bread is completely baked. The toothpick will come out of the bread without any dough on it.)

When the bread is completely baked, take the pan out of the machine and place the pan on a wire rack. Do not take the bread out until ten minutes have passed. This allows the structure of the bread to firm up so that it won't fall apart when you remove the bread from the pan.

Allow the bread to completely cool — it should take about an hour — before cutting it.

Per serving: *Calories 180; Protein 4g; Carbohydrates 32g; Dietary fiber 2g; Total fat 4.5g; Saturated fat 0.5g; Cholesterol 55mg; Sodium 190mg.*

Quinoa Onion Cheddar Bread

After learning that quinoa flour was safe for Celiacs, we started testing to see how we could incorporate it into a gluten-free recipe. (See the sidebar, "A gluten-free experience," in Chapter 3 for more information on Celiacs.) We wanted to add quinoa to improve the nutritional value of the bread. However, we weren't entirely satisfied with the flavor until we added instant minced onion and cheddar cheese — what a great bread! Pass the cabbage salad, ham, and scalloped potatoes, please.

Preparation time: *20 minutes*

Approximate cycle time: *2½ to 3 hours*

Yield: *12 to 16 slices*

Wet Ingredients

3 large eggs

1 ½ cups water

2 tablespoons vegetable oil

Dry Ingredients

2 cups white rice flour

1 cup quinoa flour

¼ cup dry milk powder

2 tablespoons sugar

1 teaspoon salt

2 teaspoons xanthan gum

1 teaspoon instant minced onions

1 ½ cups grated sharp cheddar cheese (about 6 ounces)

2 ¼ teaspoons active dry yeast

1 Be sure that all the ingredients are at room temperature.

2 Combine the wet ingredients and pour them into the bread machine pan.

3 Measure the dry ingredients, including the yeast, and mix well to blend, and then place them in the pan.

4 Place the pan in the bread machine.

5 Select the Normal, White, or Basic cycle and press Start.

If your machine is programmable, use a 20-minute knead time, a 70-minute rise time, and a 60-minute bake time. If your machine has a Bake cycle, begin by using the Dough cycle. When it ends, select the Bake cycle. If the bread is not done at the end of the baking time, reset the Bake cycle and continue baking the bread until it is done. (Use the toothpick test to determine whether or not the bread is finished.)

When the bread is completely baked, take the pan out of the machine and place the pan on a wire rack. Do not take the bread out until ten minutes have passed. This allows the structure of the bread to firm up so that it won't fall apart when you remove the bread from the pan.

Per serving: *Calories 230; Protein 9g; Carbohydrates 31g; Dietary fiber 2g; Total fat 8g; Saturated fat 2.5g; Cholesterol 65mg; Sodium 270mg.*

Gluten-Free Pizza

This is a great recipe for pizza crust. It's stiffer during the mixing time than other doughs, and it makes a perfectly crisp crust. You can make two 12-inch pizzas with this recipe.

Preparation time: *Approximately 1 hour*

Yield: *12 to 16 slices*

Wet Ingredients

4 egg whites

1 ½ cups water

3 tablespoons vegetable oil

Dry Ingredients

2 cups rice flour

1 cup tapioca flour

1 cup arrowroot flour

½ cup dry milk powder

1 ½ teaspoons salt

1 tablespoon xanthan gum

2 ¼ teaspoons active dry yeast

Your favorite pizza toppings

1 Be sure that all the ingredients are at room temperature.

2 Combine the wet ingredients and pour them into the bread machine pan.

3 Excluding your toppings, measure the dry ingredients, including the yeast, and mix thoroughly. Add them to the pan.

4 Place the pan in the bread machine.

5 Select the Dough cycle and press Start.

When the kneading is complete, press Stop on your control panel to clear the machine. Pizza dough should not rise in the machine.

Generously grease two pizza pans or cookie sheets. Remove the dough from the bread machine pan to the pizza pans, dividing it in half to form the two crusts. Grease your fingers, and spread the dough evenly, making sure it reaches into the corners of the pan. Top the pizza with your favorite pizza sauce and toppings.

Bake in a preheated 400° oven for approximately 20 minutes. Pizza is done when the bottom of the crust is a light, golden brown and the sides have pulled away from the pan.

Per serving: Calories 190; Protein 4g; Carbohydrates 36g; Dietary fiber 2g; Total fat 3.5g; Saturated fat 0g; Cholesterol 0mg; Sodium 280mg.

Bean Bread

Now here's a hearty sandwich bread. When we tasted it we wanted a slice of salami and some Havarti cheese to make a lunch, but we ended up using it for sopping up stew at dinnertime. Umm, delicious.

Preparation time: *20 minutes*

Approximate cycle time: *2½ to 3 hours*

Yield: *12 to 16 slices*

Wet Ingredients

3 extra large eggs

1 ⅓ cups water

3 tablespoons vegetable oil

Dry Ingredients

1 cup bean flour (Romano or chickpea)

1 cup brown rice flour

½ cup quinoa flour

½ cup arrowroot flour

½ cup tapioca flour

1 ½ teaspoons salt

3 tablespoons light brown sugar

1 tablespoon xanthan gum

2 ¼ teaspoons active dry yeast

1 Be sure that all the ingredients are at room temperature.

2 Combine the wet ingredients and pour them into the bread machine pan.

3 Measure the dry ingredients, including the yeast, and mix well. Place them in the pan.

4 Place the pan in the bread machine.

5 Select the Normal, White, or Basic cycle and press Start.

If your machine is programmable, use a 20-minute knead time, a 70-minute rise time, and a 60-minute bake time. If your machine has a Bake cycle, begin by using the Dough cycle. When it ends select the Bake cycle. If the bread is not done at the end of the baking time, reset the Bake cycle and continue baking the bread until it is done. (Use the toothpick test to determine if the bread is done baking.)

When the bread is completely baked, take the pan out of the machine and place the pan on a wire rack. Do not take the bread out until ten minutes have passed. This allows the structure of the bread to firm up so that it won't fall apart when you remove the bread from the pan.

Allow the bread to completely cool — it should take about an hour — before cutting it.

Per serving: *Calories 160; Protein 5g; Carbohydrates 23g; Dietary fiber 2g; Total fat 5g; Saturated fat 0.5g; Cholesterol 55mg; Sodium 280mg.*

Cream of Orange Bread

Orange and ginger complement each other perfectly in this delectable bread. It makes a wonderful gift to someone on a gluten-free diet — none if it will go to waste!

Preparation time: *20 minutes*

Approximate cycle time: *2½ to 3 hours*

Yield: *12 to 16 slices*

Wet Ingredients

3 extra large eggs

¾ cup water

¾ cup half-and-half

3 tablespoons vegetable oil

Dry Ingredients

2 cups white rice flour

¾ cup potato starch flour

¼ cup tapioca flour

3 tablespoons brown sugar

1 teaspoon salt

1 tablespoon xanthan gum

2 tablespoons grated orange peel

1 teaspoon grated lemon peel

¼ teaspoon ground ginger or cardamom

2¼ teaspoons active dry yeast

1 Be sure that all the ingredients are at room temperature.

2 Combine the wet ingredients and pour them into the bread machine pan.

3 Measure the dry ingredients, including the yeast, and mix them together. Place them in the pan.

4 Place the pan in the bread machine.

5 Select the Normal, White, or Basic cycle and press Start.

> *If your machine is programmable, use a 20-minute knead time, a 70-minute rise time, and a 60-minute bake time. If your machine has a Bake cycle, begin by using the Dough cycle. When it ends, select the Bake cycle. If the bread is not done at the end of the baking time, reset the Bake cycle and continue baking the bread until it is done. (Use the toothpick test to determine if the bread is done baking.)*

> *When the bread is completely baked, take the pan out of the machine and place the pan on a wire rack. Do not take the bread out until ten minutes have passed. This allows the structure of the bread to firm up so that it won't fall apart when you remove the bread from the pan.*

Per serving: *Calories 190; Protein 4g; Carbohydrates 30g; Dietary fiber 2g; Total fat 6g; Saturated fat 1.5g; Cholesterol 60mg; Sodium 190mg.*

Mock Swedish Limpa

The original Swedish Limpa is a Scandinavian classic. We have used the grated orange rind, molasses, and fennel to develop the same flavors as the bread made with wheat and rye flours. We think we've created a good imitation. This makes excellent toast. We happened to have some orange marmalade on hand. Can't get much better than that.

Preparation time: *20 minutes*

Approximate cycle time: *2½ to 3 hours*

Yield: *12 to 16 slices*

Wet Ingredients

3 extra large eggs

1 ⅓ cups water

3 tablespoons molasses

3 tablespoons vegetable oil

Dry Ingredients

1 cup brown rice flour

1 cup chickpea flour

1 cup tapioca flour

½ cup arrowroot

1 teaspoon salt

1 tablespoon xanthan gum

2 tablespoons grated orange peel

1 teaspoon powdered fennel

2 ¼ teaspoons active dry yeast

1 Be sure that all the ingredients are at room temperature.

2 Combine the wet ingredients and pour them into the bread machine pan.

3 Measure the dry ingredients, including the yeast, and mix them together. Place them in the pan.

4 Place the pan in the bread machine.

5 Select the Normal, White, or Basic cycle and press Start.

If your machine is programmable, use a 20-minute knead time, a 70-minute rise time, and a 60-minute bake time.

If your machine has a Bake cycle, begin by using the Dough cycle. When it ends, select the Bake cycle. If the bread is not done at the end of the baking time, reset the Bake cycle and continue baking the bread until it's done. (Use the toothpick test to determine if the bread is done baking.)

When the bread is completely baked, take the pan out of the machine and place the pan on a wire rack. Do not take the bread out until ten minutes have passed. This allows the structure of the bread to firm up so that it won't fall apart when you remove the bread from the pan.

Per serving: *Calories 150; Protein 3g; Carbohydrates 26g; Dietary fiber 2g; Total fat 4.5g; Saturated fat 0.5g; Cholesterol 50mg; Sodium 180mg.*

Banana Quick Bread

You will enjoy the mild banana flavor in this fine-textured bread. To us, the walnuts seem a must — but if you don't care for walnuts you can omit them.

Preparation time: *20 minutes*

Approximate cycle time: *1 hour and 20 minutes*

Yield: *12 to 16 slices*

Wet Ingredients

2 large eggs

2 ripe bananas

3 tablespoons vegetable oil

Dry Ingredients

⅔ cup bean flour

⅔ cup rice flour

½ cup tapioca flour

¼ cup cornstarch

¾ cup sugar

1 teaspoon baking powder

½ teaspoon baking soda

½ cup walnuts

1 Be sure that all the ingredients are at room temperature.

2 Combine the wet ingredients and pour them into the bread machine-baking pan.

3 Measure the dry ingredients, including the yeast, and mix well to blend. Place them in the pan.

4 Place the pan in the bread machine.

5 Select the Cake or Quick bread cycle and press Start.

Do not confuse the Quick bread cycle with another short cycle, like the Rapid cycle. The Quick bread cycle has no rising time. Quick breads use baking powder and/or baking soda, which leavens in a chemical reaction to moisture and heat that occurs once you start baking the bread.

When the bread is completely baked, take the pan out of the machine and place the pan on a wire rack. Do not take the bread out until ten minutes have passed. This allows the structure of the bread to firm up so that it won't fall apart when you remove the bread from the pan.

Per serving: *Calories 160; Protein 4g; Carbohydrates 21g; Dietary fiber 1g; Total fat 7g; Saturated fat 0.5g; Cholesterol 35mg; Sodium 100mg.*

Cranberry Nut Bread

You will love the texture and the flavor of this delicious bread. Take it with pride to any gathering, be it a meeting of people who can't eat gluten or the neighborhood picnic. It will receive raves no matter where you serve it or who you serve it to.

Preparation time: 20 minutes

Approximate cycle time: 1 hour and 20 minutes

Yield: 12 to 16 slices

Wet Ingredients

2 large eggs

½ cup orange juice

3 tablespoons vegetable oil

Dry Ingredients

⅔ cup bean flour

⅔ cup rice flour

½ cup tapioca flour

¼ cup arrowroot

½ cup sugar

1 teaspoon salt

1 teaspoon baking powder

½ teaspoon baking soda

Grated rind of 1 orange

1 cup of dried cranberries

½ cup coarsely chopped pecans

1 Be sure that all the ingredients are at room temperature.

2 Combine the wet ingredients and pour them into the bread machine-baking pan.

3 Measure the dry ingredients, including the yeast, and mix well to blend. Place them in the pan.

4 Place the pan in the bread machine.

5 Select the Cake or Quick Bread cycle and press Start.

Don't confuse the Quick Bread cycle with another short cycle, like the Rapid cycle. The Quick bread cycle has no rising time. Quick breads use baking powder and/or baking soda which leavens in a chemical reaction to moisture and heat that occurs once you start baking the bread.

When the bread is completely baked, take the pan out of the machine and place the pan on a wire rack. Do not take the bread out until ten minutes have passed. This allows the structure of the bread to firm up so that it won't fall apart when you remove the bread from the pan.

Per serving: Calories 210; Protein 4g; Carbohydrates 32g; Dietary fiber 2g; Total fat 7g; Saturated fat 0.5g; Cholesterol 35mg; Sodium 100mg.

Pumpkin Bread

When we think of pumpkin, we think fall or winter. But this bread will be a favorite the year around. It makes an excellent accompaniment to a chicken or turkey salad. You can serve it as a dessert perhaps with mixed fruit cocktail. Try it toasted for breakfast.

Preparation time: 20 minutes

Approximate cycle time: 1 hour and 20 minutes

Yield: 12 to 16 slices

Wet Ingredients

3 large eggs

¾ cup canned pumpkin

2 tablespoons vegetable oil

Dry Ingredients

½ cup bean flour

½ cup rice flour

½ cup sorghum

½ cup tapioca flour

¼ cup cornstarch

½ cup brown sugar

1 ½ teaspoons xanthan gum

1 teaspoon salt

1 teaspoon baking powder

½ teaspoon baking soda

1 teaspoon cinnamon

¼ teaspoon nutmeg

½ cup raisins

1 Be sure that all the ingredients are at room temperature.

2 Combine the wet ingredients and pour them into the bread machine pan.

3 Measure the dry ingredients, including the yeast, and mix them together. Place them in the pan.

4 Place the pan in the bread machine.

5 Select the Cake or Quick Bread cycle and press Start.

Don't confuse the Quick Bread cycle with another short cycle, like the Rapid cycle. The Quick bread cycle has no rising time. Quick breads use baking powder and/or baking soda which leavens in a chemical reaction to moisture and heat that occurs once you start baking the bread.

When the bread is completely baked, take the pan out of the machine and place the pan on a wire rack. Do not take the bread out until 10 minutes have passed. This allows the structure of the bread to firm up so that it won't fall apart when you remove the bread from the pan.

Per serving: Calories 180; Protein 4g; Carbohydrates 32g; Dietary fiber 2g; Total fat 4.5g; Saturated fat 0g; Cholesterol 35mg; Sodium 270mg.

Spelt Bread

Spelt, sometimes referred to as *German wheat,* is an ancient variety of wheat that was widely grown in the upland areas of Germany and France until the twentieth century. As with wheat flour, spelt flour contains gluten — that allows the dough to stretch and makes a nicely shaped loaf. Unlike wheat flour, spelt flour is usually tolerated by those with gluten sensitivities.

Preparation time: *15 minutes*

Approximate cycle time: *2½ to 3 hours*

Yield: *12 to 16 slices*

1 ½ lb loaf	2 lb loaf
¾ cup water	1 cup + 1 tablespoon water
2 tablespoons vegetable oil	3 tablespoons vegetable oil
2 tablespoons sugar	3 tablespoons sugar
1 teaspoon salt	1 ½ teaspoons salt
3 cups spelt flour	4 cups spelt flour
2 ¼ teaspoons active dry yeast	1 tablespoon active dry yeast

1 Have all the ingredients at room temperature.

2 Place the ingredients in the pan in the order listed.

3 Select a Basic, White, or Normal cycle and a medium crust color. Press Start.

Variation: You can make a cinnamon raisin bread with this recipe by adding 2 teaspoons of cinnamon and ¾ cup raisins to the 1 ½-pound loaf. If you are making the 2-pound loaf, use the same amount of cinnamon but increase the raisins to 1 cup. Be sure the raisins are a bit dry or they will disintegrate in the bread.

Per serving: Calories 130; Protein 4g; Carbohydrates 26g; Dietary fiber 5g; Total fat 3g; Saturated fat 0g; Cholesterol 0mg; Sodium 200mg.

Part IV
The Part of Tens

"Oooo, what's in here? Is that sun-dried eye of newt? How gourmet!"

In this part . . .

*E*very *For Dummies* book ends with top-ten lists. We offer you ten tips for dealing with a troublesome bread machine and ten tips for fixing your bread creations that don't turn out as you expected.

Chapter 19

Ten Tips for Troubleshooting a Bread Machine

Soon you'll be turning out breads so delicious and so easy that you and your family won't be able to live without them. And then there will come a day when your bread machine baffles you. We can hear it now, "I did everything right, but. . . ." Here are the most common bread machine–related problems — and their solutions.

None of the lights come on

First double-check that it's not your outlet by plugging the machine into other outlets. If the machine does not work in any outlet, locate your receipt so that you can return the machine to where it was purchased.

In the meantime, you have to do something with the ingredients you have in the pan, if you've gotten that far. Dump your ingredients into a large bowl, and using a wooden spoon, mix as much of the ingredients together as you can. Place the dough on a lightly floured surface. With your hands, begin to work the remaining flour into the dough and continue kneading the dough, by pulling the dough from the far side toward you with one hand and pushing that section into the dough with the palm of your other hand. Turn the dough a quarter of a turn and repeat the kneading action of pulling toward you and pushing down until the dough is smooth and elastic.

Place the dough in a lightly oiled bowl and turn to grease top. Cover; let rise until dough doubles in size before punching down and shaping. Sometimes it is hard to tell if it is double. Here's another way to determine if the dough is ready to be punched down. Push two fingers into the dough, all the way to the second knuckle and take them out. If the holes remain and do not close back up, the dough is ready to be punched down (have all the air bubbles deflated).

You can be creative and shape the dough as you so desire; cover and let it rise again before baking. You can tell if it is ready for the oven by lightly pushing in with one finger on the side of the loaf. If the indentation remains it is ready to be baked. An average baking temperature is 375° for approximately 35 minutes.

Electricity to your home is interrupted during the cycle

If the bread has already completed the kneading cycle and if your machine has a cycle that will only bake the bread without any mixing, let the dough set in the pan and continue to rise. When the dough has risen close to the top of the pan, select the Bake cycle and push Start. The bread will bake in the machine.

If your bread has already completed the kneading cycle but your machine does not have a bake only cycle, you can remove your bread from the machine and place it in a greased pan for baking. When it has risen until an indentation remains after touching, (approximately 40 minutes) bake in your conventional oven. An average baking temperature is 375° for approximately 35 minutes. If the machine has not completed kneading the dough, start the cycle again.

The bread sticks in the pan

Remove the bread any way you can, and then soak the pan with water, rinse, and wipe or drain dry. It's best not to wash the nonstick surface of the bread machine pan with dish soap or detergent. Sometimes a residue will build up that really isn't evident to our eye, but we know it's there because the bread sticks. A treatment for cleaning off the residue is to pour ¼ cup of any kind of vinegar into the pan and fill with boiling water. Allow the solution to set in the pan until it has cooled. Next time, your bread won't stick.

Another helpful hint is to let the bread remain in the pan for a few minutes before trying to remove the bread. Take the pan out of the machine and set the pan on your cooling rack, on its side; turning it from side to side will loosen the bread from the sides of the pan.

If none of these solutions help, you may have to replace your pan. With your new pan, be sure not to use soap or detergent when cleaning.

The kneading blade sticks in the pan

If you intend to remove the kneading blade from the pan, you will have to remove the blade from the pan every time you use it. As soon as the bread has been removed from the pan, fill the pan with hot water to soak. When the pan and the water have cooled, usually the blade will come off the shaft quite easily. If the blade sticks, hold the wing nut on the underside of the pan with one hand. With the other hand, hold the blade and using very little back and forth movement, pull the blade off the shaft. If you did not soak the pan immediately, you may have to soak it quite a few times before you can remove the blade.

If you absolutely cannot remove the blade from the pan, don't fret about it. But be sure you clean out under the blade with dental floss or something else that will slide between the blade and the pan.

The kneading blade comes off in the bread

This is very common and very easy to fix. A crochet hook is the best solution. As soon as you take the bread out of the machine, while it is still very warm, put the crochet hook into the center hole of the blade, catch it onto the side of the hole, and ease the blade out. If you do this while the bread is warm, it hardly disrupts the dough structure of the loaf. Unfortunately, there's no way to stop the blade from coming off into the bread. But don't worry about it. It doesn't affect the bread, the blade, or the rest of the machine one bit, as long as you quickly remove the blade from the bread.

Also, it's a good habit to always check for the kneading blade when you get done baking, so that you don't lose it. Some people have thrown it away, others have given it away, and still others have no idea where their kneading blade has disappeared to.

Your machine won't make several breads in succession

After the machine has completed the cycle that baked the bread, it will need at least 20 minutes to cool down before it will work again. If you're in a big hurry and you want to try to help the machine cool down, you can try some of our favorite methods. We have a small fan that fits over the top opening and helps to circulate the hot air out faster. We've also placed cold soda cans in the machine itself (without the pan) to help it cool down. But the best solution, and the one that helps your bread machine have a long and happy life, is to patiently wait for the machine to cool itself down.

Your crust is too dark or too thick

Look in your manual for a chart that describes what happens during the cycles. If your manual does include this type of a chart, look at the baking times in each of the cycles. You may want to choose a cycle that has a shorter baking time.

Another solution is to choose a sweet bread cycle. Sweet breads are baked at a lower temperature.

The third possibility is to take the bread out of the machine before the Bake cycle is complete. Sometimes we've had to take the bread out as much as 15 minutes before the baking is completed. A digital readout thermometer stops the guesswork. Inserted into the bread, it will read 190° if the bread is done. Always press Stop and hold the button down until the machine indicates that you've cleared the cycle. Do not unplug the machine before you've stopped it.

Your machine hesitates while it's kneading

Check what's going on immediately. Chances are good that the dough is too stiff. Add liquid.

If that's not the case, it may mean that your belt is slipping. This could mean the belt has stretched or it could mean that the gear that holds the belt has a hairline crack. You will need to have the machine repaired or replaced.

In your bread machine use and care manual there should be a toll-free number to call for a repair service nearest you. However, oftentimes the company will have only one repair service and you will have to mail your machine to that location. Be sure to find out the cost and the estimated cost of shipping before you make the decision to send your machine in for repair.

You forget to add the extras at the signal

Most bread machine manuals have a chart to show how long the kneading, rising, and baking times are. When you remember those extras you didn't add, check your manual to determine how much time has transpired in the bread machine cycle. You can remove the dough from the machine during the first part of the rising process and work the extra ingredients, like fruits and nuts, into the dough by hand. Then return the dough to the machine to continue rising.

If your dough is past the early rising stage, put your extras in a small self-sealing bag and store. They will be measured out for your next loaf. Your bread will still be delicious without the extras.

You forget how the delay timer works

After you have the ingredients in the bread pan and have selected the cycle, determine how many hours and minutes it is until you want to be able to take that bread out of the machine. Begin pressing the up arrow until that number appears on your digital screen. Press Start. The machine will delay the start time so that the time of completion will be the number of hours that you entered. And that's how the delay timer works!

Chapter 20

Ten Ways to Solve Bread Problems

In This Chapter

▶ Dealing with rising problems

▶ Making sure the crust turns out okay

Some people say that baking is an art; others say it's a science. However you view baking, you have to admit that it's easy, almost too easy, to mess up a recipe. Blame it on lack of artistry or lack of scientific precision, you're going to run into little problems once in a while when you bake. The following sections list common problems and offer some solutions.

But wait — once again let us remind you that if you check the dough for its consistency you can avoid many disappointments. We described in full detail in Chapter 5 how to do the dough consistency test. Because we think it's so important, here is another miniversion of it:

Check the dough about five minutes after the machine starts kneading; the dough should be a soft, slightly tacky ball. If it is dry, add water, one tablespoon at a time; if it is too wet, add flour, one tablespoon at a time.

The bread doesn't rise

Cut the small, dense loaf, as soon as it cools, into cubes and dry in your oven to use for croutons. At that point, you can crush the dried croutons to make breadcrumbs for baking. (See Chapter 9 for directions.)

Before your bake again, check the yeast for activity. Be sure that all the ingredients are between room temperature and 80° — no warmer, no cooler. Be sure that you're using the right amount of flour: When measuring, scoop the flour into the cup with a large spoon and level off.

In the fall and winter, your flour might be drier than usual if your home is heated. Dry flour makes the dough too dry. Dry dough is also common at high altitudes, because flour tends to dry out at elevations. Check the dough for consistency each time you bake. Never assume that because a recipe was okay last time, it's okay this time. You may need to add a tablespoon or more of water.

Bread flour has more gluten than all-purpose flour or whole-grain flour; therefore it will be more elastic and will expand easier. If you use all-purpose flour, try bread flour and compare your loaf size. Whole-grain flours will expand better if you add vital wheat gluten. (See Chapter 3 for more details.)

The bread rises too much

You may want to cut off the top, because it didn't completely bake. The air can't circulate sufficiently to bake the top if it rises too high. Usually, the rest of the loaf is very edible and enjoyable.

The bread will rise too much if the dough is too wet. Always check the dough for consistency each time you make it. Never depend on how it was the last time that you made it. You may have to add a couple of tablespoons or more of flour.

Fast-acting yeast may cause the bread to rise too much. Remember the general rule with yeast: ¾ teaspoon of active, dry yeast per cup of flour, ½ teaspoon of fast-acting yeast per cup of flour. (Bread machine yeast is fast acting.)

Salt is an important ingredient to stabilize the rate of yeast activity. If it's reduced or omitted, the loaf will overrise.

The bread doesn't bake completely

You don't need the surprise of cutting into a sweet-smelling, golden brown loaf of bread only to discover that it didn't bake all the way through. An instant-read thermometer lets you know immediately if the bread has completely baked when it reads 190° when it's inserted into the middle of the bread. If the machine has completed the cycle and the bread is not completely baked, you can finish baking the loaf in your conventional oven in the bread machine pan.

Some machines have a bake-only cycle. If yours does, you can select that cycle and continue baking your bread in the machine. However, some machines will not let you continue baking until they've completely cooled down. In this case, it's best to finish baking in your standard oven at 375° for approximately 30 minutes.

If you cut the bread before it's completely cooled, it will look doughy because the structure sets up as the bread cools off.

The bread falls in the middle

Time to get creative: Continue to make the hole larger and use the bread for a salad bowl. You can even pretend that it was intentional.

But why did it fall? When the honeycomb structure that expands your bread is too weak, the bread collapses. There are several factors that can contribute to unstable bread:

- Using all-purpose flour, which is not as strong as bread flour.

- Not checking the consistency of the dough after five minutes of kneading. Concave loaves can occur if the dough is too wet.

- Forgetting to use salt — salt controls the activity of the yeast and strengthens the dough structure.

- Using liquids that are too warm, which result in dough that is stretched too far. We call that *overproofed* dough.

The crust is tough

Toast it. This partial heat process changes the gelatinization of the starch in the bread so that the starch actually absorbs moisture from the gluten. Although the bread is now drier and in a different form, it is appears fresher and it is not tough.

If the bread is not completely baked, or it didn't bake at a high enough temperature, the crust could be tough. Try using the French Bread cycle. The temperature is hotter on that cycle.

If you would like a very tender crust, use milk for the liquid and butter for the shortening. You can even brush the baked bread with butter while it's still warm to further tenderize the crust.

If you want a harder, chewy crust, brush the bread with warm water while it's still warm.

The fruits and nuts are in the bottom of the pan

Oh well, the bread is still delicious. Maybe jam or jelly will help.

The most common reason why the fruit and nuts do not incorporate into the dough is that the dough is too stiff. There are two ways to avoid fruit-and-nuts-on-the-bottom syndrome. First, always check the condition of the dough after five minutes of kneading. If it's too stiff, add water, a tablespoon at a time. Then, check the dough a few minutes after you've added the fruit and nuts to be sure that they've worked into the dough and are not riding around on the outside, between the dough and the pan. If they don't mix into the dough during the kneading cycle, take the dough out of the machine and work the fruit and nuts into the dough with your hands. Then return the dough to the machine to rise and bake.

There's flour on the outside of the bread

Brush the flour off and serve the bread.

You probably have flour sticking to the corners of the pan. Especially with quick breads that have a shorter mixing time, the flour will stick in the corners and not be incorporated into the dough. We use a rubber spatula and help mix everything into the dough.

The bread is yeasty when it's baked in the oven

If you let your bread rise too long or if the rising place is too warm, the yeasty odor will be more noticeable and you may detect a yeasty taste. Some people really like that to happen — it brings back childhood memories of fresh bread baking in the kitchen.

The crust gets all wrinkled

If guests are coming over, glaze the bread. No one will even suspect they are eating wrinkled crust. (See Chapter 8.)

Wrinkled crust is a sign that the bread has risen too much, making the crust too thin. If you're baking the bread in your machine, try cutting back a tad on water, like maybe eliminating 1 tablespoon. If you are baking the bread in your oven, shorten the rising time. Remember to test the readiness of the dough for baking by gently pushing in with your finger on the side. When the indentation remains, it's ready to bake.

We've heard it said that the crust wrinkles if the bread is cooled in a draft. Maybe we've never baked and cooled bread in a drafty enough place, because our loaves haven't wrinkled for that reason.

Frozen dough makes bread with white spots on it

Take the attitude that you planned for it to happen this way. Consider it unique.

As the dough was thawing, not enough air circulated to evaporate the moisture. The white marks are caused from the condensation of the liquid on the dough as it comes to room temperature. The trick is to have enough air circulating around the dough to remove the excess moisture, but not too much air, which makes the dough overly dry. You can accomplish this task by taking the frozen item out of the freezer wrapping and loosely covering it with plastic wrap while it is defrosting and coming to room temperature.

Index

YOUR ONLINE RESOURCE
WWW.DUMMIES.COM

Discover Dummies Online!

The Dummies Web Site is your fun and friendly online resource for the latest information about *For Dummies®* books and your favorite topics. The Web site is the place to communicate with us, exchange ideas with other *For Dummies* readers, chat with authors, and have fun!

Ten Fun and Useful Things You Can Do at www.dummies.com

1. Win free *For Dummies* books and more!
2. Register your book and be entered in a prize drawing.
3. Meet your favorite authors through the IDG Books Worldwide Author Chat Series.
4. Exchange helpful information with other *For Dummies* readers.
5. Discover other great *For Dummies* books you must have!
6. Purchase Dummieswear® exclusively from our Web site.
7. Buy *For Dummies* books online.
8. Talk to us. Make comments, ask questions, get answers!
9. Download free software.
10. Find additional useful resources from authors.

Link directly to these ten fun and useful things at
http://www.dummies.com/10useful

For other technology titles from IDG Books Worldwide, go to
www.idgbooks.com

Not on the Web yet? It's easy to get started with *Dummies 101®: The Internet For Windows® 98* or *The Internet For Dummies®* at local retailers everywhere.

Find other *For Dummies* books on these topics:
Business • Career • Databases • Food & Beverage • Games • Gardening • Graphics • Hardware
Health & Fitness • Internet and the World Wide Web • Networking • Office Suites
Operating Systems • Personal Finance • Pets • Programming • Recreation • Sports
Spreadsheets • Teacher Resources • Test Prep • Word Processing

IDG BOOKS WORLDWIDE BOOK REGISTRATION

Register This Book and Win!

We want to hear from you!

Visit **http://my2cents.dummies.com** to register this book and tell us how you liked it!

- Get entered in our monthly prize giveaway.

- Give us feedback about this book — tell us what you like best, what you like least, or maybe what you'd like to ask the author and us to change!

- Let us know any other *For Dummies*® topics that interest you.

Your feedback helps us determine what books to publish, tells us what coverage to add as we revise our books, and lets us know whether we're meeting your needs as a *For Dummies* reader. You're our most valuable resource, and what you have to say is important to us!

Not on the Web yet? It's easy to get started with *Dummies 101*®: *The Internet For Windows*® *98* or *The Internet For Dummies*® at local retailers everywhere.

Or let us know what you think by sending us a letter at the following address:

For Dummies Book Registration
Dummies Press
10475 Crosspoint Blvd.
Indianapolis, IN 46256

BESTSELLING
BOOK SERIES